The

MARRIAGE LICENSE BONDS
of
NORTHAMPTON COUNTY
VIRGINIA

- 1706-1854 -

Copied and Indexed by:
Stratton Nottingham

Southern Historical Press, Inc.
Greenville, South Carolina

Please direct all correspondence and book orders to:
SOUTHERN HISTORICAL PRESS, Inc.
PO Box 1267
Greenville, SC   29602-1267

Originally printed: Onancock, VA 1929
ISBN #978-1-63914-161-6
Printed in the United States of America

PREFACE

Accawmack, one of the eight original shires, originally included the present counties of Accomack and Northampton. In 1642/3 the name was changed to Northampton, and about 1663 was divided, the upper part retaining the name of Accomack, and the lower part being called Northampton. Northampton County has the oldest continuous records in the country, dating from 1632 without a break. The records are in an excellent state of preservation - Those from 1632 to 1663 include the records of Accomack as well as Northampton, and are in the Clerk's Office of Northampton County.

In 1850 the use of marriage bonds ceased, and licenses were issued. The Marriage Register in Northampton does not start until 1854; the original licenses from 1850 to 1860 are bound in a small volume and filed in the Clerk's Office with the Bonds. In order to bring the record up to the Marriage Register these have been included. There is on file in the office a volume marked "Marriage Records 1791-1854" This is a record of Ministers returns. The Bonds for some of these marriages are missing, and when this is the case the Minister's notes or returns have been included in this volume.

The Marriage Bond seldom gives the names of the parents of either party, but frequently notes of consent from parents or guardian supplies this information, and these notes have also been included.

* Indicates marriages for which there are no bonds, and which were abstracted from the original licenses 1850-1860

** Marriages for which there are no bonds or licenses, but which are listed in vol. marked "Marriage Records 1791-1854"

? Investigate as to race.

The following marriages are indexed both ways, but are, in most cases, unquestionably the same. ** indicate the way the marriages are listed by the Clerk from the Ministers returns in "Marriage Records 1791-1854", but it is reasonable to assume that the names of the contracting parties as they appear in the Bonds are correct. It would be well, however, to prove these marriages before accepting either as definite.

Clark, Thomas & Adah Ward, 8 Dec. 1806
**Black,Thomas & Adah Ward _____ 1806

Travis, Dennard & Rebekah Costin, 14 Sept. 1808
**Morris, Dennard & Rebekah Costin, _____ 1808

Kellam, Stephen & Elizabeth Belote, 10 May 1845
**Kelly,Stephen & Elizabeth Belote, 10 May 1845

Kellam, Charles & Rosey Ann Wingate,5 Jan. 1838
**Kilmon,Charles & Rosey Ann Wingate,7 May 1836

Meccown,John & Grace Jones, 22 June 1818
**McCowan, John & Grace Jones, 25 June 1818

Bool, James & Mary Mears, 24 Dec. 1821
**Bull,James & Mary Mears, 26 Dec. 1821

Martin, Thomas & Mahala Fletcher,10 Sept. 1831
**Bird, Thomas & Mahala Fletcher, ___ Sept.1831

Mason, George & Susanna Wilkins, 17 Aug. 1805
**Watson, George & Susanna Wilkins,_____ 1805

Moore, William H. & Mary Isdell, 11 Feb. 1850
**Ward,William H. & Mary Isdell, 13 Feb. 1850

Robertson, William & Mary Abdell, 30 Jan 1838
**Roberts, William & Mary Abdell, 30 Jan. 1838

Tyler, Thomas & Ann Bishop, 1 Jan. 1800
**Taylor, Thomas & Anne Bishop, ___ 1799

Vichus, Thomas & Sally Freshwater, 14 Dec. 1818
**Biccus,Thomas & Sally Freshwater, 24 Dec. 1818

Whitehead, William & Margaret Warrington 3 Dec.1821
**Warrington,William & Margaret Warrington, 6 Dec.1821

Wilson, John & Rosey Goffigon, 8 Dec. 1813
**Nelson, John & Rosey Goffigon _____ 1813

Peak, Robert & Sukey Jarvis Flood, 25 July 1807
**Floyd,Robert & Sukey Jarvis Floyd, _____1807

The compiler wishes to acknowledge his appreciation
of the universal courtesy and consideration shown him by Mr. George
T. Tyson, Clerk, and by Mr. H. H. Adams and Mrs Hugh Roberts, his
Deputies.

Abbott, Zephaniah & Margaret Howell, 20 Mar. 1804 - William Howell
    sec.

Abdell(Abdeel,Abdil,Abdale), Abel & Rachel Johnson, 14 Sept. 1807,
    William D. James sec.
*Abdell, George D., of Accomack, & Mary F. Hallett, ward of William
    T. Fitchett, 1 Feb. 1853
Abdell, Hancock & Keziah Dalby, 7 Mar. 1780, Henry Warner sec.
Abdell, Preson & Nancy Lewis, 25 Mar. 1840, John B.Wescoat sec.
Abdell, Shepherd & Margaret Kendall, 15 Oct. 1811, John Jacob sec.
Abdell, William & Elizabeth Barecraft, dau. William Barecraft, dec.
    28 Mar. 1848, John Belote sec.

Abdeel(Abdell,Abdil,Abdale), Abel & Nancy Dixon, dau. Tilney Dixon,
    17 June 1779, Luke Heath sec.
Abdeel, Ezekiel & Sarah Dalby, dau. Waterfield Dalby, 16 Sept.1779,
    con. of Abel Abdeel, father of Ezekiel.
Abdeel, Henry & Sarah Tankard, wid. John Tankard, 26 Apr. 1781,
    William Belote sec.
Abdeel, John & Elizabeth Kelly, 29 Dec. 1791, Severn Abdeel sec.
Abdeel, William & Levicy Gooday, 11 Apr. 1786, Moses Roberts sec.

Abdil(Abdell,Abdale,Abdeel),George & a daughter of Moses Roberts,
    born 24 June 1779 - 20 Apr. 1802, John Harrison sec. Con.
    of Moses Roberts
Abdil, Henry & Hetty Stott, 1 Oct. 1796, Thomas Dowty sec.
Abdil, Preeson & Polly Kee, 30 July 1795, Nicholas Bloxom sec.
Abdil, Thomas & ___(no name)___ 9 Aug. 1794, William Garris sec.

Abdale (Abdell,Abdeel,Abdil), William & Amy Pettit, 25 Apr. 1794,
    William Chance sec.

Acthison, Samuel & Esther Respass,dau. John Respess, 16 Aug.1771,
    John Lewis Fulwell sec.

Addison, Arthur & Tabitha Joyne, 22 May 1756, Stratton Cobb sec.
    Con. of Edmund Joyne, father of Tabitha.
Addison, Arthur & Esther Pagboth, 8 Mar. 1786, Severn Kellum sec.
Addison, Arthur & Elizabeth Cook, 10 Apr. 1787, Henry Harmanson sec.
Addison, Arthur & Rosey James, 3 Feb. 1812, Andrew James sec.
Addison, Edward W. & Miss Elizabeth West, 11 Oct. 1826, Charles
    West sec.
Addison, John & Peggy White, 27 Dec. 1802, Wm.P.Harmanson sec.
Addison, John & Ann E. Kellam, dau. Col. H. Kellam, 30 Nov. 1842,
    Kendall F. Addison sec.
Addison, Kendall & Palmer Rodgers, 26 June 1787, Wm.Satchell,Jr.
    sec.
*Dr. Kendall F. Addison & Arinthia S. Wilkins, dau. William E.
    Wilkins, 12 May 1851
Addison, Thomas & Margaret Waltham, wid. 14 Oct. 1775, Edward
    Turner sec.
Addison, Thomas,Jr. & Peggy Savage, Dau. Nathaniel Savage, dec.
    11 Jan. 1780, John Turner sec.

Addison, Thomas E. & Rosey W. Savage, 23 Nov. 1816, Wm.Savage sec.

Adams, John & Sarah Kendall, 21 Feb. 1816, Caleb B. Upshur sec.

Aimes (Ames), William & Patsey Bool, 20 Dec. 1796, Richard Coleburn sec.

Allen, Thomas, of Baltimore, & Elizabeth Massey, born 1771 - 11 Dec. 1789, John Ohara, of Philadelphia sec. Con. of Anne Massey, mother of Elizabeth

Ames(Aimes), James & Rachel Johnson, sister of the wife of Levin Beach, 26 Mar. 1811, Levin Beach sec.
Ames, John & Ann Hunt, 16 Jan. 1809, Amos Underhill sec.
Ames, Levin S. & Margaret Brittingham, 22 May 1838, Elijah Brittingham sec.
Ames, Mark & Peggy Pool, Free Negroes, 30 Sept. 1840, Benjamin J. Dalby sec.
*Ames, Nelson & Peggy Brickhouse, his ward, Free Negroes, 9 June 1851
Ames, Richard & Nancy Milby, 4 Mar. 1805, John P. Johnson sec.
Ames, Shadrack & Matilda Christian, wid. 28 Feb. 1775, Adiel Milby sec.
Ames, Shadrack T. & Sarah S. Gardiner, dau. Walter C. Gardiner, dec. 4 Aug. 1830, John Simkins sec.
Ames, Teagle & Margaret Belote, ward of Alexander W. Ward, 10 Jan. 1831, Alexander W. Ward sec.
Ames, Thomas & Sally Christian, 21 May 1800, John P. Johnson sec.
Ames, Thomas & Leanna Long, 11 Mar. 1822, John N. Brickhouse sec.
Ames, Thomas & Mary Clark, dau. William Clark, dec. 12 Dec. 1842, Alexander W. Ward sec.
Ames, William C. L. & Sally A. Henderson, dau. John T. Henderson, 13 June, 1848, William B. Savage sec.

Andrews, Isaac & Tamar A. Savage, dau. William Savage, Sr., 14 June 1824, William Savage sec.
Andrews, Isaac & Joanna Heath dau. Seth D. Heath, 5 Mar. 1827, John R. Fisher sec.
Andrews, Isaac & Juliet I. Parker, 9 June 1842, Alex. W. F. Mears sec.
Andrews, Jacob & Margarett Joyne, 19 Aug. 1752, William Joyne sec.
Andrews, Jacob & Catharine Harmon, 2 May 1808, William James sec.
Andrews, Major & Hannah Bell Powell, Orph. of George Powell, 30 Jan. 1774. Nathaniel Powell sec.
Andrews, Major & Nancy Custis, 24 June 1795, John Boggs sec.
Andrews, Major & Patsey Cox, 16 Oct. 1804, George Belote sec.
Andrews, Robert, of Accomack, & Betsy Stratton, dau. Benjamin Stratton, dec. 11 Dec. 1788, Thomas Parker, of Accomack, sec. Con. of William Stratton, brother of Betsy.
Andrews, Shepherd & Nancy Dowty, 27 Dec. 1819, Thomas Johnson, Jr. sec. Con. of Zob: Dowty, father of Nancy.
Andrews, Southey & Adah Carpenter, 18 Jan. 1819, John Dowty sec. Con. of John Carpenter, father of Adah.

Andrews, William & Bridget Heath, dau. William Heath, dec. 20 Apr.
     1781, John Dalby, Jr. sec.
Andrews, William & Sarah Hunt, 23 July 1787, John Wheeler sec.
Andrews, William & Sally Waterfield, 20 June 1791, John Wheeler sec.
Andrews, William & Adah Dennis, 14 Aug. 1792, John Dalby sec.
Andrews, William & Drusilla Floyd, 19 Mar. 1808, Nath'l.Widgeon sec.
Andrews, William W. & Margaret Dowty, ward of John Adams, 17 Oct.
     1831, John Adams sec.
Andrews, William W. & Polly S. Parsons, dau. William Parsons, Sr.,
     dec., 8 Dec. 1838, Custis T. Williams sec.

Anderson, Edward W. & Sarah A.H.Young, dau. George H. Young, dec.,
     25 Apr. 1837, William B. Anderson sec.
Anderson, Matthew & Rosey Collins, 8 Apr. 1794, John Graves sec.

Arbuckle, William, of Accomack, & Athalia Hall, dau. John Hall,
     20 May 1765, John Hall sec. Con. of James Arbuckle as to
     William.

Armistead, Ellison & Susanna Christian, dau. Michael Christian, 5
     Apr. 1780, Griffin Stith, Jr. sec.
Armistead, Francis, of Gloster County, & Sarah Smith, 29 Oct.
     1715, Richard Nottingham sec.

*Ashby, James & Elizabeth S. Johnson, wid. Geo. F.Johnson, 10
     Mar. 1851
Ashby, Washpan (Washbourn) & Ann Smith, ward of George Smith,
     8 Oct. 1838, George Smith sec.
Ashby, William & Margaret A.T.Turner, 10 June, 1846, John B.
     Turner sec. Con. of Teagle J. Turner, father of Margaret.

Avery, Isaac & Esther Preeson, wid. 4 May 1768, William Kendall sec.
Avery, Isaac & Margaret Stringer, dau. Hillary Stringer, 7 June
     1785, George Fisher sec.
Avery, Isaac W. & Sally T. Savage, wid. George Savage, 14 Dec.
     1821, Peter S. Bowdoin sec.

Ayres, Edmund & Cassa Johnson, 8 Mar. 1800, William Johnson sec.
Ayres, Richard J. & Leah W. Johnson, dau. John Johnson, sec. 20
     Dec. 1827, William P. Johnson sec.
Ayres, Thomas & Ann Taylor, 29 Sept. 1846, John S. Turpin sec.

Bachurst, James & Bridget Stott, 2 Dec. 1782, William Stott sec.

Badger, Ezekiel & Mary Dunton, 22 May 1790, Michael Dunton sec.
Badger, Thomas W. & Sally Dixon, 10 Oct. 1808, Harrison Thomas sec.
Badger, Thomas W. & Margaret Churn, 28 Dec. 1818, Benj.F.Dunton sec.

Bagwell, George T. & Elizabeth M. Johnson, ward of Egbert G. Bayly,
     19 Dec. 1848, John W. F. Gunter sec.
Bagwell, Hely D. & Mrs Elizabeth A. Mears, 14 Dec. 1835, Leonard
     B. Nottingham sec.

Bain, William & Judith Stevenson, 31 Aug. 1785, Robert Hewitt sec.
Bain, William & Susanna Dunton, 16 July 1793, Thomas Dunton sec.
Bain, William & Betsey Robins, 8 June 1797, Coventon Simkins sec.

Bailey(Bayly), Edmund & Rachel Upshur, 14 Sept. 1790, James
    Upshur sec.

Baker, Elijah & Ann Widgeon, wid. John Widgeon, 5 Nov. 1787,
    John Dennis sec.
Baker, Savage & Edith Heath, wid. Augustus C.E.Heath, 11 Dec. 1837,
    Thomas E. Brickhouse sec.
Baker, Savage & Lavinia Williams, dau. Peter Williams, 8 May 1843,
    Peter Williams sec.
? Baker, Thomas & Betsey Bingham, 5 Dec. 1805, Nathan Drighouse sec.
? Baker, Thomas & Mary Bevans, dau. John Bevans, 29 Jan. 1825, John
    Bevans sec.
Baker, Timothy & Jane Wilkins, dau. John Wilkins,Sr., 27 Nov. 1766,
    Edmund Glanville sec.

Ball, David B. & Sally Parsons, dau. Marriot Parsons, dec., 5
    Jan. 1842, Leonard B. Nottingham sec.
Ball, John & Margaret Warrington, 5 Apr. 1830, Smith Nottingham
    sec. Con. of George Warrington, father of Margaret.
Ball, Luther & Esther Wheeler, 26 Dec. 1826, John Bishop sec.

Baptist, Edward & Maria S. Satchell, 14 Mar. 1820, John Simkins
    sec.

Barecraft, James & Sally Floyd, 18 May 1813, Edmund Fletcher sec.
*Barcraft, John T. & Arinthia J. Harman, dau. Kely Harman dec.,
    10 July 1850
Barecraft, William & Elizabeth Speakman, dau. Thomas Speakman,
    19 Feb. 1781, Stuart Saunders sec.

Barnes, James & Sally Peck, 25 Aug. 1790, Benjamin Griffith sec.
    Con. of Elizabeth Pake, mother of Sally.
Barns, John & Elizabeth Jacob, dau. Esau Jacob, 26 Dec. 1776,
    Thorowgood Smith sec.

Barlow, Thomas & Jane Mapp, wid. 6 Feb. 1765, Samuel Holbrook
    sec.
Barlow, Thomas & Anne Stott, 9 May 1775, John Burton sec.
Barlow, Thomas & Elizabeth Rascoe, 26 Sept. 178_, Griffin
    Stith sec.

Barrott, John W. & Isetta Rooks, 11 Oct. 1842, William Lewis
    sec. Con. of Sally Rooks, mother of Isetta.
Barrett, John W. & Mary Nottingham, dau. Thomas W.Nottingham,
    31 Dec. 1845, Thomas W. Nottingham sec.

Batson, Ralph & Sarah Moor, wid., 6 Dec. 1749, Thomas Michael
    sec.

Bayly(Bailey),Edward & Nancy Pitts, 21 Sept. 1802, Major S.Pitts sec.
    Con. of Hezekiah Pitts, father of Nancy.

Bayly, Edward L. & Pamala E.J.Powell, ward of Miers W. Fisher, 13
    Nov. 1834, Miers W. Fisher sec.

Bayly, Edmund W. & Sally Ker, ward of Leonard B. Nottingham, 25 May
    1847, Leonard B. Nottingham sec.

Bayly, John H. & Margaret S. Wilson, 4 Nov. 1816, Edward H.C.Wilson
    sec. Con. of William W.Wilson, father of Margaret.

Bayly, Peter & Sukey Bevans, dau. Sam. Bevans, Free Negroes, 22
    Nov. 1825, Sam Bevans sec.

Bayly, Rodney N. & Sally A.S.Brickhouse, dau. George Brickhouse,
    18 Dec. 1838, Edmund W. Underhill sec.

Bayly, Col. Thomas M. & Mrs Jane O. Addison, 4 Oct. 1826,
    Richard D. Bayly sec.

?Beavans(Bevans),Hezekiah & Mary Morris, 31 July, 1798, Revel
    Morris sec.

? Beavans, John & Mary Ann Carter, 2 Jan. 1822, Mac Collins sec.

? **Beavans, Moses & Nancy West _____1807

? Beavans, Peter & Louisa Toyer, dau. George Toyer, 11 Mar.1823,
    George Toyer sec.

? Beavans, Sam & Molly Press, 19 Aug. 1797, Abraham Lang sec.

? Beavans, Solomon & Esther Casey, 24 Sept. 1796, Edmund Press sec.

Beazley, Ephraim H. & Sally Warren, dau. John Warren, Sr., dec.,
    19 Feb. 1849, Peter Williams sec.

Beach (Beech),James & Esther Hall, 9 Dec. 1811,John Scott,Sr.,sec.

Beach, James & Betsey Dann, dau. Silas Dann, dec., 4 July 1829,
    Robert A. Joynes sec.

Beach, James & Elizabeth Robins, wid. John Robins, 17 Dec. 1844,
    John M. Henderson sec.

Beach, Levin & Sally Johnson, 11 Apr. 1808, Silas Dan sec.

Beach, William T. & Margaret S. Churn, dau. William Churn, 7
    June 1848, Arthur E. Roberts sec.

? Becket, Abraham & Sarah Thompson, 26 Oct. 1797, Jacob Thompson
    sec.

Becket, Arthur, Free Negro, son of Sarah Becket, & Ann, a slave
    belonging to Matthew Floyd, 14 Jan. 1839, Alfred Parker
    & Sarah Becket sec.

? Becket, Isaac & Betsey Bivans, 28 Dec. 1816, Saul Becket sec.

? Becket, Joshua & Sally Stevens, 21 May 1803, Jacob Thompson sec.

*Becket, Peter & Ann Read, Free Negroes, 21 Nov. 1851

Becket, Smith & Fanny Collins, Free Negroes, 12 Mar. 1839, Smith
    S. Nottingham sec.

?**Becket, Solomon & Sarah Liverpool, ___ July 1800

? Becket, Solomon & Adah Liverpool, 7 July 1801, Josiah
    Liverpool sec.

? Becket, Solomon & Abigail Stevens, 19 Feb. 1803, Jacob Thomp-
    son sec.

Bedell, James & Caroline Evans, 16 June, 1835, William Snead sec.
    Con.of Nancy Evans, mother of Caroline.

Beech(Beach),Reubin & Mary Wilkins, dau. Patrick Wilkins, dec. 6 Jan. 1779, William Waterfield sec.

Belote, Abel & Susan West, 24 Nov. 1818, Caleb B. Upshur sec.

Belote, Abbot & Betsey Abdeel, wid., 8 July 1822, David Ewing sec.

Belote, Benjamin & Elizabeth Joynes, dau. Robert A. Joynes, 13 Jan. 1834, Robert A. Joynes sec.

Belote, Edward & Mary Nottingham, dau. Jacob Nottingham, 25 Nov. 1760, Addison Nottingham sec.

Belote, George & Molly Westcoat, 24 May 1798,William Parramore sec.

Belote, George & Margaret Ross, dau. Ann Ross, 12 Jan. 1830, Teackle J. Turner sec.

Belote, George T. & Rosaline Costin, ward of Miers W. Fisher, 24 Dec. 1838, Miers W. Fisher sec.

Belote, Hezekiah & Nancy Eshon, 4 June 1817, Samuel West sec. Con. of Nathaniel West as to Nancy.

Belote, Hezekiah & Susan Kendall, wid. John W. Kendall, 26 Nov. 1828, Thomas Smith, Jr., sec.

Belote, Hezekiah & Lucretia Harmanson, orphan of Henry Harmanson, 1 Jan. 1833, Seldon Ridley sec.

Belote, Hezekiah & Betsy Taylor, wid. John Taylor, 18 Oct. 1837, Smith Belote sec.

Belote, Hezekiah & Margaret Ann Bool, wid. Edward Bool, 16 Apr. 1845, W. J. Fitchett sec.

Belote, John & Frances Fitchett, alias Frances Williams, dau. Robert F. Williams, dec., 22 May 1832, Azariah Williams sec.

Belote, John & Ann Darby, dau. Shadrack Darby, dec. 14 May 1834, Hezekiah P. James sec.

Belote, John & Maria C. Savage, dau. William F. Savage, dec.,24 Dec. 1849, Peter B. Savage sec.

Belote, Jonas & Susanna Holt, wid. Stuart Holt, 21 May 1791, George Moore sec.

Belote, Kendall & Sucky Widgeon, 31 July 1793, John Widgeon sec.

Belote, Kendall & Sukey Lingo, ward of Thomas Smith, Jr., 10 Dec. 1832, Thomas Smith, Jr. sec.

Belote, Laban & Esther Dalby, 20 Dec. 1793, Reuben Westerhouse sec. Con. of John Dalby,Sr., father of Esther.

Belote, Laban,Jr. & Susan Dolby, 11 Dec. 1833, John Ewell sec. Con. of James Dolby, father of Susan.

Belote, Perry L. & Peggy Smith, 16 Dec. 1806, Arthur Cobb sec. Con. of William Smith, father of Peggy & of Noah Belote, father of Perry L.

Belote, Robert & Elizabeth Richardson, ward of William Roberts, 14 July 1828, William Roberts sec.

Belote, Smith & Margaret A.J.Gunter, dau. Rev. Stephen S.Gunter, dec., 20 Apr. 1836, Thomas Smith, Jr. sec.

Belote, Smith & Catharine P. Gunter, ward of Smith Belote, 20 May 1843, John S. Gayle sec.

Belote, Walter & Nancy Westcot, 13 Sept. 1802, George Belote, Jr. sec.

Belote, Walter & Esther Warren, dau. Seth Warren, dec. 10 Dec. 1834, Hezekiah Dalby sec.

Belote, William & Sarah Tankard, dau. John Tankard,dec. 16 Apr. 1779, Thomas Parramore sec.

Bell, Anthony & Tabitha Harman, 14 Sept. 1807, Thomas Widgeon sec.
Bell, Bayly & Mary C. Dunton, 11 May 1840, Joseph E. Bell sec.
Bell, Edmund & Polly Hanby, 27 Dec. 1802, William Parkerson sec.
    Con. of Joseph Hanby, father of Polly.
Bell, Ezekiel & Anne Carpenter, wid., 3 May 1748, Philip Jacob sec.
Bell, George & Susey Bell, 19 Dec. 1790, Anthony Bell sec.
Bell, George & Elizabeth Scott, 23 July1808, William Bell sec.
Bell, George & Margaret W. Colonna, dau. Major Colonna, dec., 25
    Jan. 1832, Lorenzo D. Mears sec.
Bell, George, Jr. & Elizabeth P. Badger, dau. Thomas W. Badger,
    5 Feb. 1833, Thomas W. Badger sec.
Bell, Jeptha & Louisa Bell, dau. Jesse Bell, 11 Jan. 1830, Jesse
    Bell sec.
Bell, Jesse & Nancy Richardson, born 1788, dau. Kendall Richardson,
    13 Dec. 1811, James Tatum sec.
Bell, Jesse & Mary Tatum, dau. James Tatum, 3 May 1828, James
    Tatum sec.
Bell, John & Sally Taylor, 12 Mar. 1804, John H. Harmanson sec.
Bell, John F. & Margaret Jane Nelson, 9 Dec. 1845, Benjamin J.
    Dalby sec. Con. of Hezekiah Dalby, Gdn. of Margaret Jane.
Bell, Joseph E. & Rosey Clegg, ward of Edmund Watson, 10 Nov.
    1834, Edmund Watson sec.
Bell, Nathaniel & Elizabeth Turpin, 20 Dec. 1786, Thomas Upshur,
    Jr. sec. Con. of Thomas Upshur "to marry my cousin
    Elizabeth Turpin".
Bell, Robert & Abigail Grice, dau. Thomas Grice, 12 Nov. 1771,
    Thomas Grice sec.
Bell, Robert & Mary Jarvis, dau. William Jarvis, 17 June 1772,
    William Jarvis sec.
Bell, Robert & Maria Isdell, his ward, orph. of Matthew Isdell,
    dec. 11 Feb. 1828, Hezekiah P. Wescoat sec.
** Bell, Savage & Elizabeth Spires ____ Nov. 1822
Bell, Smith, son of Edmund, & Peggy Wescoat, dau. Edmund P.
    Wescoat, 10 Mar. 1828, Edmund Bell & Edmund P. Wescoat sec.
Bell, Thomas & Sarah Gascoyne, 28 Sept. 1780, Robert Bell sec.
Bell, Thomas & Tinney Chance, 18 Nov. 1797, Southy Webb sec.
    Con. of William Chance, father of Tinney.
Bell, William, Jr. & Esther Scott, 4 Sept. 1797, Rickard Dunton,
    Jr. sec.

Benson(Benston), Azariah & Sarah Cutler, 15 Dec. 1796, Michael
    Dunton sec.
Benson, Edmond & Rachael Richardson, 3 July 1815, Daniel Luke sec.
Benson, James & Elizabeth Stott, 21 Dec. 1802, Laban Stott sec.
Benson, James & Elizabeth Dowty, wid. William Dowty, 16 June,
    1828, Thomas W. Badger sec.
Benson, James & Sally Roberts, dau. Teackle Roberts, dec. 27
    Mar. 1841, William J. Fitchett sec.
Benson, Nathaniel & Polly Willis, dau. Josiah Willis, born 22
    Jan. 1799 - 11 June 1823 (no sec.)
Benson, Patrick & Elizabeth Kellpy, 29 Jan. 1816, George
    Parkinson sec.

Benson, Samuel, of Accomack, & Nancy Savage, 11 Sept. 1812, Joshua
    Garrison sec.

Benston(Benson), James & Betsey Benston, 21 May 1804, William Only
    sec.

Bennett, Covey, Jr. & Miss Mary A. Gilden, 18 June 1849, George
    Waterfield sec.

Benthall, Caleb & Elizabeth Stripe, dau. Moses Stripe, 21 May 1779,
    John Nelson sec.
Benthall, Daniel & Adah Warren, 19 Feb. 1795, Nath'l. Goffigon sec.
Benthall, Daniel & Betsey Moor, dau. Isaac Moor, dec. 4 July 1791,
    George Moor sec.
Benthall, John & Elizabeth Goffigon, wid. 8 Jan. 1753, John Flood
    sec.
Benthall, Nathaniel & Elizabeth Nottingham, dau. Richard Nottingham,
    2 Apr. 1793, Richard Nottingham sec.
Benthall, Nathaniel & Peggy Odear, 24 Mar. 1796, Richard Evans sec.

Berry, John H., ward of Thomas B. Williams, & Louisa Y. West, dau.
    Nathaniel West, 9 Aug. 1841, Thomas B. Williams & Nath'l.
    West sec.

? Bevans(Beavans), Revel & Rachel Bevans, 6 Aug. 1817, John Bevans
    sec.
Bevans, Samuel S. & Mary Collins, Free Negroes, 29 Dec. 1829,
    Samuel Bevans sec.
Bevans, Samuel & Matilda Stephens, dau. Adah Read, Free Negroes,
    10 Mar. 1841, John Kendall & Adah Read sec.
? Bevans, Thomas, son of John, & Nancy Jeffery, wid. Littleton
    Jeffery, 19 Sept. 1827, John Bevans sec.

**Biccus, Thomas & Sally Freshwater, 24 Dec. 1818

**Biggs, Christopher & Jenny Trower, _____ 1804
Biggs, Christopher & Tinney Speakman, dau. Thomas Speakman,
    11 Mar. 1829, Thomas Speakman sec.
Biggs, James & Nice Courser, 13 Sept. 1796, Henry Wilkins sec.
Biggs, John & Tabitha Goffigon, wid. 31 Mar. 177__, William
    Biggs sec.
Biggs, John & Catherine Floyd, 16 Dec. 1817, Samuel Floyd sec.
    Con. of James Floyd, father of Catherine.
Biggs, Thomas & Ann Warren, 9 Dec. 1794, William Scott sec.
Biggs, William & Elishe Smaw, dau. John Smaw, 9 Mar. 1769,
    James Biggs sec.

? Bingham, Henry & Ritter Collins, 13 June 1794, Ralph Collins
    sec.
? Bingham, Littleton & Rosey Becket, 18 Sept. 1804, Moses
    Bingham sec.
? Bingham, Moses & Esther Collins, 24 Nov. 1819, Caleb Downing,
    Jr. sec. "This is to certify that Esther Collins is 25

years old the 23 of this month.   This from her father, Rafe
Collins.

Bird(Byrd), John & Margaret Meholloms, 26 Nov. 1792, Peter Dowty sec.
Bird, Thomas & Catherine West, 13 May 1825, George Grey sec.
**Thomas Bird & Mahala Fletcher, 1 Sept. 1831

Bishop, George & Polly Bird, 13 Feb. 1837, William F.Bishop sec.
Bishop, John & Anne Dixon, orph. of William Dixon, 4 Oct. 1775,
    Ralph Dixon sec.
Bishop, John & Rachell Wilson, 13 May 1809, William Kendall sec.
Bishop, John & Gracy Fitchet, 1 Sept. 1845, James S.Wilson sec.
Bishop, William,Jr. & Elizabeth Graves, dau. William Graves, 29
    Jan. 1765, George Graves sec.
Bishop, William & Lurana Mehollomes, dau. Thomas Mehollomes, 16
    Jan. 1828, Thomas Mehollomes sec.

Blake, Joshua & Esther Warrem, dau. Devorex Warren, 18 Mar. 1775,
    Major Brickhouse sec.

**Black, Thomas & Adah Ward _____ 1807

Blacknell, John & Margaret Jarvis, 9 Oct. 1789, John Williams sec.
    Con. of William Jarvis, father of Margaret.

Blair, John & Sarah Mapp, dau. Samuel Mapp, dec. 18 May 1768, John
    Mapp sec.
Blair, John & Mary Darby, 22 Jan. 1772, John Mapp sec.

Bloxom, Nicholas & Peggy Abell, 2 May 1793, William Garris sec.
Bloxom, Samuel & Lucretia Willis, ward of Keley Stott, 3 Aug.
    1824, Keley Stott sec.
Bloxom, William & Kesiah Core, wid. Charles Core, 25 June,1788,
    Kendall Addison sec.
Bloxom, William & Mary Johnson, wid. Robinson Johnson, 3 Aug.
    1790, William Wescoat sec.
Bloxom, William & Elizabeth Pettit, 9 Sept. 1816, Christr Gayle
    sec.

Boggs, George & Margaret Stringer, 11 Feb. 1795, Thomas Dunton sec.

Boisnard, Edward R. & Anne Holland, 4 Feb. 1818, Nathaniel
    Holland sec.
Boisnard, John, of Accomack, & Esther Robins, dau. Edward Robins,
    Esq., dec., 17 Feb. 1789, John Robins sec.
Boisnard, John & Nancy Kendall, 8 Aug. 1798, Joseph Moore sec.

Bolling, Robert, of the County of Buckingham, & Mary Burton, 3
    June, 1763, William Waters, of the City of Williamsburg,
    sec. Con. of William Burton, Gent. father of Mary.

Bonwell, Arthur & Susanna Toleman, 16 Jan. 1794, William Toleman
    sec.

Bonwell, Amos & Tabitha J. Thompson, dau. Elizabeth Collins, 17 Dec.
1845, James M. Bool sec.

**Rev. Charles Bonnwell & Nancy Scott, 6 Jan. 1816

Bonwell, Charles S. & Lucy Jane Smith, dau. John Smith, alias John
C. Smith, 11 Dec. 1843, Alex. W.F.Mears sec. Con. of John
Smith, father of Lucy Jane.

Bonwell, James, of Accomack, & Mary Robins, 21 May 1783, Arthur
Robins sec.

Bool, David N. & Sally Bell, dau. Edmund Bell sec., 23 Nov. 1840,
Jacob Spady sec.

Bool, Edward & Margaret Ann Ward, ward of William Wyatt, Jr., 13
Nov. 1832, William Wyatt, Jr. sec.

Bool, Ezekiel & Mahala Stott, 15 May 1819, Spencer Bool sec. Con.
of Laban Stott, father of Mahala.

**Bool, George & Mary Thompson _____ 1798

Bool, George & Ann Spady, 9 Apr. 1827, John Roberts sec.

Bool, James & Mary Mears, 24 Dec. 1821, Robert Sanford sec. Con.
of William Mears, father of Mary.

*Bool, James M. & Elizabeth Rayfield, 26 Feb. 1852

Bool, John & Priscilla Addison, 11 June, 1776, Hezekiah Pitts sec.
Con. of Thomas Addison, father of Priscilla.

Bool, Jonathan & Peggy Bool, 8 June 1801, Teackle Turner sec.

Bool, Jonathan & Sally Dunton, 22 Oct. 1818, Samuel West sec.

Boole, Major & Patience Turner, wid. John Turner, 28 Feb. 1781,
Richard Boole sec.

Bool, Major & Eliza Roberts, orph. of Francis Roberts, 3 Aug. 1831,
James Pratt sec.

Bool, Michael & Adeline Dunton, dau. Rickards Dunton, 13 July 1840,
Michael Bool & Richard Miles sec.

Bool, Nicholas & Elizabeth Nottingham, 18 Aug. 1802, Edmund Bell
sec.

Bool, Richard & Margaret Addison, 31 May 1787, Jonathan Stott sec.

Bool, Spencer & Charlotte Stott, 5 June 1821, Thomas Snead sec.

Booth, John & Esther Cowdry, 30 Apr. 1792, James Johnson sec. Con.
of William Cowdry, father of Esther.

Booth, William, born 29 Feb. 1798, son of Easter Booth, & Elizabeth
Floyd, alias Elizabeth Roberts, 10 Dec. 1821, Stephen
Wilkinson sec.

Boswell, Abraham & Elishe Jacob, dau. Esau Jacob, 15 Mar. 1763,
Esau Jacob sec.

Boswell, Abraham & Mary Dixon, wid. 19 Aug. 1774, Jacob Moor sec.

Boswell, James, of Gloucester, & Margaret Jacob, 31 Dec. 1770,
Edmund Glanville sec.

Borrows(Burris,Burros),Thomas & Sally Richardson, 16 Nov. 1807,
Levi Richardson sec.

Bow, Moses, Mariner, & Margaret Savage, dau. Capt. Thomas Savage,
23 Sept. 1710, Hillary Stringer sec.

Bowdoin, John & Grace Stringer, 10 Jan. 1754, Littleton Eyre sec.

Bowdoin, Peter & Susanna Preeson, 13 May 1733, Custis Kendall sec.

Bowdoin, Peter & Leah Teackle, 1 Aug. 1801, John Robins sec.

Bowdoin, Peter S. & Susan M. Jacob, 17 Oct. 1818, Peter Bowdoin sec.

Bowdoin, Preeson & Sarah Eyre, 19 Feb. 1759, Severn Eyre sec. Con.
of Littleton Eyre, father of Sarah.

Bowdoin, Severn E. & Laura A. Upshur, dau. Ann B. Upshur, 21 Apr.
1834, Ann B. Upshur sec.

Boyle, Charles D. & Charlotte Jenkins, wid. George Jenkins, 9 Aug.
1847, Jackson B. Powell sec.

Boyd, Alexander & Sally Goffigon, dau. Peter Goffigon, dec. 24
Jan. 1780, William Stockley sec. Con. of Tabitha Biggs,
mother of Sally.

Bozeman, John S. & Elizabeth Kelly, dau. Jesse Kelly, dec. 14 Aug.
1849, Joseph J. Parsons sec.

Bratten, Isaac & Nancy Nottingham, dau. Jacob Nottingham, 27 Dec.
1788

Bradford, Abel & Susan Gildon, 29 Nov. 1836, Teackle J. Turner sec.
Con. of John Gildon, father of Susan.

*Bradford, Abel & Tamarzene White, dau. Teackle S. White, dec. 23
July, 1850

Bradford, Brown & Peggy Johnson, dau. Obedience Johnson, 14 Mar.
1788, Nathaniel Darby sec.

Bradford, Charles & Nancy Abdeel, 7 Mar. 1788, Robert Rodgers sec.

Bradford, Ezra & Ann Smith, 29 Dec. 1784, George Pitts sec.

Bradford, Ezra & Sally Waltham, 3 June 1795, Coventon Simkins sec.

Bradford, George & Elizabeth Boswell, 31 Jan. 1797, Richard
Nottingham sec.

Bradford, George & Sarah Willis, 5 Apr. 1822, Johannes Johnson sec.

Bradford, George & Mrs Nancy Dennis, 19 May 1827, James Charnock
sec.

Bradford, George & Betsy Kilman, 20 June 1837, William Savage,Sr.,
sec.

Bradford, George & Mrs Elizabeth M. Christian, 30 Mar. 1842,
Patrick Warren, Jr. sec.

Bradford, John & Esther P. Ridley, dau. William W. Ridley, 28 Dec.
1846, William W. Ridley sec.

Bradford, John Brown & Peggy Addison, 3 July 1810, Thomas
Addison sec.

Bradford, Nathaniel G. & Esther Ridley, wid. William P. Ridley,
12 Apr. 1847, John W. Leatherbury sec.

Bradford, William, ward of Newton Harrison, & Mrs Mary Williams,
wid. John Williams, 12 June, 1837, William W.Wilson sec.

Brickhouse, Albert S. & Margaret S. Mears, dau. Thomas C. Mears,
15 Nov. 1836, Thomas C. Mears sec.

Brickhouse, Elan L., ward of Thomas S.Brickhouse, & Elizabeth P.
Fitchett, dau. Chs Fitchett, dec., 4 Sept. 1828,

Thomas S. Brickhouse sec.

Brickhouse, George & Mary Belote, dau. Edward Belote, dec., 21 Nov. 1781, Richard Nottingham sec.

Brickhouse, George,Jr. & Ann Sanford, 20 Dec. 1815, William White,Jr. sec. Con. of James Sanford, father of Ann

Brickhouse, George & Sally B. Nelson, wid. Ch^S Nelson, 23 June, 1846, Louis P. Rogers sec.

Brickhouse, John & Susanna Nottingham, dau. Thomas Nottingham,Sr., 19 Feb. 1785, Robert Brickhouse sec.

Brickhouse, John N.,Jr. & Catherine C. Ames, 22 Nov. 1817, Thomas S. Brickhouse sec. Con. of Thomas Ames, father of Catherine.

Brickhouse, John(of George) & Polly Taylor, wid. Barth^W Taylor, 12 Dec. 1825, Edward R. Turner sec.

Brickhouse, Robert & Sarah Nottingham, 11 Mar. 1785, John Williams sec.

Brickhouse, Smith & Peggy G. Dunton, 23 Mar. 1808, Elias Dunton sec. Con. of Arthur R. Savage as to Peggy.

Brickhouse, Smith & Miss Susanna G. Dunton, 19 Aug. 1824, Henry G. Dunton sec.

Brickhouse, Smith L. & Elizabeth W. Nottingham, dau. Maj. Smith Nottingham, 7 Apr. 1834, Smith Nottingham & John N. Brickhouse sec.

Brickhouse, Theophilus H. & Elizabeth S. Brickhouse, dau. Thomas S. Brickhouse, 7 Mar. 1846, Southey S. Wilkins sec.

Brickhouse, Thomas E. & Elizabeth N. Luker, wid. John Luker, 21 Dec. 1835, James Saunders sec.

Brickhouse, Thomas S. & Nancy Waterfield, 29 Nov. 1803, John Stratton sec. Con. of John Brickhouse father of Thomas S., and of Richard Waterfield, Gdn. of Nancy.

Brittingham, George W. & Mrs Emily Jacob, wid. John C. Jacob, 22 Dec. 1836, George F. Wilkins sec.

Brian(Bryan),Henry & Nancy Dunton, 14 Dec. 1818, William Dunton sec.

Brown, Allen & Nancy Smith, 6 Apr. 1808, Thomas Dillon sec.
Brown, Allen & Nancy Dowty, 10 July 1816, Matthew H.Dunton sec.
Brown, Allen & Jenny Davis, wid. 11 Mar. 1822, Charles Dillon sec.
Brown, Allen & Rachel Williams, wid. Thomas Williams, 8 Jan. 1838, John Segar sec.
Brown, Chas. T. & Margaret Ames, 17 July 1844, Smith Richardson sec. Con. of Rachel Ames, mother of Margaret.
Brown, Nathaniel & Nanny Dillion, wid. 9 Feb. 1778, William Saunders sec.

Broadwater, William, orph. of Robert P. Broadwater & ward of Obed Adams & Ann Hall, dau. Robert Hall, dec., 11 Jan. 1828, Shepherd A. Joynes sec.

Bruff, John W. born 7 Apr. 1813, son of Joseph Bruff of Bay Side, Talbot County, Md., & Sarah J.W.Floyd, dau. Elijah Floyd, dec., _____ 1838 circa., James R. Garrison sec.

Bryan(Brian), Nathaniel & Esther Mapp, 20 Dec. 1797, Nathaniel
    Holland sec.

Bryant, Henry & Nancey Holland, 28 Mar. 1764, Daniel Eshon sec.

**Bull, James & Mary Lears, 26 Dec. 1821
Bull, John & Sarah Ann Wingate, ward of William S. Floyd, 24 Dec.
    1838, William S. Floyd sec.
Bull, Richard & Kesiah Bool, 10 Dec. 1738, George Ashby sec.

Bullock, Thomas & Athaliah Underhill, 11 Oct. 1774, Thomas Under-
    hill sec.
Bullock, Thomas & Mary Mehollams, wid., 12 Jan. 1778, Thomas
    Cowdry sec.
Bullock, Thomas & Nancy Wingate, 30 May, 1798, Wm.B.Wilson sec.

Bunting, George, of Accomack, & Elizabeth Johnson, dau. Moses
    Johnson, dec. 6 Aug. 1770, Moses Johnson sec.
Bunting, Halloway & Priscilla Turner, 21 May, 1787, Thomas Clark
    sec. Con. of John Furbush Turner, father of Priscilla.
Bunting, Halloway & Sally White, 10 July 1797, Arthur Savage sec.
Bunting, James & Sally Harman, 28 Dec. 1816, Reuben Gooday sec.
Bunting, James & Margaret Dunton, dau. John Dunton, sec. 28 Dec.
    1840, James Dalby & Thomas Dalby sec.
Bunting, John S., ward of John W. Leatherbury & Dreusilla Jacob,
    8 Dec. 1828, Nathaniel H. Winder & John W.Leatherbury sec.
Bunting, John S. & Rachel Abdell, dau. Abel Abdell, dec., & ward
    of Alexander W. Ward, 12 July 1830, Alexander W. Ward sec.
Bunting, Jonathan & Nancy White, dau. Obedience White, dec. 9 Dec.
    1791, Halloway Bunting sec.
Bunting, Levin & Anne Bunting, dau. Solomon Bunting, 13 Dec. 1771,
    Solomon Bunting sec.
Bunting, Samuel & Margaret Savage, 9 Dec. 1820, Benjamin N. Scott
    sec. Con. of William Savage, father of Margaret.
Bunting, Shephard & Mary Dennis, 9 Sept. 1812, Nathaniel West sec.
    Con. of Sukey Dennis, mother of Mary.
Bunting, Solomon & Polly Pitts, wid., 30 May 1776, George Bonewell
    sec.
Bunting, William & Anne B. Poulson, ward of Robert Ashby, 10 Dec.
    1821, Robert Ashby sec.

Bundick & Ann Custis West, 19 Nov. 1811, Charles West sec.

Burton, John & Bridget Dalby, dau. Thomas Dalby, 21 Jan. (not
    dated - Bundle marked "1772)
Burton, John & Ann Simkins, 20 Feb. 1800, Coventon Simkins sec.
? Burton, Peter & Betsy Drighouse, dau. Nathan Drighouse, 13 Oct.
    1829, Nathan Drighouse sec.
Burton, Thomas & Maria Parvin, 3 June 1818, Zacheus Parvin sec.
Burton, William, Jr. & Elizabeth Eyre, 25 Dec. 1721, George
    Harmanson & Zerrubbable Preeson sec.

Nathaniel Burgess, of Norfolk County, & Anne Goffigon, dau. Peter

Goffigon, dec., 14 Jan. 1772, John Nottingham sec.

Burris(Borrows,Burras), Nathaniel & Frances Goffigon, 13 Jan. 1817,
    John Goffigon sec.
Burris, Nathaniel & Mary Ann Scott, wid. Benjamin N. Scott, 5 Jan.
    1835, Nathaniel L. Goffigon sec.
*Burris, Nathaniel G,Mary Ann Powell, ward of Daniel Fitchett, 3
    Nov. 1851

Burras(Borrows,Burris), Anthony & Mary Robert Bell, wid. Robert Bell,
    12 Feb. 1790, Thomas Jarvis sec.

Butler, Thomas & Frances Costin, 19 Feb. 1778, Abraham Costin sec.

Byrd (Bird), William & Polly Richardson, 12 Nov. 1821, Thomas
    Meholloms sec.

Cable, Thomas & Sorrowful Margaret Kendall, 25 May 1723, Gawton
    Hunt & Edward Carter sec.

Campbell, Nicholas & Ann Pigot, dau. Salem Pigot dec. 21 Dec. 1779,
    John Dolby sec.
Campbell, Simon & Joannah Roberts, 10 May 1736, George Holt sec.
Campbell, William J. & Mary A.H.Brittingham, dau. Elijah Brittingham,
    26 Mar. 1828, Elijah Brittingham sec.
Campbell, William J., widower, & Elizabeth W. Young, spinster, dau.
    John Young, dec., 24 Aug. 1840, William W. Cutler sec.
*Campbell, William T. & Eleanore S. Floyd, dau. Lavenia A. Floyd,
    27 Feb. 1851

Caple, John & Ann Phabin, dau. Paul Phabin, dec., 20 Dec. 1788,
    William Phaben sec.
Caple, William & Anne Luke (not dated - Bundle marked 1786-7)
    John Roberts sec.
Caple, William & Esther Odear, 14 Aug. 1787, John Graves sec.
    Con. of Major Caple father of William, & of William Odear
    father of Esther.

Carvey, Richard & Sarah Walter, 1 Oct. 1722, John West &
    Sorrowfull Margaret Kendall sec.

? Carter, Benj: & Betsey Drighouse, his ward, 26 Nov. 1823, Charles
    Pool sec.
Carter, Edward & Mary Mapp, 12 Jan. 1725, Esther Mapp & John Mapp sec.
Carter, James, Jr. & Adah Collins, Jr. 12 Oct. 1818, Jacob Wooser sec.
?Carter, Major & Juliet Ann Scisco, 20 Dec. 1824, Peter Thompson sec.
? Carter, Thomas & Sophia Jeffries, 7 Dec. 1803, Peter Toyar sec.

Cary, Obed & Esther Nottingham, 16 Dec. 1783, Seth Powell sec.
Cary, William & Esther Matthews, 8 Mar. 1768, Arthur Simpkins sec.

Carpenter, Aden & Elizabeth Dunton, 23 Jan. 1849, William T.Nottingham
    sec. Con. of Rickarts Dunton, father of Elizabeth.
Carpenter, Charles, Jr. & Elizabeth Matthews, dau. John Custis
    Matthews, 15 Apr. 1758, John Custis Matthews sec.
Carpenter, Charles & Bridget Matthews, 8 Nov. 1768, Hezekiah Brick-
    house sec.
Carpenter, Charles & Susanna Waltham, 18 Sept. 1782, John Carpenter
    sec.
Carpenter, James & Miss Nelly Fletcher, 15 Dec. 1824, Shepherd B.
    Floyd sec. Con. of James Fletcher, father of Nelly
Carpenter, James S. & Anne Dennis, dau. Archibald Dennis, 11 Oct.
    1834, James Isdell sec.
Carpenter, James S. & Adeline Bool, wid. Michael Bool, 22 Nov. 1843,
    Michael Dennis sec.
Carpenter, John & Lucy Gault, dau. Dicky Gault, 22 Sept. 1787,
    William Jacob sec.
Carpenter, John & Adah Floyd, 14 Nov. 1796, William Roberts,Jr. sec.
    Con. of Matthew Floyd as to Adah.
Carpenter, John, Jr. & Fanny Scott, 11 Mar. 1799, John Carpenter,Sr.
    sec. Con. of John Scott, father of Fanny.
Carpenter, John & Peggy Floyd, 10 Apr. 1809, John Floyd sec.
Carpenter, John B. & Mary Harrison, 1 Jan. 1830, James S. Carpenter
    sec. Con. of Abel Harrison, Hog Island, father of Mary.
Carpenter, John B. & Sally Fletcher, dau. William Fletcher, 18 Jan.
    1849, James S. Carpenter sec.
*Carpenter, James B. & Mary Martin, 2 Dec. 1852
Carpenter, James C. & Eliza Clay, ward of Peter Williams, Jr., 12
    June 1826, Peter Williams, Jr. sec.
*Carpenter, John P. & Mary Harrison, 12 Sept. 1853
*Carpenter, Lewis & Ann Ward, dau. Susan Ward, 18 Nov. 1851
Carpenter, Samuel G. & Elizabeth W. Wilson, ward of Sally J.Nelson,
    9 Jan. 1826, William Goffigon sec.
Carpenter, William & Tabitha Goffigon, dau. Peter Goffigon, 28
    May 1781, Michael Dunton sec.

Carmine, Elijah & Camilla White, 28 June 1798, John White sec.
Carmine, James & Elishe Trower, 14 May 1808, Henry Fitchew sec.
Carmine, John & Polly Abdill, 25 May 1801, John Nottingham,Sr. sec.
Carmine, William & Nancy Belote, 13 Mar. 1797, Ezra Bradford sec.
Carmine, William & Elizabeth Abdell, 30 Dec. 1826, George C.
    Wescoat sec.
Carmine, William T. & Lavenia Rayfield, dau. Harrison T. Rayfield,
    dec., 8 Jan. 1845, Joshua G. Stewart sec.

Casey, John & Ann Willis, 8 Jan. 1820, Marriott Willis sec.
*Casey, John T. & Malinda Odear, dau. William Odear, dec. 25 Nov.
    1850

Charnock(Charnick), Abel & Peggy Collins, 14 Mar. 1803, Emanuel
    Hozier sec.
Charnock, Eli & Jenny Dennis, 12 May 1817, John Ross sec.
Charnock, George & Margaret S. Bonewell, dau. John K. Bonewell

31 Mar. 1834, Thomas J. Bonewell sec.

Charnock, James & Sally Robinson, 16 Jan. 1832, Samuel Watson sec.

Charnock, John T. & Harriet Williams, dau. Peter Williams, dec. 11 Jan. 1845, Benjamin Nottingham sec.

Charnock, John T. & Leah Spady, wid. John Spady(of John),dec., 19 Jan. 1850, Major Richardson sec.

Charnick(Charnock), John & Polly Roberts, 23 Dec. 1833, John Speakman sec.

Charnick, John & Fanny Rippin, dau. Thomas Speakman,dec., 27 Dec. 1837, James Willis sec.

Charnick, William H. & Mary P. Ames, dau. William Clark, 22 Jan. 1848, Covington Bennett sec.

Chandler, Lucius Henry & Susan Ann Kendall, 9 Dec. 1833, John Goffigon, Sr. sec.

?Christian, James & Charlotte Bingham, 18 Sept. 1810, Benjamin Gardner sec.

Christian, Michael & Patience Michael, 30 Dec. 1747, George Holt sec. Con. of Joachim Michael, father of Patience.

Christian, Michael & Elizabeth Barlow, 20 Feb. 1770, Robert Polk sec.

Christian, William & Matildah Johnson, dau. Kelly Johnson, dec. 6 Jan. 1764, Obadiah Johnson sec. Con. of Butifiler Johnson, mother of Matildah.

Christian, William S., ward of Miers W. Fisher & W. B. Upshur, & Susan Wilkins, dau. George F. Wilkins, 11 June, 1845, William B. Upshur & George F. Wilkins sec.

Christian, William & Kasiah Blair, 7 June, 1750, John Flood sec.

Church, Peter & Eliza Collins, dau. Ritta Collins, Free Negroes, 24 Dec. 1828, George Upshur sec.

Church, Solomon & Arinthia Stevens, Free Negroes, 15 Jan. 1850, Tully R. Wise sec. Con. of Letty Samson, mother of Arinthia.

Church, Littleton & Louisa Thompson, Free Negroes, 20 July 1826, William Stephens sec.

Churn, Severn & Tamar Mehollams, Born 2 Jan. 1770, 13 Jan. 1791, Archibald Dowty sec.

Churn, Thomas & Catharine Fletcher, dau. William Fletcher dec. 13 Dec. 1830, Thomas W. Badger sec.

Churn, William, ward of George C. Wescoat, & Dunarara Roberts, ward of Joshua K. Roberts, 19 Jan. 1826, Joshua K. Roberts & Geo. C. Wescoat sec.

Churn, William W, & Sally Powell, wid. of James Powell, 11 Jan.1831, William Churn sec.

Churn, George E., son of Thomas Churn,dec., & Rosey Scott, dau. of Ann Carpenter, dec. 30 Dec. 1849, James Dennis sec.

Clay, Jacob & Elizabeth Hickman, 20 Aug. 1816, Thomas Powell sec. Certificate from Bowdoin Abdell that Elizabeth Hickman is 21 years of age.

Clay, Thomas & Sally Freshwater, 2 Nov. 1796, Peter Bowdoin sec. Con. of William Freshwater, father of Sally.

Clay, William & Nancy Fitchett, dau. Joshua Fitchett, dec. 8 Jan. 1782, John Wheeler, Jr. sec.

Clark, Thomas & Elizabeth Warren, 23 Mar. 1787, William Godwin sec.
Clark, Thomas & Adah Ward, 8 Dec. 1806, James Ward sec.
Clark, William & Polly Parker, 28 Sept. 1810, Keley Stott sec. Con. of Hezekiah Pitts, Gdn. of Polly.

Clegg, Hillery & Mary Elligood, 14 Dec. 1786, John Tyson sec.
Clegg, Hillary & Peggy Knight, dau. William Knight, dec. 29 Nov. 1788, Westerhouse Widgeon sec.
Clegg, Isaac & Anne Belote, wid. 8 May 1764, Benjamin Dixon sec.
Clegg, Isaac & Peggy Major, dau. William Major, 25 Feb. 1756, Patrick Harmanson sec.
Clegg, Isaac & Esther Jacob, wid. 17 June 1763, John Waterfield sec.
Clegg, Isaac & Agnes Piper, 2 Dec. 1783, John Dalby sec. Con. of Josiah Piper, father of Agnes.
Clegg, James E. & Elizabeth W. Mears, dau. William Mears, 30 Oct. 1843, William Mears sec.
Clegg, Major & Nancy Mehollams, 18 Jan. 1800, Johannes Johnson sec.
Clegg, Major & Patience Benthall, 9 Oct. 1794, Peter Clegg sec.
Clegg, Peter & Rosanna Milby, 2 July 1784, Thomas Waterfield sec. Con. of Coventon Simkins as to Peter.
Clegg, Peter M. & Lovely Watson, 31 July 1810, John S. Heath sec. Con. of Edmund Watson, father of Lovely.
Clegg, Robert & _____ Scott, wid. William Scott, 21 Dec. 1784, Arthur Evans sec.
Clegg, Robert & Polly Bloxom, 24 Dec. 1798, Stuart Saunders sec.
Clegg, William & Susanna Dixon, dau. John Dixon, 20 Nov. 1779, John Widgeon, Sr. sec.
Clegg, William & Elizabeth Spady Speakman, dau. William Speakman, 23 Dec. 1845, William Speakman sec.

Clowes, Peter & Margaret F. Mears, dau. Richard Mears, dec. 13 Dec. 1830, Thomas P. Wise sec.

Cobb, Arthur & Peggy Edmunds, 1 Dec. 1803, Dickie Dunton sec.
Cobb, Nathan F. & Esther Fletcher, wid. Charles Fletcher, 13 Sept. 1842, William W. Andrews sec.
Cobb, Nathan F., Jr. & Sally Dowty, ward of John H. Powell, 2 Dec. 1848, John W. Dowty sec.
Cobb, Southy & Anne Pratt, 29 Aug. 1787, William Rippin sec.
Cobb, William H. & Betsey Peake, 17 Jan. 1822, John Bull sec. Con. of Southy Cobb, father of William H.

Coleburn, John F. & Eliza C. Williams, dau. Peter Williams, 14 Feb. 1848, Peter Williams sec.
Coleburn, Thomas A. & Maria S. Holland, dau. Nathaniel Holland, 20 Mar. 1834, Nathaniel Holland sec.
Coleburn, Richard & Peggy Boole, 20 Dec. 1796, William Aimes sec.

**Coldy, Robert & Mary Gale, 1 Dec. 1821

Colonna, Michael & Elizabeth A. Evans, dau. Lucinda Evans, 16 Aug.
    1848, Samuel H. Parsons sec.
Colona, William P. & Miss Sarah D. Pitts, 27 Feb. 1826, George C.
    Wescoat sec.

*Collins, Caleb & Sabra Stephens, dau. Adah Stephens, Free Negroes,
    9 June 1851
*Collins, Jacob, son of Margaret Collins & Susan Weicks, dau. Jenny
    Weicks, now Jenny Collins, Free Negroes, 3 Sept. 1851
? Collins, James & Betsey Stevens, 23 Dec. 1822, Jacob Collins sec.
    Con. of Littleton Collins, father of Betsy.
Collins, James & Eliza Wilkerson, 22 May 1837, James Wilkins sec.
*Collins, James & Margaret Weicks, Free Negroes, 27 Dec. 1351
Collins, John & Anne Clegg, 21 Nov. 1786, Hillary Clegg sec.
?Collins, John & Nanny Sabers, 11 Aug. 1790, Peter Warren sec.
Collins, John & Grace Costin, 12 Sept. 1796, John Tyson sec.
?Collins, John & Betsey Jeffries, 3 Feb. 1803, Samuel Beavans sec.
Collins, John & Nancy Pratt, 7 Oct. 1813, Nathaniel Bishop sec.
? Collins, John & Comfort Beavans, 19 Feb. 1823, Mac Collins sec.
Collins, John & Jenny Brickhouse, dau. Esther Brickhouse, Free
    Negroes, 29 Dec. 1830, William Stevens sec.
Collins, John & Adah Bevans, Free Negroes, 30 Oct. 1830, Nath'l.
    J. Winder sec.
Collins, John & Mary Juliet Scott, dau. John Scott, dec., 4 June
    1834, Obediah Scott sec. Con. of Sally Scott, mother of
    Mary Juliet.
*Collins, John & Mary Jane Upshur, Free Negroes, 6 Mar. 1851
Collins, Joseph & Betsey Anderson, 31 Jan. 1799, John Collins sec.
Collins, Leonard & Emeline Howell, dau. Mary Howell, Free Negroes,
    17 Feb. 1841, Mary Howell sec.
? Collins, Lighty & Lear Drighouse, 3 Jan. 1795, Thomas Lewis sec.
? Collins, Mac & Betsey Shepherd, 27 Nov. 1809, Abraham Lang sec.
?Collins, Nathaniel & Salley Stockley, 6 Oct. 1807, Anthony Bell
    sec.
? Collins, Nathaniel & Molly Sample, 16 Aug. 1810, Isaiah Carter
    sec.
Collins, Nathaniel & Molly Widgeon, 24 Mar. 1812, Westerhouse
    Widgeon sec.
Collins, Nathaniel & Margaret Collins, Free Negroes, 5 Dec. 1849,
    Frederick Moses sec.
?Collins, Patrick & Sukey Becket, 14 Nov. 1807, William Drigus sec.
?Collins, Patrick & Comfort Francis, dau. William Francis, Jr.,
    26 Dec. 1829, Jacob Collins(long Jake) & William Francis,Jr.
    sec.
? Collins, Ralph & Tamar Bingham, 20 Dec. 1799, John Simkins sec.
? Collins, Severn (also Severn Weeks) & Nancy Beavans, dau. John
    Beavans, 25 Mar. 1823, Mac Collins & John Beavans sec.
*Collins, Severn, son of Eliza, & Margaret Collins., dau. Jenny,
    Free Negroes, 8 Aug. 1850
Collins, Victor & Ann Maria Read, Free Negroes, 21 Dec. 1839,
    Smith S. Nottingham sec.
Collins, William & Susan Parsons, ward of Thomas Hallet, 14 May
    1827, Thomas Hallet sec.

? Collins, William & Betsy Thompson, wid. William Thompson, 11 June
   1838, John S. Brickhouse sec.

Comer, Michael & Margaret Griffeth, 3 Jan. 1778, William Rippin sec.

Commines, William & Peggy Wilson, 4 Jan. 1803, John Commines sec.
   Con. of Ann Wilson, mother of Peggy.
Comines, William & Elizabeth Garrett, 13 Sept. 1813, Harrison
   Nottingham sec.

Cook, Giles, of the County of Gloucester, & Margaret Savage, dau.
   Esther Savage, 3 Oct. 1750, William Tazewell, Jr. sec.
Cook, John & Molly Graves, 9 Dec. 1799, Robertson Custis sec.

Coopeland, William & (no name)   19 Sept. 1721, Thomas Savage,
   Sr. & Thomas Savage, Jr. sec.

*Copes, James S. & Margaret S. Saunders, dau. Samuel Saunders, 1
   Nov. 1852
Copes, Leonard B. & Elizabeth Bell, 22 Nov. 1848, Lafayette
   Harmanson sec. Con. of Polly Bell, mother of Elizabeth.
Copes, Thomas & Jenney Luke, 12 Mar. 1804, Zachariah Wise sec.
Copes, Thomas & Fanny Warren, 6 Jan. 1815, John Upshur, Jr. sec.
Copes, Thomas & Sally Saunders, 21 Jan. 1817, James Floyd sec.
Copes, Thomas, Sr. & Damia Hickman, 17 May 1817, William G. Pitts
   sec.

Core, Caleb & Sarah Parramore, 27 Sept. 1793, Kendall Belote sec.
Core, Caleb & Susey Hickman, 28 Aug. 1806, Richard Dunton sec.
Core, Charles & Betty Dolby, 12 Jan. 1768, Edmund Core sec.
Core, Edmund & Sarah Garris, dau. Thomas Garris, 15 Dec. 1760,
   John Downing sec.
Core, Eleazer & Keziah Rodgers, 15 Jan. 1783, Stuart Holt sec.
Core, John & Susanna Baker, 20 Dec. 1785, William Wilkins, Sr.
   sec.
Core, Posthumos & Susanna Henderson, 12 Mar. 1750, Jacob Henderson
   sec.
Core, William H. & Margaret Wheeler, dau. Thomas A. Wheeler, 10
   Dec. 1832, Thomas A. Wheeler sec.

Costin, Abraham, Jr. & Peggy Costin, 21 July 1798, Francis Costin
   sec.   Con. of Francis Costin, father of Peggy.
Costin, Abraham & Mary Goffigon, 7 Jan. 1806, Thomas Nottingham
   sec.
Costin, Coventon & Mary Taylor, ward of Thomas S. Evans, 8 Jan.
   1827, Thomas S. Evans sec.
Costin, Elijah & Charlott Trower, 6 Oct. 1817, Laurance Enholm
   sec.
Costin, Elijah & Rosy S. Spady, wid. Southy Spady, 30 Oct. 1830,
   Silas Jefferson sec.
Costin, Francis & Susanna Elliot, dau. Thomas Elliot, 7 Dec.
   1764, Thomas Elliot sec.
Costin, Francis & Mary Pratt, 9 Oct. 1820, Thomas Moore sec.

Costin, **Henry** & Rachel Saunders, dau. James Saunders, dec., 14 Feb. 1782, Stuart Saunders & Eligood Ayres, sec. Con. of Tabitha Saunders, mother of Rachel.

Costin, **Henry** & Margaret Dennis, 20 May 1817, Abram Costin sec.

Costin, Isaac & Nancy Nottingham, 1 Jan. 1819, John Evans sec. Con. of William Nottingham, father of Nancy.

Costin, Jacob & Sophia Savage, 1 Feb. 1733, James Forse sec.

Costin, James H. & Margaret Spady, dau. Southy Spady, 10 Mar. 1828, Silas Jefferson sec.

Costin, John & Elizabeth Fitchett, 6 Aug. 1793, Henry Giddens sec. Con. of Joshua Fitchett, father of Elizabeth.

Costin, John & Nancy Evans, 5 Sept. 1800, John Evans sec.

Costin, John & Louisa Griffin, 10 Dec. 1810, Patrick Warren sec. Con. of B. Griffith as to Louisa.

Costin, John & Maria Ellis, 23 July 1821, William Dixon, Sr. sec.

Costin, Matthew & Mary Joynes, wid. 24 Nov. 1891, William Satchell, Jr. sec.

Costin, Patrick F. & Anne Nottingham, ward of James Saunders, 9 Dec. 1822, James Saunders sec.

Costin, Samuel & Elizabeth Griffith, 13 Dec. 1785, Thomas Widgeon sec.

Costin, Samuel & Polly Roberts, 19 Jan. 1796, Parker Willis sec.

*Costin, Samuel & Mary T. Whitehead, dau. Thomas Whitehead, 10 Mar. 1851

Costin, Seth & Pricilla Elliott, dau. Jeremiah Elliott, 16 Dec. 1839, James Hampleton sec.

Costin, Stephen & Peggy Kellam, 12 June 1838, Victor A. Nottingham sec.

Costin, William & Anne Trower, dau. Robert Trower, dec., 23 Mar. 1773, William Trower sec. Con. of Matthew Costin, father of William.

Costin, William & Lucretia Dixon, 12 Jan. 1791, Griffin Stith sec. Con. of Elizabeth Dixon.

Costin, William, Jr. & Elizabeth Thurstin, 6 Aug. 1811, Peter Williams sec.

Costin, William G. & Elizabeth S. Brickhouse, dau. Smith Brickhouse, dec. 18 Dec. 1833, John N. Brickhouse sec.

Costin, William G. & Ann S. Dalby, dau. Hezekiah Dalby, 25 Nov. 1837, Hezekiah Dalby sec.

Costin, William T. & Nancy Roberts, dau. Thomas Roberts, Sr., 21 Nov. 1838, Thomas S. Brickhouse sec.

Cottingham, Elisha D. & Harriet S. Nicholson, wid. Levin H. Nicholson, 16 Apr. 1844, Sylvester Kelly sec.

Cottingham, Henry & Miss Elizabeth G. Smith, 3 Dec. 1824, Elijah Brittingham sec.

Cottingham, Henry & Elizabeth Wilkins, dau. Benjamin Wilkins, dec. 5 Dec. 1827, William B. Nottingham sec.

*Cottingham, William H., son of Henry Cottingham, & Mary Ann Casey, dau. John Casey, dec. 9 June 1851

Cotral(Cottrel,Cottrell), James & Elizabeth Stephens, dau. Susan, Free Negroes, 26 Jan. 1848, Jesse N. Jarvis & Elizabeth

Stephens sec.

?Cottrel, John & Betsey Fletcher, 22 May 1810, Thomas Fletcher sec.
Cottrell, John S. & Elizabeth Carpenter, dau. John Carpenter,Sr.,
    1 Jan. 1849, James Dennis sec.

Cowdry, Savage & Mary Barlow, 15 June 1758, Thomas White sec.
    Con. of Rev. Henry Barlow.
Cowdry, Thomas & Sarah Jacob, dau. Esau Jacob, 11 Nov. 1769,
    Edmund Glanville sec.

Cowles, John & Rachel Stephens, 1 Mar. 1787, William Stith sec.

Cox, Moses, of the County of Norfolk, & Jeaca Mills, 24 Mar. 1749,
    Con. of William Mills, father of Jeaca.
**Cox, Samuel & Susanna Beloat _____ 1798
Cox, Samuel & Nancy Whitehead, 14 Nov. 1820, Charles Bonwell sec.

Craik, John & Rosey Cutler, 9 Jan. 1804, William Parkinson sec.

Craig, William A., ward of Thomas E. Addison & Ann W. Gunter, ward
    of Stephen S. Gunter, 12 Apr. 1824, Thomas E. Addison &
    Stephen S. Gunter sec.

Croswell, William & Elishe Stripe, 25 Nov. 1786, Nath'l.Eshon sec.

Cullin, Samuel & Polly Rippin, 10 Apr. 1792, Southy Cobb sec.

Culpepper, Jesse & Edith S. Brickhouse, ward of Elam L. Brickhouse,
    10 Sept. 1838, Elam L. Brickhouse sec.

Custis, Henry, of Accomack, & Betty Downing, dau. Arthur Downing,
    dec. 29 Aug. 1763, John Downing, Jr. sec.
Custis, John & Anne Kendall, 3 Mar. 1732, Thomas Cable sec.
Custis, John W. & Miss Margaret W. Addison, 5 July 1826, John R.
    Wise sec. Con. of J. Addison, father of Margaret.
Custis, Robinson & Mary Savage, 6 Aug. 1793, Thomas Dunton sec.
Custis, Thomas, of Accomack, & Anne Kendall, 24 June, 1717, Sarah
    Custis, of Northampton, sec.
Custis, Dr. Thomas V. & Peggy Dixon, 2 July 1803, Coventon
    Simkins sec. Con. of Samuel W. Brown & wife "our daughter
    Peggy Dixon".
Custis, Thomas & Ann Parsons, 21 May 1808, William White sec.
Custis, Thomas O. & Betsy Powell, wid. Jesse Powell, 11 May 1846,
    William G. Johnson sec.
Custis, William & Elizabeth Willet, 20 Dec. 1803, Robinson Custis
    sec.
Custis, William S. & Eleanor D. Wise, 13 Dec. 1832, Samuel L.
    Floyd sec. Con. of John Addison, Gdn. of Eleanor.

Cutler, Peter & Rosey Finney, 1 Sept. 1818, James Johnson sec.
Cutler, Richard & Margaret Dann, 21 Feb. 1819, John Adams sec.
Cutler, Rich: & Delitha A. Wilkins, 30 Apr. 1831, John Wilkins,
    Jr. sec. Con. of Delitha Wilkins, Gdn. of Delitha A.

Dalby(Dolby),Benjamin & Mary Core, 19 July 1786, William Dalby sec.

Dalby, Benjamin & Sarah Bull, 17 Dec. 1789, John Satchell sec.

Balby, Benjamin J. & Mary Ann Kendall, dau. Dr. John Kendall, dec.,
     17 June, 1830, William J. Campbell sec.

*Dalby, Branson W. & Margaret Ann Hall, dau. Thomas Hall, dec., 18
     Mar. 1852

Dalby, Henry & Susanna Sturgis, 9 May, 1787, John Darby sec.

Dalby, Hezekiah & Nancy Nottingham, 20 Dec. 1815, Samuel Collins
     sec. Con. of Richard Nottingham, father of Nancy.

Dalby, James & Betsey Griffin, 3 Aug. 1805, Dickie Dunton sec.

Dalby, James B. & Elizabeth Leatherbury, wid. James M. Leatherbury,
     28 Oct. 1845, William T. Nottingham sec.

Dalby, James & Catharine Mears, dau. John Mears, dec. 9 Dec. 1845,
     James Dennis sec.

Dalby, John & Leah Dunton, 1 Jan. 1789, Michael Dunton sec.

Dalby, John & Abigail Bell, 10 Nov. 1789, William Roberts sec.

Dalby, John, Jr. & Elizabeth Barlow, wid. Thomas Barlow, 2 Mar. 1790,
     John Dalby sec.

Dalby, Littleton & Bridget Fisher, 28 Aug. 1794, Stewart Pettit sec.

Dalby, Nathaniel & Miss Nancy Wilkins, 14 Oct. 1824, George F.
     Outten sec.

Dalby, Samuel & Peggy Watch(Walch?) 9 June 1814, Timothy Austin sec.

Dalby, Severn & Sukey Spady, wid. William Spady, 2 Aug. 1821, Thomas
     Dalby sec.

Dalby, Spencer & Nancy Watson, dau. Littleton Watson, 4 Apr. 1780,
     Levin Parkerson sec.   S.

Dalby, Thomas & Delitha Bunting, 27 Dec. 1837, James/Carpenter sec.

Dalby, Thomas & Mary Robinson, wid. William Robinson, 23 Dec. 1846,
     James Dennis sec.

Dalby, Thomas,Esq. & Catharine Harmanson, dau. John Harmanson, 8
     Oct. 1789, William Stith sec.

Dalby, William & Sarah Eshon, 12 Feb. 1785, Obed Cary sec.

Dalby, William & Martha Bool, wid. Nicholas Bool, 29 Aug. 1788,
     William Bloxom sec.

Dalby, William & Susanna Kendall, 26 Dec. 1805, Major Andrews sec.
     Con. of George Boggs as to William Dalby.

Dalby, William L. & Sarah S. Ames, wid. Shadrack T. Ames, 14 Aug.
     1847, James B. Dalby sec.

Dann, Samuel & Mrs Naomi Wheeler, 10 Dec. 1838, William H.
     Wescoat sec.

Dan, Silas & Mary Sherwood, 10 July 1802, Michael Savage sec.

Darby, John & Esther Harmanson, dau. John Harmanson, Sr., 31 Dec.
     1777, William Harmanson sec.

Darby, John & Esther Christian, 14 May 1782, Griffin Stith,Jr.sec.

Darby, Walter W. & Juliet Robins, dau. Thomas Robins,Sr. dec. 2
     Aug. 1837, George Gray sec.

Dashiel, George & Elizabeth Fairfax, 10 Sept. 1740, Thomas Preeson
     sec.

Dashiell, George & Rose Fisher, dau. Maddox Fisher, dec. 12 Aug.
     1760, Thomas Dolby sec.

Davis, Levin & Susanna Westerhouse, 31 Dec. 1778, George Bonewell sec.
Davis, Robert & Sarah Andrews, 4 Aug. 1786, William Waterfield sec.
     Con. of Andrew Andrews, father of Sarah.

Davidson, Edward & Jenney McMeth, 23 May 1801, John Wescoat,Jr.sec.

Dawson, Thomas & Louisa Costin, 7 May 1816, William Jarvis,Jr. sec.

Dell, Thomas & Mary Reeve, 30 Nov. 1723, Peter Rasco & Henry
     Speakman sec.

Delpeach, James & Peggy Sampson, wid. 29 Sept. 1743, John Marshall
     sec.
Delastatious(Dillastions), Ezekiel & Frances Smith, ward of Silas
     Jefferson, 12 Mar. 1823, Silas Jefferson sec.

Dennis, Archibald & Sally Dennis, 13 Oct. 1804, John S. Scott sec.
Dennis, Archibald & Betsey Dennis, 29 Sept. 1810, Arthur Cobb sec.
Dennis, Archibald & Lucy Poulson, 21 Jan. 1812, John Wheelor sec.
Dennis, Archibald & Leah Window, 4 May 1813, Samuel Dalby sec.
Dennis, Archibald & Rachel Benson, wid. Edmund Benson, 3 July 1838,
     Montcalm Oldham sec.
Dennis, James & Nancy Isdell, dau. James Isdell, 23 Dec. 1864,
     James Dalby sec.
Dennis, John & Susanna Widgeon, wid. Levin Widgeon, 15 Dec. 1786,
     Robert Greenaway sec.
Dennis, Joseph & Livinia Birch, 24 Apr. 1788, Thomas Griffith sec.
Dennis, Laban & Jenney Bunting, 14 Jan. 1811, Archibald Dennis sec.
Dennis, Littleton & Elizabeth Upshur, dau. John Upshur, Gent., 3
     Dec. 1788, James Upshur sec.
Dennis, Major & Mary Robins, 3 Aug. 1802, Hezekiah Dennis sec.
Dennis, Major & Nancy Nottingham, 1 May 1805, Johannes Johnson sec.
     Con. of Ann Nottingham, mother and Gdn. of Nancy.
Dennis, Michael & Molly Jackson, 12 Jan. 1788, David James sec.
Dennis, Michael & Ansley James, 28 Feb. 1805, John Nottingham sec.
Dennis, Michael & Mary Dennis, dau. Archibald Dennis, 28 Dec. 1829,
     Archibald Dennis sec.
Dennis, Teackle & Polly Hale, 20 Jan. 1791, John Dalby sec.
Dennis, William & Susanna Whitehead, dau. John Whitehead, dec.
     29 Sept. 1791, Jacob Moor sec.
Dennis, William & Ann Caple, 8 Jan. 1800, William Wingate sec.
Dennis, William & Betsey Spady, 13 Nov. 1826, Shepherd Abdill sec.

Denwood, Levin, of the Province of Maryland, & Isbell Stringer, 12
     Mar. 1744, John Kendall sec. Con. of Littleton Eyre as to
     Isbell.

Dickerson, Peter & Mary Waterfield, wid. 20 Apr. 1774, Walter
     Hyslop sec.
Dickerson, Samuel & Adah Heath, 24 Feb. 1802, George Heath sec.

Dillon, Charles & Lucy Moore, 17 June 1802, Charles Fitchett sec.

Dillon, Charles & Elizabeth Stripe, 22 Mar. 1806, David Eshon sec.
Dillon, Thomas & Bridget Widgeon, 3 Dec. 1803, Charles Dillon sec.
Dillon, William & Nancy Fisher, 4 June 1798, Arthur Roberts sec.

**Dillastions(Delastations),Thomas & Elizabeth Trower,14 Sept.1848

Dix, Isaac & Ann Jacob, dau. John Jacob, 12 Jan. 1830, George F.
     Outten sec.
Dix, William A., son of Levin Dix, & Elizabeth S. Scott, dau.
     William W. Scott, 1 May 1838, William W. Scott sec.

Dixon, Benjamin & Elizabeth Nelson, 5 May 1776, Thomas Widgeon sec.
Dixon, Benjamin & Fanny Fletcher, 13 Jan. 1806, George Abdell sec.
Dixon, Christopher & Sabra Simkins, 22 Sept. 1783, William Simkins
     sec.
Dixon, Christopher & Jenney S. Trower, 12 Sept. 1803, William
     Knight sec. Con. of John Elliott, Gdn. of Jenney, dau. of
     Elizabeth.
Dixon, John & Bridget Thomas, 11 Sept. 1781, Isaac Bell sec.
     Con. of John Thomas, father of Bridget.
Dixon, John & Lucretia Costin, 2 Aug. 1786, Abraham Costin sec.
Dixon, John & Nelly Costin, 18 July 1791, Jacob Moor sec. Con.
     of Abraham Costin, father of Nelly.
Dixon, John W. & Molly Lewis, 13 May 1811, William Nottingham,Jr.
     sec. Con. of Margaretta Lewis, mother of Molly.
Dixon, Thomas & Elizabeth Holmes, wid. 17 Aug. 1790, Azariah
     Williams sec.
Dixon, Thomas & Betsey Smith, dau. Richard Smith, Sr., 23 June
     1791, Thomas Smith sec.
Dixon, Thomas & Anne Nottingham, 7 Mar. 1793, Levin Nottingham
     sec.
Dixon, William & Esther Kendall, 29 Dec. 1784, Teackle Jacob sec.
Dixon, William & Betty Dunton, wid. Jacob Dunton, 14 Mar. 1787,
     James Powell sec.
Dixon, William & Ann D. Garrison, 2 June 1807, Jeptha Johnson sec.
     Con. of Sarah Savage, mother of Ann D. Garrison.
Dixon, William & Sukey Costin, 10 Oct. 1808, William Costin sec.
Dixon, William W. & Mary P. Fitchett, 16 July 1831, John Barnard
     sec. Con. of Martha Fitchett, mother & Gdn. of Mary P.
*Dixon, William W. & Gracy Bishop, wid. John Bishop, 16 June,
     1851

Dolby(Dalby),Benjamin & Anne Ra_____:___Feb. 1705/6,
     Richard Smith sec.
Dolby, Henry & Rachel Andrews, 7 Nov. 1772, William Waltham sec.
Dolby, Isaac & Peggy Matthews, 14 Aug. 1759, John Dolby,Jr. sec.
     Con. of John Custis Matthews, father of Peggy.
Dolby, Isaac & Catharine Dolby, 25 May 1798,Matthew Harmanson sec.
Dolby, James & Anne Griffith, 16 Nov. 1789, William Dalby sec.
Dolby, James & Ann Elizabeth Williams, 30 Nov. 1848, John E.
     Winder sec.
Dolby, John & Susanna Jacob, dau. Isaac Jacob, 25 Feb. 1769,
     John Burton sec. Con. of Robert C. Jacob.

Dolby, John & Keziah Westerhouse, 10 Oct. 1769, Edmund Glanville sec.
Dolby, Joseph & Jane Luke, wid., 19 May 1764, John Dolby sec.
Dolby, Thomas, Jr. & Margaret Haze, 19 Aug. 1772, Joseph Dolby sec.
    Con. of Thomas Dolby, Gdn. of Margaret Haze.
Dolby, Thomas & Pricilla Rogers, 8 June 1795, William Roberts,Jr. sec.

Donnell, John, of Baltimore, & Anna Teackle Smith, 10 Oct. 1798,
    Isaac Smith sec.   Con. of Isaac Smith, father of Anna T.

Dorman, William & Peggy Dunton, 24 Nov. 1795, Thomas Hall sec.

Dorsey, Hill, of Anne Arundel County, Md., & Elizabeth B. Jacob, 13
    Oct. 1812, George Parratt sec. Con. of William H. Dorsey,
    Gdn. of Hill & of John K. Evans, Gdn. of Elizabeth B.

*Doughty(Dowty), Archibald & Mary Ann Kelly, dau. Charles Kelly.
    16 July 1850
Doughty, James C. & Margaret S. Johnson, 12 Dec. 1842, Richard J.
    Ayres sec. Con. of Frances L. Mears, mother of Margaret
    and wife of Thomas C. Mears.
Doughty, William J. & Harriet Cotterel, dau. Capt. John Cotterel,
    dec., 20 Dec. 1841, Major Dowty sec.

Dowty(Doughty),Addison & Tabitha Dalby, 15 July 1778, Hezekiah
    Dalby sec.
Dowty, Addison & Seymour Heath, 13 July 1779,
Dowty, Archibald & Nancy Edmunds, 24 Sept. 1788, Peter Dowty sec.
Dowty, Babel & Betsey Hickman, 6 July 1798, Joseph Hanby sec.
Dowty, Eli & Nancy Floyd, 9 Jan. 1815, Arthur Cobb sec.
Dowty, Elisha & Elishe Jacob, 21 Oct. 1772, Hezekiah Dowty sec.
    Con. of Thomas Jacob, father of Elishe.
Dowty, James & Susanna James, dau. Andrew James, 6 Dec. 1821,
    Andrew James sec.
Dowty, James P., son of James Dowty, & Sarah A. Dunton, dau. Benj.
    F. Dunton, dec. 1 Mar. 1847, James Dowty sec.
Dowty, James, son of Major Dowty, dec. & Mary Rogers, dau. John
    Rogers, dec., 9 Jan. 1850, Edward R. Waddey sec.
Dowty, John & Sally Carpenter, 24 Oct. 1821, Shepherd B. Floyd
    sec.
Dowty, John W. & Susan Smith, dau. Thomas Smith, dec., 22 Dec.
    1845, Southey Rew sec.
*Dowty, John A., son of James Dowty,Sr. & Emily Godwin, wid.
    Griffin Godwin, 27 Aug. 1851
Dowty, Littleton & Susanna Smith, 12 Mar. 1821, George E.
    Christian sec.
Dowty, Major & Adah Andrews, wid. Southy Andrews, 30 June, 1822,
    George Hickman sec.
Dowty, Major, & Elizabeth Mears, dau. John Mears, 30 Jan. 1841,
    Jacob Spady sec.
Dowty, Martin & Sally Dunton, dau. Richard Dunton, 21 July 1845,
    Rickards Dunton & Martin Dowty sec.
Dowty, Michael & Peggy Jones, 21 Dec. 1790, Zerobabel Jones sec.
Dowty, Michael & Ann Dixon, ward of John W. Dixon, 9 Mar. 1824,

John W. Dixon & George F. Wilkins sec.

Dowty, Michael & Ann Nelson, dau. John Nelson,Jr., 30 Sept. 1830, George T. Yerby sec.

Dowty, Peter & Sinah Edmunds, 8 Mar. 1787, Elisha Dowty sec.

Dowty, Rowland,Jr. & Mary Bratten, 8 Dec. 1817, James Dowty sec. Con. of Isaac Bratten, father of Mary.

Dowty, Thomas & Sarah Belote, wid. William Belote, 7 June, 1791, William Satchell, Jr. sec.

Dowty, Thomas & Susanna Turner, 2 Aug. 1797, George Turner sec.

Dowty, Thomas & Susan Clegg, 27 Dec, 1813, Zachariah Wise sec.

Dowty, William & Elizabeth Edmonds, 15 Dec. 1823, Teackle Roberts sec. Con. of Thomas Edmonds, father of Elizabeth.

Downes(Downs),Daniel & Charlotte Costin, 10 Jan. 1825, Christopher Fitchett sec.

Downs, Henry & Maria Costin, wid. John Costin, 17 Nov. 1830, John M. Savage sec.

Downes, Nathaniel, ward of James B. Nottingham, & Dianna Hallett, dau. Thomas Hallett, 11 Nov. 1844

Downs, Thomas & Anne Williams, 7 Feb. 1783, Joseph Warren sec.

Downs, Thomas & Margaret Biggs, 31 Oct. 1809, Southy Goffigon sec.

Downs, Thomas & Elizabeth Nottingham, 5 June 1820, James Goffigon sec.

*Downes, Thomas A. & Arinthia S. Spady, ward of Thomas F. Spady, 9 Dec. 1850

Downs, William & Elizabeth Warren, 27 Dec. 1798, William Wilkins sec.

Downs, William & Esther Warren, 2 Sept. 1809, David Topping sec.

Downes, William & Margaret Rippin, dau. Thomas Rippin,dec., 2 Jan. 1837, Severn Wilkins sec.

Downing, Caleb & Lucy Thompson, dau. Isaac Thompson, 30 June, 1821, Isaac Becket sec.

Downing, Edmund W. P. & Mary Bell, 11 Dec. 1809, James Sanford sec.

Downing, John & Edey Nottingham, 25 Jan. 1791, William Bain sec.

Downing, William & Martha Jacob, dau. Philip Jacob, dec. 14 Jan. 1772, John Wise sec.

? Drighouse, George & Peggy Land, 2 Mar. 1798, Abraham Lang sec.

? Drighouse, Nathan & Elizabeth Bingham, 23 Jan. 1794, Reubin Read sec.

? Drighouse, Nathan & Polly Jeffry, 24 July 1810, Abraham Lang sec.

? Drighouse, William & Ann Bingham, 25 Sept. 1802, Samuel Beavans sec.

Driskeel, Moses & Margaret Joynes, 4 Nov. 1795, John Dalby sec.

*Drummond, James & Emily Bevans, dau. Tom Bevans, Free Negroes, 9 Feb. 1852

Drummond, William & Nanny Dunton, dau. Elias Dunton, Sr., 7 July 1759, John Waterfield sec.

Drummond, William S. & Molly Savage, 7 June, 1809,William Savage sec.

Drysdale, Thomas & Mary Anne Smith, 22 Nov. 1796, William Eyre sec.
Con. of Isaac Smith, father of Mary Anne.

Dunton, Benjamin & Anne Jacob, dau. Hancock Jacob, 15 Sept. 1778,
William Waterfield sec.
Dunton, Benjamin & Sarah Garrison, 3 June 1797, Dickie Dunton sec.
Dunton, Benj: F, & Sally Churn, 27 Mar. 1816, Thos: S.Brickhouse sec.
Dunton, Benjamin & Ann S.Topping, 22 Nov. 1820, Daniel Topping sec.
Dunton, Benjamin & Mary T. S. Tankard, 25 Mar. 1828, George L. E.
Tankard sec. Con. of Dr.John Tankard, father of Mary.
Dunton, Carvey, of Accomack, & Margaret Robins, 20 Nov. 1792,
Arthur Robins sec.
Dunton, Custis M. & Caroline E.Harmanson, 14 Apr. 1845, William P.
Nottingham sec.
Dunton, David A., ward of Thomas B. Williams & Bell Sarah Nottingham,
dau. Jacob Nottingham, dec., 19 May 1845, Edw:P.Roberts sec.
Dunton, Edward M. & Ann S. Stewart, dau. James Stewart, 13 Sept.
1842, Joshua G. Stewart sec.
Dunton, Elias & Esther Waterfield, wid. 6 Oct. 1750, Southy Satchell
sec.
Dunton, Elias & Fanney Nottingham, 25 Nov. 1811, Thomas Nottingham
sec.
Dunton, George & Sally Benston, 25 Oct. 1808, William Andrews sec.
Dunton, George & Margaret Richardson, 11 July 1814, John B.Thomas sec.
Dunton, George W. & Arinthia B. Downing, dau. Dr. Edm^d W. P.
Downing, 19 Dec. 1831, John C. Jacob sec.
Dunton, Hancock & Sally Godwin, 16 Feb. 1802, Charles S.Satchell sec.
Dunton, Isaac & Elizabeth Toleman, 4 Apr. 1785, Obed Cary sec.
Dunton, Isaac & Hannah White, 19 Dec. 1809, William White sec.
Dunton, Jacob & Betty Satchell, dau. Southy Satchell, dec. 24 May
1763, William Satchell sec.
Dunton,James M. & Susan Fitchett, dau. William Fitchett, 2 May
1842, John Y. Johnson sec.
*Dunton,James S. & Mary B. Churn, 24 Oct. 1853
Dunton, John & Sukey Mills, 22 Dec. 1800, William Graves sec.
Dunton, John & Nancy Roberts, 27 Aug. 1816, Teackle Roberts sec.
Dunton, John R. & Emeline Dunton, ward of Alexander W. Ward, 12
Sept. 1831, Alexander W. Ward sec.
Dunton, Levin & Agness Grice, 25 June 1785, William Ward sec.
Dunton, Matthew & Polly N. Brickhouse, 14 Apr. 1807, Thomas Jacob,
Jr. sec. Con. of George Brickhouse as to Polly N.
Dunton, Michael & Rosey Matthews, dau. John Custis Matthews, dec.,
26 May 1779, Con. of Martha Matthews, mother of Rosey.
Dunton, Michael, & Anne Nottingham, wid., 22 Jan. 1780, John
Stratton, Jr. sec.
Dunton, Michael, Jr. & Peggy Griffin, 13 Dec. 1791, Kendal
Belote sec.
Dunton, Michael & Sarah Bell, wid. Thomas Bell, 3 July 1792,
Nathaniel Holland sec.
Dunton, Rickard, Jr. & Sinah Benthall, 20 Oct. 1803, George Ben-
thall sec.
Dunton, Richard T. & Vianna Wescoat, dau. Edmund Wescoat, 2 Jan.
1849, John E. Winder sec.

Dunton, Ricketts & Ann Jacob, wid., 18 Aug. 1722, John Stringer &
Edward Carter sec.

Dunton, Rickards, Jr. & Sophia Harmanson, 7 Sept. 1774, William
Waltham sec.

Dunton, Rickards, Jr. & Rosanna Clegg, 13 Aug. 1796, John Macgowan
sec.

Dunton, Rickards, Jr. & Lucy Carpenter, 5 May 1807, Littleton
Kendall sec.

Dunton, Rickards & Charlotte Harrison, 26 Apr. 1808, Caleb Core sec.

Dunton, Rickards, Jr. & Susan Simkins, 24 Dec. 1817, Henry B.
Kendall sec.

Dunton, Rickards & Harriet Hall, dau. Thomas Hall, 20 Dec. 1827,
Henry B. Kendall sec.

Dunton, Samuel W. & Margaret G. Badger, 5 July 1841, George Bell sec.
Con. of Thomas W. Badger, father of Margaret G.

Dunton, Selby & Elizabeth Kellam, 16 Apr. 1808, Laban Hickman sec.

Dunton, Sevårn & Mary Bryan, 10 Apr. 1792, William Stith sec.

Dunton, Såvern & Sally Dunton, wid. George Dunton, 13 Oct. 1821,
William Richardson sec.

Dunton, Smith L. & Ann A. Ward, dau. Littleton Ward, dec. 3 Mar.
1834, George D. White sec.

Dunton, Southy & Peggy Dalby, 20 Dec. 1790, Thomas Underhill sec.
Con. of John Dalby, father of Peggy.

Dunton, Thomas & Sukey Bell, 16 July 1794, John Goffigon sec.

Dunton, Thomas & Polly Hanby, 26 Mar. 1800, Thomas Dalby sec.

Dunton, Thomas & Sarah Joynes, 19 Feb. 1808, John R. Waddey sec.

Dunton, Waterfield & Susanna Waterfield, 17 May 1756, Isaac
Dunton sec. Con. of Jacob Waterfield, father of Susanna.

Dunton, William & Nancy Bryan, wid. Henry Bryan, 10 Dec. 1827,
James Dunton sec.

Dunton, William M. & Rosa Fitchett, ward of James Dowty, 13 Feb.
1832, James Dowty sec.

Dunton, William M. & Harriet S. Andrews, dau. Isaac Andrews, 13
Feb. 1837, Isaac Andrews sec.

Dun, William & Mary Godferry, 1 Oct. 1709, Robert Howson sec.

Duncan, Thomas & Ann Susan Wheelor, dau. Thomas Wheelor, 27 June
1826, Thomas A Wheeler sec.

East, Southy W. & Elizabeth Yetman, wid. John Yetman, 26 Mar. 1824,
    Edmund W. P. Downing sec.

Edmonds(Edmunds),John & Ann Benston, 21 Aug. 1826, Shep^d Andrews sec.
Edmonds, John & Rosy Dennis, orph. of Michael Dennis & ward of John
    Adams, 29 Dec. 1830, John Adams sec.
Edmunds, Thomas & Peggy Hanby, 3 Feb. 1798, Joseph Hanby sec.
Edmunds, Thomas & Rosey Dennis, 22 Oct. 1800, Joseph Hanby sec.
Edmunds, William,Jr. & Susan Scarborough, 4 Dec. 1815, Edmund
    Scarborough sec.

Ellet, Thomas & Sally Widgeon, 1 Aug. 1801, William Carpenter sec.
    Con. of Daniel Fitchett, Gdn. of Sally.

Elliott, John J. & Caroline Wingate, dau. Hickson Wingate, 5 May
    1845 - William S. Wilkins sec.
Elliott, John T. ward of William S. Smith, & Margaret E. Downes,
    ward of John E. Nottingham,15 Jan. 1834 William S. Smith
    & John E. Nottingham sec.
Elliott, John & Mary Abdeel, wid. 30 Aug. 1792, Henry Smaw sec.
Elliott, John & Polly Nolen, 18 Dec. 1801, Levin Scott sec.
Elliott, John T. & Mary B. Snead, 16 Jan. 1808, Major Pettit sec.
    Con. of Adah Snead, mother of Mary B.
Elliott, John T. & Juliet Upshur, 22 Feb. 1814, Caleb B. Upshur sec.
Elliott, John W. & Louisa Travis, 1 Dec. 1834, Nathaniel Hickman
    sec. Con. of Dennard Travis, father of Louisa.
Elliott, Thomas & Keziah Turner, 10 Aug. 1784, Robert Oag sec.
Elliott, Thomas W. & Susan Evans, orph. of John Evans & ward of
    Nathaniel Hickman, 12 Aug. 1834, Nathaniel Hickman sec.
Elliott, Thomas W. & Susan Ann Speakman, dau. Shepherd Speakman,
    9 Nov. 1840, John McCown sec.
Elliott, Thomas W. & Nancy Smith, orph. of Hannah Smith, 12
    Sept. 1845, William T. Fitchett sec. Con. of Daniel
    Fitchett, Gdn. of Nancy.
Elliott, William & Rose Johnson dau. John Johnson dec. 16 July
    1774, John Johnson sec.
Elliott, William C. & Rachel Hill, 11 Aug. 1823, George Eshon sec.
Elliott, William & Peggy Costin, wid. Henry Costin, 25 Mar. 1833,
    Nathaniel Hickman sec.
Elliott, William W. & Harriet Rolly, dau. William Rolly, 9 Oct.
    1848, John T. Hallett sec.

Ellegood(Elligood),John & Elinor Jacob, 1 Apr. 1727, William
    Brooke & Joseph Sheppard sec.
Ellegood, John & Susanna Wilkins, wid. 12 May 1748, Benj.Scott sec.
Ellegood, John & Esther Wilkins, 19 Mar. 1752, Alexander Kemp sec.
    Con. of John Wilkins.
Ellegood, John, of the County of Worcester, Md., & Nanny Powell,
    dau. Abel Powell, dec. 15 Mar. 1764, Addison Nottingham sec.
Elligood, Jonathan & Esther Floyd, wid. William Floyd, 28 Jan.
    1788, Nathaniel Wilkins, Jr. sec.
Ellegood, Peter Norly & Margaret Forse, wid. 25 Nov. 1735.

Ellegood, William, of Worcester County, Md. & Sarah Powell, 14 Sept. 1768, Addison Nottingham, sec.

Esdel(Isdell,Isdel,Isdale), Edward & Elizabeth Floyd - (not dated - Bundle marked 1786-7) Elizabeth wid. of Charles Floyd, William Roberts sec.

Esdell, George & Esther Green, dau. George Green, 23 June 1715, William Nottingham sec.

Eshon, Daniel & Elizabeth Wheelor, 23 Nov. 1808, Charles Dillon sec.

Eshon, George & Mary Wise 27 Dec. 1820, Charles Bonwell sec.

Eshon, Thomas & Caty Roberts, dau. William Roberts, dec., 20 May 1845, Charles Kelly sec.

Evans, Arthur & Adah Kemp, wid. 12 Sept. 1777, Robert Bell sec.

Evans, Arthur & Nelly Dixon, 21 June 1796, Nathan Griffeth sec.

Evans, Edward & Louisa Bowdoin, 4 June 1805, John K. Evans sec. Con. of Peter Bowdoin, father of Louisa.

Evans, Isaac & Lucinda Evans, 11 Aug. 1817, Hancock Jacob sec.

Evans, John & Peggy Simkins, 7 Feb. 1774, Thomas Underhill sec. Con. of William Simkins, father of Peggy.

Evans, John & Santekey Moore, 17 Nov. 1800, Isaac Nottingham sec.

Evans, John & Ann Toleman, 2 June 1802, Thomas Dunton sec.

Evans, John K. & Margaret Jacob, 7 Apr. 1807, Robert Jacob sec.

Evans, John & Susan Mills, 3 July 1816, Abram Costin sec. Con. of Abram Costin, Gdn. of Susan & of William L. & Ann Evans.

Evans, John & Catherine Dowty, 24 Dec. 1817, Thomas Dowty sec.

Evans, John & Betsy Spady, wid. Thomas Spady, 13 Apr. 1840, William W. Elliott sec.

Evans, Levin & Anne Mary Pitts, 17 May 1755, Littleton Wilkins & John Fraser sec.

Evans, Richard & Elizabeth Goffigon, 31 Dec. 1782, Alexander Boyd sec. Con. of Tabitha Bigs, mother of Elizabeth.

Evans, Thomas & Mary Milbourn, 29 May 1827, Angelo A. Townsend sec. Con. of Thomas Milbourn, father of Mary.

Evans, Thomas & Sally Milbourn, dau. Thomas Milbourn, 2 Nov. 1830, Thomas Milbourn sec.

Evans, Thomas S. & Mary Ann P. Ridley, dau. William W. Ridley, 11 May 1832, William W. Ridley sec.

Evans, Thomas E. & Juliet S. Upshur, ward of Abel P. Upshur, 28 Jan. 1839, Smith S. Nottingham sec.

Evans, Thomas & Laura E. Custis, ward of Sylvester M. Kelly, 19 June 1841, Sylvester Kelly sec.

Evans, William & Adah Widgeon, 26 Aug. 1765, Thomas Bullock sec.

Evans, William & Rebecka Wood, wid. William Wood, 21 May 1790, Thomas Suttie sec.

Evans, William S. & Sophia Moore, 2 Mar. 1805, John Evans sec.

Evans, William S. & Nancy Fitchett, 8 Feb. 1809, James Travis sec. Con. of Joshua Fitchett, father of Nancy.

Evans, William & Miss Sally Costin, 8 Sept. 1824, William Dixon sec. Con. of William Evans as to William & of Joseph Warren as to Sally.

Ewing, David & Ann Hopkins, wid. William Hopkins, 1 Aug. 1821,
    William P. Copes sec.
Ewing, Gustavus & Elizabeth James, wid. 7 June 1760, John Harmanson
    sec.
Ewing, John & Jane Holbrook, 28 Nov. 1785, Maddox Andrews sec.
Ewing, John & Polly McDaniel.29 Feb. 1812, Nath'l. Freshwater sec.
Ewing, John & Margaret A. Matthews, 14 July 1826, William Matthews
    sec.
Ewing, Victor & Margaret Matthews, 27 Jan. 1817, Preeson Savage sec.

Ewell, John & Esther A. Belote, 26 Jan. 1830, Thomas Smith,Jr. sec.
    Con. of Laban Belote, father of Esther A.

Eyre, Ellegood & Esther Saunders, dau. James Saunders, 17 Mar. 1777,
    Benjamin Wilkins sec.
Eyre, John & Ann Upshur, 24 Feb. 1800, Littleton Upshur sec.
Eyre, Littleton & Bridget Harmanson, 15 Jan. 1734, William Tazewell
    sec. Con. of Gertrude Harmanson, grandmother of Littleton
    Eyre.
Eyre, Neech & Anne Mifflin, 12 Mar. 1732, Peter Bowdoin sec.
Eyre, Neech & Isabell Harmanson, 21 Mar. 1734, John Stratton sec.
Eyre, Thomas & Mary Ann Dunton, dau. Matthew H. Dunton, 8 Jan. 1838
    Matthew H. Dunton sec.
Eyre, William L. & Mary B. Savage, 10 Mar. 1828, John Eyre sec.

Fathery(Fatherly) Ebinezer & Amy Barret, 8 Feb. 1784, Southy
    Goffigon sec.
Fathery, Jacob & Esther Bell, 20 Sept. 1787, Robert Brickhouse sec.
Fatherly, Jacob & Elizabeth Haley, ward of Azariah Williams, 13
    Jan. 1840, Azariah Williams sec.
Fatherly, Jacob & Elizabeth Gildon, wid. William Gildon, 1 June
    1846, William T. Good sec.
Fatherly, John & Sally Bearcraft, 8 Apr. 1816, William Frost sec.
Fathery , Matthew & Weltha Woodward, 30 Jan. 1799, Jacob Mills sec.
Fatherly, Matthew & Rachel Frost, 26 Dec. 1809, William Frost sec.
Fatherly, Matthew & Nancy Wilson, 14 Nov. 1814, John Wilson, Jr.
    sec.
Fatherly, William & Susan Matthews, dau. William Matthews, 11 Nov.
    1834, Thomas Young sec.

Finney, Edward O. & Margaret S. Thomas, dau. John B. Thomas, 9
    June, 1828, John B. Thomas sec.
Finney, William, of Accomack, & Joanna Stott, wid. 24 Dec. 1746,
    Peter Hogg sec.
Finney, William R. & Rosey Johnson 10 Dec. 1810, Arthur R.
    Savage sec.

Firkettle, Hamon & Frances Cowdery, 13 May 1709, Hillary Stringer
    & Josias Cowdry sec.

Fisher,Caleb & Elizabeth Downing, dau. Zerobabel Downing, 6 Sept.
    1774, William Downing sec.

Fisher, Caleb & Elizabeth West, 2 Oct. 1793, Elijah Baker sec.

Fisher, Edwin J. & Anna M. Cutler, wid. William W. Cutler, 12 Dec. 1848, Miers W. Fisher sec.

Fisher, Esme & Margaret Roberts, wid., 16 Apr. 1765, Thomas Fisher, Jr. sec.

Fisher, George & Susanna Joynes, 13 Oct. 1789, William Fisher sec.

Fisher, James & Mary White, dau. William White, 13 Dec. 1791, George Meholloms sec.

Fisher, James & Sally Frost, 18 Jan. 1804, Robinson Custis sec.

Fisher, John R. & Melinda D. Heath, 8 Feb. 1819, William R. Fisher sec.

Fisher, John R. & Edney Henderson, 4 Jan. 1840, Miers W. Fisher sec.

Fisher, Miers W. & Mrs Juliet B. Harmanson, 6 Oct. 1829, John Ker sec.

Fisher, Reubin & Mary M. Ross, dau. John Ross, dec. 18 Feb. 1835, George T. Belote sec.

Fisher, Samuel P. & Susan Pettit, ward of William M. Pettit, 13 June 1825, William M. Pettit sec.

Fisher, Thomas & Sarah Turner, wid. 1 Aug. 1754, William Major,Jr. sec. Con. of Thomas & Susanna Knight as to Sarah.

Fisher, Thomas & Margaret Christian, 15 May 1770, Joachim Michael sec. Con. of Michael Christian, father of Margaret.

Fisher, William & Rose Christian, dau. William Christian, 25 Sept. 1776, Thomas Fisher, Sr. sec. Con. of John Michael, Sr., Gdn. of Rose.

Fisher, William & Sally Johnson, dau. Powell Johnson, dec. 12 Feb. 1789, William Wilkins, Sr. sec.

Fisher, William R. & Esther Williams, orph., 11 Mar. 1822, Samuel P. Fisher sec. Con. of Margaret Williams, Gdn. of Esther.

Fitchett, Charles & Peggy Powell, dau. George Powell, Sr. 22 Nov. 1797, Joshua Fitchett sec.

Fitchett, Christopher & Leah Costin, dau. William Costin, 8 Sept. 1823, William Costin sec.

Fitchett, Daniel & Ann Widgeon, 24 Dec. 1821, Southy Spady sec. Con. of Nancy Widgeon, mother of Ann.

*Fitchett, Edward G. & Elizabeth Kelly, dau. Obed Kelly, 23 July 1850

*Fitchett, Edward C. & Mary W. Dunton, dau. Thomas S. Dunton, 24 Jan. 1853

Fitchett, George P. & Mary S. Williams, dau. & ward of Margaret Williams, 30 Aug. 1830, Samuel L. Floyd sec.

Fitchett, Henry & Ann Heritage, 21 Dec. 1789, William Clay sec.

Fitchett, Jacob & Mary Bull, wid. Richard Bull, 29 Dec. 1830, John Ewell sec.

*Fitchett, James & Miss Elizabeth Jane Bell, dau. Jesse Bell, dec. 13 Dec. 1852

Fitchett, James M. & Susanna Rogers, orph. of John Rogers, 13 Feb. 1809, George Bell sec.

Fitchett, Jonathan & Elizabeth Nottingham, 15 Jan. 1783, John Nottingham sec.

Fitchett, Jonathan & Nancy Tyson, dau. Nathaniel Tyson, 30 Nov. 1787, Nathaniel Tyson sec.

*Fitchett, John R. & Fannie O. Simkins, dau. Dr. Jesse J. Simkins, 30 June, 1851

Fitchett, Joshua & Sukey Dixon, 12 Nov. 1782, Ralph Dixon sec.

Fitchett, Joshua, Jr. & Polly Dixon, 25 July 1801, Severn Savage sec.

Fitchett, Nathaniel P., son of Thomas Fitchett, & Sally H. Jacob, ward of John Addison, 13 Dec. 1834, Richard H. Read sec.

Fitchett, Nehemiah & Elizabeth Flood, 15 July 1752, John Flood sec.

Fitchett, Nehemiah & Rachel Stringer, wid. 22 July 1762, John Smaw sec.

Fitchett, Patrick H. & Susan Williams, dau. Samuel Williams, dec. 1 Jan. 1830, John Spady, Jr. sec.

Fitchett, Ralph D. & Mary E. Fitchett, dau. Thomas Fitchett, Sr., 23 Oct. 1828, Thomas Fitchett, Sr. sec.

Fitchett, Robert & Sally Warren, 25 Nov. 1782, Henry Smaw sec.

Fitchett, Robert & Frances Wilkins Widgeon, 27 Dec. 1790, Joshua Fitchett sec. Con. of William Wilkins, Gdn. of Frances.

Fitchett, Robert & Fanny Giddens, 19 July 1806, Isaac Nottingham sec.

Fitchett, Robert & Patsey Odear, 11 Dec. 1809, William S. Evans sec.

Fitchett, Robert & Elizabeth Clay, wid. James Clay, 8 Nov. 1824, Thomas Moore sec.

Fitchett, Robert & Elizabeth Griffith, wid. William Griffith, 22 Dec. 1840, George Odear sec.

Fitchett, Robert W. & Elizabeth A. Griffith, ward of John H.Griffith, 11 Feb. 1850, John H. Griffith sec.

Fitchett, Severn F. & Martha Goffigon, ward of Severn E.Nottingham, 22 May 1838, Severn E. Nottingham sec.

Fitchett, Thomas & Hannah Powell, 14 Sept. 1805, Joshua D.Fitchett sec.

Fitchett, Thomas D. & Lucy Ann Nottingham, dau. Jacob Nottingham, dec., 8 Dec. 1834, George P. Fitchett sec.

Fitchett, Thomas, Jr. & Mrs Elizabeth Fitchett, wid. Robert Fitchett 1 Jan. 1836, Thomas R. Jarvis sec.

Fitchett, Thomas J. & Elcana B. Parsons, dau. Sally Parsons, 21 Dec. 1848, Samuel H. Parsons sec.

Fitchett, William & Sally Hunt, 27 June, 1815, Arthur Simkins sec.

Fitchett, William & Elizabeth Elligood, 15 June 1818, John Adams sec.

Fitchett, William J. & Mary W. Ward, orph. of Tully S. Ward, dec., 31 Dec. 1836, William H. Bell sec. Con. of Jane W. Harrison, mother of Mary W.

Fitchett, William P. & Elizabeth Ann Williams, 27 Oct. 1838, Thomas K. Dunton sec. Con. of Martha Fitchett, mother of William P. & of Ann J. Williams, mother of Elizabeth Ann.

Fitchew(Fitzhugh), Henry & Betsy Wilson, 23 Oct. 1797, Matthew Floyd sec.

Fitchew, Henry & Cassey Nottingham, 17 Dec. 1800, Custis Kendall sec.

Fitchew, John & Molly Luke, 25 Aug. 1795, John Dolby sec.

Fitzhugh(Fitchew), Dr. Philip Aylett & Miss Georgianna Tankard, 16 Apr. 1849, George P. Scarborough sec.

Fletcher, Charles & Esther Harrison, 1 Aug. 1822, Major Dowty sec.

Fletcher, Charles W. & Margaret Scott, dau. John Scott, 17 Sept. 1838
     Charles W. Fletcher sec.
Fletcher, James & Nancy Churn, 13 Jan. 1796, William Fletcher sec.
Fletcher, Jesse & Betsey Barecraft, 18 Dec. 1806, John Scott sec.
Fletcher, John T. & Rachel P. Horton, ward of John T. Fletcher,
     10 June 1850, Nathan F. Cobb sec.
Fletcher, Nathan R. & Margaret E. S. Johnson, dau. Jeptha Johnson,
     9 Oct. 1840, Jeptha Johnson sec.
Fletcher, Richard T. & Sally Webb, 7 May 1845, James S. Webb sec.
     (James S. Webb father of Sally)
Fletcher, Samuel & Mary Parkerson, wid. George Parkerson, 2 July
     1834, John Robins sec.
Fletcher, Stephen & Susanna Churn, 12 Mar. 1790, Archibald Dowty sec.
Fletcher, William & Sarah Churn, 13 Jan. 1796, James Fletcher sec.
Fletcher, William & Mary Stakes, 6 Sept. 1799, William Hanby sec.
Fletcher, William H. & Esther Mears, wid. of James Mears, 16 May
     1835, Samuel C. Fletcher sec.

Floyd, Berry & Lavinia Ann Nottingham, ward of Benjamin N. Scott,
     & orph. of Levin Nottingham, 23 Dec. 1829, Severn
     Nottingham sec.
Floyd, Charles & Sarah Williams, dau. Jacob Williams,dec., 8 Dec.
     1762, Thomas Wilson sec.
Floyd, Charles & Elizabeth Tankard, dau. John Tankard, 3 Mar. 1778,
     John Tankard sec.
Floyd, Frederick & Comfort Downing, 30 Aug. 1800, Johannes Johnson
     sec.
? Floyd, Ishaman & Sally Liverpool, 8 July 1820, Josiah Liverpool sec.
Floyd, John & Mary Floyd, dau. Matthew Floyd, 14 Feb. 1765, John
     Harmanson sec.
Floyd, John, Jr. & Mary Brickhouse, dau. John Brickhouse, 21 Aug.
     1773, John Brickhouse, Sr. sec.
Floyd, John & Nancy Smith, 28 Mar. 1794, William Bain sec.
Floyd, John K. & Ann Stoackley Teackle, 26 July 1802, Thomas Lytt:
     Savage sec. Con. of Thomas Teackle, father of Ann.
Floyd, John & Molly Savage, 12 Jan. 1818, Michael Savage,Sr. sec.
Floyd, Matthew & Sarah Robins, wid. 22 Dec. 1790, Coventon
     Simkins sec.
Floyd, Matthew & Nancy Wilson, 31 July 1794, William Roberts sec.
Floyd, Matthew & Peggy Roberts, 29 Dec. 1802, William Rooks sec.
Floyd, Matthew & Nancy Clay, 19 Nov. 1816, Thomas Powell sec.
Floyd, Matthew & Elizabeth Wilkins, 9 Dec. 1816, Edward Joynes sec.
Floyd, Matthew, & Nancy Williams, 17 July 1821, Azariah Williams
     sec. Con. of Peter Williams,Jr. Gdn. of Nancy.
**Floyd, Matthew & Anne Willis, 19 July 1821
Floyd, Major & Nancy Willis, 11 Oct. 1800, Matthew Floyd sec.
Floyd, Major & Sally Moore, 16 Dec. 1817, William E. Nottingham sec.
**Floyd, Robert & Sukey Jarvis Floyd, _____ 1807
Floyd, Samuel L. & Mary R. Wise, dau. Dr. Tully R. Wise, dec.,
     16 Oct. 1829, Nathaniel H. Winder sec.
Floyd, Shephard B. & Susan Freshwater, 5 Sept. 1813, William
     Stokely sec. Con. of William Stokely, Gdn. of Susan

Floyd, William & Esther Kendall, dau. John Kendall, dec. 14 Apr. 1772,
Samuel Williams sec.

Floyd, William & Sukey Kendall, 23 Dec. 1801, Reuben Frost sec.

Floyd, William & Frances Hallet, 7 May 1805, John Hallet sec.

Floyd, William & Mary Custis, 28 Dec. 1813, Major Floyd sec.

Floyd, William & Margaret Joynes, ward of Daniel Fitchett, 10 Dec.
1827, Daniel Fitchett sec.

Floyd, William S. & Ann T. Smith, dau. Isaac Smith, 13 Jan. 1834,
Isaac Smith sec.

Floyd, William H. & Sarah Ann Stockley, dau. Charles B. Stockley,
23 Sept. 1839, Charles B. Stockley sec.

Flood, John & Frances Warren, wid. 11 July 1752, Nehemiah Fitchett
sec.

Flood, Samuel & Sarah Chance, 20 Apr. 1787, Eyres Stockley sec.

Formicola, Serafino, of York County, & Matilda Newman, 12 July 1774,
Teackle Robins sec.

Foushee, William, of the Borough of Norfolk, & Isabella Harmanson,
6 Mar. 1775, John Staughton Harmanson sec.

Fox, John & Priscilla Widgeon, wid. 22 May 1824, Littleton Upshur
sec.

Fox, William & Adah Andrews, 13 Feb. 1804, Jacob Roberts sec.

Fox, William & Ann W. Travis, wid. Elliott Travis, 3 Sept. 1834,
Thomas Powell sec.

Fox, William G. & Esther Ann Fox, dau. John D. Fox, 21 Feb. 1846,
John D. Fox sec.

? Francis, John & Ibby Shephard, wid. 28 Dec. 1792, Abraham Lang
sec.

? Francis, Thomas & Tabby Press, 26 Dec. 1796, Edmund Press sec.

? Francis, Thomas & Chrysanna Collins, 11 Aug. 1825, William
Francis sec.

? Francis, William & Polly Jacob, 30 Dec. 1791, Abraham Lang.

? Francis, William, Jr. & Margaret Bingham, 26 Dec. 1829, Severn
Wickes sec.

Fraser, Collin & Ellenor Waterfield, 11 Jan. 1769, John Waterfield,
Jr. sec.

Freshwater, Edward & Susan Harrison, dau. Newton Harrison, 27 Dec.
1831, Newton Harrison sec.

Freshwater, Edward & Fanny Richardson, 30 May 1843, James Williams
sec.

Freshwater, Jacob, & Mary Nelson, dau. John Nelson dec. 24 Mar.
1763, John Wilkins, blacksmith, sec.

Freshwater, Nathaniel & Elizabeth Clegg, 14 Apr. 1802, John
Simkins sec. Con. of James Powell as to Elizabeth.

Freshwater, William, Jr. & Nancy Mills, 11 Nov. 1786, Southy
Spady sec.

Freshwater, William & Betsey Wilkins, 11 Nov. 1800, Wm. Scott sec.

?Freeman, Absolem & Polly West, 17 Apr. 1805, Samuel Stevens sec.

*Frost, Francis & Emma S. Dunton, dau. Rickards Dunton, 29 June,1852
Frost, John & Betsey Knight, 1 Mar. 1791, Severn Nottingham sec.
Frost, John & Tabby Dowty, 12 Aug. 1799, Thomas Jacob sec.
Frost, John, Jr. & Frances Wise, 31 Dec. 1817, Stephen Wilkins sec.
Frost, John & Smarta Wilson, 9 July 1818, Thomas Peed sec.
Frost, Joseph & Elenor Walker, 27 Nov. 1782, Stuart Saunders sec.
    Con. of John Walker, father of Elenor.
Frost, Josephus S. & Elizabeth Susan Scott, dau. John Scott, dec.
    22 May 1846, Obediah Scott sec.
Frost, Nathaniel & Peggy Williams, 18 Dec. 1798, William Scott sec.
Frost, Reubin & Emily Wingate, dau. Daniel Wingate, 27 Dec. 1842,
    Daniel Wingate sec.
Frost, Robert & Esther Rippin, dau. William Rippin, dec., 4 July
    1836, Severn Wilkins sec.
Frost, Robert _ Sarah Ann Wingate, dau. Daniel Wingate, 5 Aug. 1839,
    Daniel Wingate sec.
Frost, Capt. William & Sally Russell, 1 June 1308, John Boggs sec.
    Con. of Robert Greening & wife as to Sally

Fulwell, John Lewis & Margaret Costin, dau. Jacob Costin, 24 June,
    1761, Nathaniel Savage sec.
Fulwell, Victor Augustus & Elizabeth Simkins, 12 Sept. 1795, William
    Simkins sec. Con. of Coventon Simkins, Gdn. of Elizabeth.

Galt, Dickey & Leah Benthall, dau. Azel Benthall, 13 Jan. 1761, Azel
    Benthall sec.

Gale, Chris & Mary Ann Stevens, 20 Dec. 1798, David Topping, sec.
    Con. of Rachel Cowles as to Mary Ann.
Gale, Christopher & Ann Stevens, 22 May 1802, John R. Waddy sec.
Gale, Christopher & Margaret Abbot, 3 Dec. 1808, Joshua Garrison sec.
Gale, Joseph & Peggy Gale, 14 Apr. 1801, Richard Dunton sec.
Gale, Joseph & Margaret Cook, 22 May 1794, David Topping sec.

Gardner, Walter C. & Elizabeth Fulwell, 2 May 1804, Arthur Simkins
    sec.
? Gardner, William & Tinsey Bingham, 25 Nov. 1797, Isaac Stevens sec.

Garris, Isaiah & Lavinia Terrier, ward of James M. Wilson, 13 June
    1842.
Garris, William & Elizabeth Gooldsburry, 24 Sept. 1796, Coventon
    Stott sec.

Garrison, Abell & Margaret Floyd, dau. John Floyd, 8 Aug. 1775,
    John Widgeon sec.
Garrison, Bagwell & Catharine Mathews, 21 Mar. 1809, John Ames sec.
Garrison, George & Sarah Dunton, 13 Dec. 1735, Dicky Dunton sec.
Garrison, James & Sally Jacob, 7 Aug. 1797, Richard Jacob sec.
Garrison, James R. & Susan P. Tankard, 14 Dec. 1833, Elijah Floyd
    sec. Con. of John Tankard, father of Susan P.

Garrison, William B. & Susan S. Mears, dau. Richard Mears, dec., 14
    Feb. 1833, Thomas Young sec.
Garrison, William B. & Margaret S. Johnson, dau. Richard Johnson, dec.
    1 Mar. 1836, George L. Garrison sec.

*Garrett, Charles & Leana Bool, dau. George Bool, dec. 10 Jan. 1853.
Garret, George & Susan Bird, 24 Dec. 1825, William Carmine sec.
Garrett, Richard & Polly Robins, 9 Sept. 1816, Major F. Richardson
    sec.
Garrett, Robert M. & Susan C. Winder, dau. John H. Winder, 2 June
    1835, Levin Y. Winder sec.

Gascoigne(Gascoyne), Thomas & Sarah Andrews, 8 Jan. 1722, Thomas
    Johnson & John White sec.
Gascoigne, William & Anne Harmanson, dau. Matthew Harmanson, 17
    Jan. 1769, Dickey Galt sec.

Gascoyne(Gascoigne), Henry & Sarah Upshur, wid. 14 Apr. 1752, Esau
    Jacob sec.
Gascoyne, Henry & Sarah Stott, dau. Laban Stott, 13 July 1773,
    Joachim Michael sec.

George, Willis & Catharine Smith, 29 Dec. 1800, Thomas James sec.
    Con. of Major Pettit, Gdn. of Catharine.

Gibb, Flavious J. & Emmy J. Hoshier, 17 Aug. 1843, John T. Johnson
    sec.
Gibb, Zorobabel & Ann Evans, 16 Mar. 1827, Henry B. Kendall sec.
    Con. of John Evans, father of Ann

Gibbons, Jonathan, of the State of Delaware, & Frances Gault, 8
    Feb. 1792, John Carpenter sec. Con. of Sarah Jacob,
    Mother of Frances.

Giddens, Benjamin & Betsey West, Free Negroes, 16 Feb. 1826,
    Samuel Scisco sec.
Giddens, Daniel & Sally Custis, Free Negroes, 29 Dec. 1824,
    Benjamin Giddens sec.
Giddens, Henry & Milly Moor, 16 Feb. 1786, Jacob Fathery sec.
Giddens, Henry & Betsey Evans, 20 Dec. 1794, John Simkins sec.
    Con. of John Evans, father of Betsey.
Giddens, Henry & Betsey Jones, 24 Feb. 1823, Thomas Eshon sec.
    Con. of George Eshon, Gdn. of Henry.
Giddens, Henry & Elizabeth Matthews, wid. Teackle Matthews,
    25 July 1826, James Young sec.
Giddens, Henry , widower, & Sally Williams, dau. James Williams,
    14 Sept. 1829, James Williams sec.
Giddens, Thomas & Betsey Harrison, 18 July 1801, Johannes
    Johnson sec.

Gilmour, William & Mary Ann Drysdale, 15 Apr. 1799, Isaac Smith
    sec.

Gilson, George & Kesiah Abdell, dau. .bel Abdell, 11 June 1838,
      Samuel Bunting sec.

Gilding(Gildon,Gilden), Charles & Peggy Turner, 22 Dec. 1798, Chris-
      topher Gale sec.
Gilding, Charles & Sally Jacob, 5 Nov. 1803, Teackle Roberts sec.
Gilding, John & Nancy Core, 4 Aug. 1803, Severn Nottingham sec. Con.
      of Robins Mapp, Gdn. of Nancy.

Gildon(Gilding,Gilden), John & Rosey Clack, 12 Nov. 1827, William W.
      Ridley sec.
Gildon, William C., son of John, & Elizabeth Clarke, ward of Little- n
      ton K. Godwin, 14 Oct. 1828, John Gilden & Littleton K.
      Godwin sec.

Gilden(Gilding,Gildon), Charles & Mary Dixon, dau. John Dixon, 8
      June, 1771, Richard Smith sec.

Glanville, Edmund, of York County, & Anna Katharine Thurmar, wid.,
      30 Oct. 1758, John Dolby, Jr. sec.
Glanville, Edmund & Margaret Scott, dau. Zerobabel Scott, 24 Dec.
      1778, Walter Hyslop sec.

Gleeson(Gleason), James & Adah Bell, dau. Joab Bell, 8 Oct. 1793,
      George Bell sec.
Gleeson, John & Elizabeth Dodd, 10 Jan. 1770, Robert Polk sec.
Gleason, John & Elizabeth Bullock, 10 May 1785, William Jeffries
      sec.
Gleeson, John, Sr. & Rachel Fitzgerald, 24 May 1798, John Carpenter,
      Sr. sec.
Gleason, Peter & Sally Francis, dau. John Francis, 5 Feb. 1825,
      John Francis sec.
Gleason, William C. & Polly Bell, dau. George Bell, 13 Dec. 1823,
      George Bell sec.

Godwin, Archibald & Vianna Gray Jacob, wid. 9 July 1776, William
      Wood sec.
Godwin, Charles & Elizabeth Wilson, wid. Thomas Wilson, 1 Jan. 1836,
      John Tyson sec.
Godwin, Daniell & Elishaba Benthall, 12 Jan. 1724, Devorax Godwin
      & George Lucar sec. Con. of George Lucar & wife as to
      Elishaba.
Godwin, Daniel & Susanna Preeson, 5 Feb. 1724, Thomas Savage,Sr.
      & Godfrey Pole, Gent. sec.
Godwin, Daniel & Sarah Cowdry, 30 Sept. 1779, Archibald Godwin sec.
Godwin, Devorax & Sally Floyd, 3 Mar. 1807, Ezekiel Badger sec.
Godwin, Devorax & Margaret Jacob, dau. Teackle Jacob, 16 June,
      1838, Teackle Jacob sec.
Godwin, Devorax & Elizabeth B. Nicholson, 4 May 1842, John Ker sec.
Godwin, Devorax & Maria Underhill, wid. Michael Underhill, 6 Jan.
      1846, Southy Wilkins sec.
Godwin, Edwin & Mary B. Nottingham, 3 July 1821, Thomas N. Will-
      iams sec.
 Godwin,Devorax & Esther Bailey,dau.Isaac Bailey,dec. 27 Aug.1763
 Daniel Eshon sec.

Godwin, Edmund & Nancy Grey Godwin, 23 Oct. 1797, Archibald Godwin sec.
Godwin, Edmund S. & Susan T. Mehollanes, dau. Thomas Mehollanes, 14
    Apr. 1834, Thomas Mehollanes sec.
Godwin, Edmund S. & Rosey P. Mears, dau. Jamima Mears, 9 Jan. 1837,
    John G. Turner sec.
Godwin, Griffin F. & Emily Wilkins, 31 Oct. 1846, James H.Stewart
    sec. Con. of Hetty Wilkins, mother of Emily.
Godwin, John, Born 19 Aug. 1800, son of Laban Goffigon, & Polly
    Haggoman, dau. Robert Haggoman, 19 Aug. 1823.
Godwin, Joseph P. & Arinthia Roberts, 1 Jan. 1848, Thomas Smith,
    Jr. sec. Con. of Sally Roberts, mother of Arinthia.
Godwin, Laban & Letty Floyd, 18 Feb. 1800, George Holt sec. Con.
    of John Floyd, father of Letty.
Godwin, Laban & Ann A. Ward, 22 Feb. 1828, George T. Yerby sec.
Godwin, Littleton & Ann Dalby, 9 Nov. 1801, John Dalby sec.
Godwin, Littleton & Sukey Johnson, 18 Oct. 1813, John Warren sec.
Godwin, Smith P. & Ann Powell, ward of Joseph W. Thomas, 18 May,
    1833, Joseph W. Thomas sec.

Goffigon, Edwin & Louisa C. Spady, 1 Jan. 1839, Jacob E.Nottingham
    sec.
*Goffigon, Frederick J. & Mary E. Nottingham, dau. James B. Notting-
    ham, 15 Oct. 1851
Goffigon, James & Mary Floyd, 27 Sept. 1755, Anne Holt, wid. sec.
Goffigon, James & Polly Goffigon, 21 Dec. 1802, Obediah Hunt sec.
    Con. of Nathaniel Goffigon, father of Polly.
Goffigon, John & Nancy Bell, dau. Robert Bell, dec. 19 May 1792,
    Con. of William Jarvis, Gdn. of Nancy. William Jarvis sec.
Goffigon, John & Sally Goffigon, 18 Apr. 1796, John Nelson sec.
Goffigon, John & Diana D. Segar, ward of John Segar, 15 Nov. 1821,
    John Segar sec.
Goffigon, John,Sr. & Susan Goffigon, 9 Jan. 1832, Nath'l.Goffigon
    sec.
Goffigon, Nathaniel & Frances Dunton, 19 Dec. 1772, Samuel
    Actchison sec. Con. of Levin Dunton,Sr.,father of Frances.
Goffigon, Nathaniel S. & Emily Goffigon, dau. James Goffigon, 27
    Nov. 1837, James Goffigon sec.
Goffigon, Obed, & Mary Trower, dau. John Trower, 14 Sept. 1829,
    John Trower sec.
Goffigon, Capt. Peter & Sarah Costin, 6 Apr. 1781, Walter Hyslop
    sec. Con. of Abraham Costin, father of Sarah.
Goffigon, Southy & Margaret Evans, 18 Nov. 1769, James Drummond
    sec.
Goffigon, Southy & Esther Goffigon, 23 Nov. 1805, Samuel Williams
    sec. Con. of Nathaniel Goffigon, father of Esther.
Goffigon, Thomas & Bridget Elliott, wid. William Elliott, 10 Mar.
    1781, William Rascoe sec.
Goffigon, Thomas & Peggy Wilson, 23 July 1785, Daniel Benthall sec.
Goffigon, William & Polly Dixon, 14 Apr. 1806, Custis Hyslop sec.
Goffigon, William J. & Arinthia S.G.Burris, ward of John Goffigon,
    Sr., 11 Sept. 1837, John Goffigon, Sr. sec.

Goodday, Reuben & Betsey Kendall, 20 Jan. 1808, Henry Smaw sec.

Goodday, Reubin & Hetty Harman, 2 Apr. 1816, Revil Watson sec.

Graves, John & Anne Wilson, 26 Nov. 1785, John Stoyt sec. Con of
    Peter Graves, father of John
Graves, John, Jr. & Molly Pratt, 28 Jan. 1799, William Wilson sec.
Graves, William & Mary Murray, 7 Feb. 1778, John Scott sec.
Graves, William & Peggy Warren, 23 Dec. 1800, John Dunton sec.
Graves, William & Sukey Warren, 2 Aug. 1808, Marriot Parsons sec.

Gray(Grey),John & Delitha Heath, 31 Oct. 1816, Robert A. Joynes sec.
    Con. of Patience Heath, mother & Gdn. of Delitha.

Grey(Gray), George & Mahala Byrd, 27 June, 1825, Thomas Byrd sec. Con.
    of Peggy Byrd, mother of Mahala.

Green, George, of Accomack, & Ann Benson, 19 Dec. 1798, George
    Kellam, of Accomack, sec.
Green, Hilary & Tamar Pitts, wid. 12 Apr. 1757, Holloway Bunting sec.

Greenway(Greenaway), Robert & Susanna Rippin, 9 Apr. 1798, James
    Dolby sec.
Greenway, Robert & Elizabeth Bearcraft, 15 Feb. 1817, Thomas G.
    Scott sec.
Greenaway, Robert & Leah Scott, 28 June, 1788, Nathaniel Goffigon sec.

Griffin, Moses & Nancy Costin, 13 Jan, 1800, Nathan Griffin sec.

Griffeth(Griffith), Benjamin & Lilly Miller, 9 Dec. 1783, John
    Harwood sec.
Griffith, Benjamin & Rachel Havard, 11 Jan. 1808, John Winder sec.
Griffith, Benjamin & Sally Travis, orph. of Elliott Travis, 11 Oct.
    1832, Con. of Dennard Travis, Gdn. of Sally. Thomas
    Powell sec.
Griffith, Charles & Sally More, 28 Apr. 1817, John Moore sec. Con.
    of Mathew & Ann More, mother & father of Sally.
Griffith, Jeremiah & Elizabeth Dixon, dau. William Dixon, 1 Sept.
    1832, Christopher Dixon sec. Con. of Moses Griffith,
    father of Jeremiah.
Griffith, John & Nancy Costin, wid William Costin, 4 June, 1791,
    John Pratt sec.
Griffeth, John & Nancy Williams, 13 May 1809, William Stockley sec.
Griffith, John, Jr. & Mary Frost, 26 Dec. 1815, William Frost sec.
Griffith, John, Jr. Ann Griffith, dau. John Griffith, Sr., 8 Sept.
    1828, John Griffith, Sr. sec.
Griffith, John H. & Elizabeth Ridley, dau. William W. Ridley, 9
    Apr. 1838, William W. Ridley sec.
Griffith, Littleton & Peggy Wilson, 13 Dec. 1813, Isaiah Willis sec.
Griffith, Littleton & Polly Collins, 9 June, 1817, John Collins sec.
Griffeth, Moses & Elenor Ellegood, 13 May 1752, John Ellegood sec.
Griffeth, Nathan & Sally Costin, 27 May 1797, Moses Griffith,Jr. sec.
Griffith, Nathan & Fanny Griffith, 8 Feb. 1838, Thomas S. Evans sec.
    Con. of Moses Griffith, father of Fanny.

Griffith, Thomas & Mary A. Kelly, 13 Feb. 1836, James B. Nottingham
    sec. Con. of Ann Kelly, mother of Mary A.
Griffith, Thomas L. & Elizabeth Parkerson, 23 Dec. 1837, William
    W. Wilson sec. Con. of George P. Fitchett, Gdn. of Elizabeth.
Griffith, Thomas & Mary Jacob, dau. John Jacob,Sr. dec. 15 Sept.
    1841, Joshua Nottingham sec.
Griffith, Thomas & Mary Ann Saunders, dau. John Saunders, dec. 4
    May 1844, David B. Ball sec.
Griffith, William & Sally Snail, 22 June 1791, John Graves,Jr. sec.
Griffith, William & Sally Williams, 24 May 1799, Azariah Williams
    sec.
Griffith, William & Elizabeth Griffith, dau. Moses Griffith, 20
    Sept. 1828, George Odear sec.
Groten, Kendall & Leah Spady, 15 Aug. 1815, Joshua Garrison sec.
Groten, Kendall & Betsey Wilson, 26 Mar. 1818, Silas Jefferson sec.
Groten, Thomas & Elizabeth Custis, 12 Dec. 1796, George Scott sec.

*Gunter, Benjamin T. & Frances Ellen Fisher, dau. John R. Fisher,
    22 Jan. 1853
Gunter, John W. F., son of Stephen S. Gunter, dec. & Sarah A.
    Johnson, dau. William P. Johnson, dec., 12 Dec. 1836,
    Smith Belote sec. Con. of Margaret R. Johnson, mother
    of Sarah A.
Gunter, Joseph S. M. & Louisa B. Johnson, dau. William P.Johnson,
    30 Dec. 1837, Thomas Pearson sec.
Gunter, Joseph S. M. & Esther A. Ewell, wid. John Ewell, 2 Aug.
    1845, John Sterling, sec.
Gunter, Stephen & Tamar Pearson (18 years old) 7 Jan. 1814, Isaac
    Lewis sec. Tamar dau. of Thomas Pearson, dec. Con. of
    Adah Stott, wife of Jonathan Stott, mother of Tamar.
Gunter, Stephen C. & Miss Tabitha S. Belote, ward of Laban Belote
    12 Feb. 1849, Laban Belote sec.

?Gusties, Abel & Abigail Stephens,   6 Sept. 1806, York
    Stepney sec.

?Gustin, Isaac & Jenney Bingham, 13 Nov. 1804, Jacob Floyd sec.
? Gustin, Jacob & Sarah Morris, 28 July 1820, John Simkins sec.

? Gutrie, Eson, of Accomack, & Absel Pool, 23 Dec. 1803, Moses
    Bucner sec.

Guy, Henry & Adah Harmanson, 18 Oct. 1755, John Harmanson sec.
Guy, Henry & Adah Harmanson, 6 Jan. 1778, John Burton sec.
    Con. of John Harmanson, Gdn. of Adah.
Guy, John & Susanna Burton, dau. John Burton, Gent. dec., 27
    Sept. 1760, Griffin Stith sec. Con. of John Kendall,
    "kinsman"of Susanna Burton.
Guy, John & Elizabeth James, dau. Thomas James, 14 Feb. 1791,
    Coventon Smith sec.
Guy, Matthew & Margaret Harmanson, dau. John Harmanson, Esq.,
    dec., 25 Dec. 1787, John Kendall, Jr. sec.

Hack, Peter, of Accomack, & Sally Upshur, 23 Oct. 1786, John Upshur,
Jr. sec. Con. of John Upshur, Jr., father of Sally

Haggoman, John, Jr. & Betty Jacob, 11 Mar. 1755, Henry Tomlinson sec.
Con. of Hancock Jacob, father of Betty.
Haggoman, Robert & Catharine Snead, 10 Mar. 1786, Maddox Andrews sec.
Haggoman, Robert & Mary MacDaniel, 7 May 1799, Rickards Dunton,Jr.sec.
Haggoman, William & Margaret Michael, wid. 13 Jan. 1755, John
Haggoman, Jr. sec.

Hale, James & Esther Scott, 9 Sept. 1791, John Dennis sec.

Haley, Benjamin & Peggy Dawson, 17 Nov. 1803, Isaac Nottingham,sec.
Haley, Benjamin & Patsy Collins, dau. Nathaniel Collins, 18 Nov.
1845, Walter W. Widgeon sec.
Haley, Robert & Peggy Costin, 30 July, 1807, Zorobabel Roberts sec.
Haley, Robert & Miss Nancy Mills, 2 Sept. 1824, James Costin sec.
Haley, William, ward of John W. Elliott, & Margaret Ann Costin, 9
Oct. 1848, John T. Hallett sec. Con. of Coventon R. Costin,
father of Margaret.

Hallett, Michael & Eliza Jacob, ward of John Simkins, 11 Oct. 1824,
John Simkins sec.
Hallett, Thomas & Sally Trower, 14 Aug. 1815, John Trower sec.
Hallett, Thomas D. & Sally Trower, 12 Nov. 1817, George Powell sec.
Hallett, Thomas & Tamer Trower, 13 May 1822, Michael Hallett sec.
Hallett, William & Clear Dixon, 4 Aug. 1775, John Biggs sec.
Con. of John Dixon.

Hall, Daniel Roles & Susanna Guy, wid. John Guy, 5 Feb. 1772,
Samuel Atchison sec.
Hall, Daniel R. & Susanna Wilkins, 22 Nov. 1780, John Stratton,
Jr. sec.
Hall, John R. & Lucretia Bell, 3 June 1816, William Dunton sec.
Certificate from George Brickhouse that Lucretia Bell
is over 21.
Hall, Robert & Esther Evans, age 17 years, orph. of Thomas
Evans, 10 July 1793, William Roberts sec. Con. of John
Elliott, Gdn. of Esther.
Hall, Thomas & Esther Dunton, 8 Oct. 1793, Edward Bishop sec.
Hall, Thomas E. & Lisha Jones, 29 Dec. 1825, John McCowan sec.
Hall, William & Lucretia Jones, 29 Dec. 1823, James Saunders sec.
Con. of James H. Jones, father of Lucretia. Endorse-
ment on back refers to Lucretia as "sister"of James H.
Jones.

Hampton(Hamilton,Hampleton),Bowdoin & Betsey Hosier, 16 May, 1816,
Major Abdeel sec.

Hamilton(Hampton,Hampleton),Andrew & Ann Preeson, wid. 6 Mar.1706,
William Waters sec.
Hamilton, Andrew & Peggy Whelor, 25 Dec. 1806, Nath'l.Jones sec.
Hamilton, Andrew & Mary G. Williams, 2 Dec. 1823, John Moore sec.
Hamilton, Bowdoin & Susey Robins, 26 Dec. 1797, William Robins sec.

Hampleton(Hampton,Hamilton),James & Susan Bell, dau. Thomas Bell,dec.
  16 Dec. 1839, Elias Roberts sec.
Hampleton, James & Betsey Thurston, ward of Thomas K. Dunton, 11
  Sept. 1843, Thomas K. Dunton sec.
Hampleton, John & Mary Bell, dau. Thomas Bell, dec., 3 Mar. 1838,
  Thomas S. Brickhouse sec.
Hampleton, William & Miss Molly Rippin, ward of John Wilkins, 13 Dec.
  1824, John Wilkins sec.
Hampleton, William & Margaret Williams, dau. John Williams, dec.,
  15 Dec. 1832, Legustus Roberts sec.
Hampleton, William & Keziah Bell, dau. John Bell, 8 Jan. 1850, Edw.
  T. Robins sec.

Hammon, Phillip & Mary Collever, 13 Jan. 1708/9,Samuel Palmer,sec.

Hanby, John & Leah Taylor, 13 Mar. 1809, Edmund Bell sec.
Hanby, John & Sukey Taylor, wid. George Taylor, 12 Apr. 1830, John
  M. Wilkins sec.
Hanby, John J. & Rosina J. Dalby, dau. James Dalby, 11 Jan. 1841,
  Devorax Warren sec.
Hanby, Joseph & Bridget Dalby, 19 Jan. 1791, Isaac Bull sec.
Hanby, Thomas & Sukey Odear, 13 May 1815, Peter Williams sec.
Hanby, William & Adelia Moore, wid. 19 May 1788, Walter Hyslop sec.
Hanby, William & Elizabeth James, 15 Dec. 1792, William Toleman sec.
Hanby, William,Jr. & Polly James, 21 Oct. 1797, Thomas Addison sec.
Hanby, William & Rosey Scott, 22 Aug. 1798, John Speakman sec.
Hanby, William & Joanna Williams, 20 Apr. 1802, Azariah Williams sec.
Hanby, William & Mary Ann Wescoat, 10 Dec. 1833, Smith Bell sec.
  Con. of Edmund Wescoat, father of Mary Ann.
Hanby, William & Elizabeth Wescoat, dau. Edmund Wescoat, 24 Oct.
  1842, Thomas Smith, Jr. sec.

Handy, William W. & Sally T. B. Upshur, dau. John Upshur,Sr., 7 Oct.
  1834, William L. Savage sec.

Hart, Stephen & Susanna Nottingham, 6 Oct. 1777, John Hamilton sec.
  Con. of Richard Nottingham, father of Susanna.

Harmanson, Henry & Rose Harmanson, 7 May 1736, William Tazewell sec.
Harmanson, Henry & Lucretia Rispas, 14 Feb. 1764, Con. of John
  Rispas, father of Lucretia.
Harmanson, Henry & Elizabeth Robins, 27 May 1789, Robert Nottingham
  sec.
Harmanson, Henry,Jr. & Sarah Robins, 19 Apr. 1794, Henry Harmanson,
  Sr. sec.
Harmanson, John & Isabell Harmanson, 8 Oct. 1723, Thomas Harmanson
  sec.
Harmanson, John H. & Catharine Coleburne, 27 Feb. 1806, John
  Simkins sec. Con of George Coleburne, Gdn. of Catharine.
Harmanson, John & Margaret Wilkins, 13 Oct. 1823, Johannis Johnson
  sec.
Harmanson, John H. & Juliet B. Holland, 1 Nov. 1823, Nath'l.
  Holland sec.

Harmanson, Matthew & Rachel Roberts, 9 Apr. 1740, Thomas Cable, Wm.
    Tazewell, George Holden & Thomas Preeson sec.
Harmanson, Matthew & Catherine Robins, 3 Jan. 1791, Matthew Guy sec.
    Con. of Henry Harmanson, father & Gdn. of Catherine.
Harmanson, Matthew & Elizabeth Kendall, 13 Dec. 1798, Henry Harmanson
    sec. Con. of Lucretia Kendall "to marry my daughter E.B.Kendall".
Harmanson, Patrick & Elishe Kendall, wid. 14 Mar. 1758, John Harmanson
    sec.
Harmanson, William & Margaret Mapp, 13 Sept. 1774, John S.Harmanson
    sec.
Harmanson, William & Joanna Satchell, 31 Dec. 1777, John Savage,Jr.
    sec.
Harmanson, William P. & Sally Wilson Smith, 26 Nov. 1803, William
    Fisher sec.
Harmanson, William & Miss Margaret C. Mapp, 19 Dec. 1825, George F.
    Wilkins sec. Con. of Margaret Mapp, mother of Margaret C.

Harrison, Abel, & Mary Carpenter, 20 Dec. 1797, John Carpenter sec.
Harrison, Abel & Polly Miles, 10 Oct. 1808, Southey Webb sec.
Harrison, Abel & Nancy Chance, 20 Mar. 1812, William G.Harrison sec.
Harrison, Arthur & Kitty Lewis, 10 Aug. 1813, Arthur Cobb sec.
    Con. of Arthur Cobb as to Kitty.
Harrison, Carvey & Caroline Joynes, dau. Thomas Joynes, dec., 28
    Oct. 1842, Victor A. Nottingham sec. Con. of Leah Joynes,
    mother of Caroline.
Harrison, Carvey & Nancy Nottingham, dau. Harrison Nottingham,
    10 Nov. 1848, Leonard B. Nottingham sec.
Harrison, Isma & Ann Dillion, dau. Charles Dillion, 19 Nov. 1832,
    Charles Dillion sec.
Harrison, James & Susan Chance, 19 Dec. 1816, William Smith sec.
Harrison, Jesse & Jane Ward,wid. Tully S.Ward,dec., 24 Apr. 1832,
    Edward R. Turner, sec.
Harrison, Keley & Caty Ashby, 9 Mar. 1818, Revel Watson sec.
Harrison, Newton & Tamar Edmunds, 26 Dec. 1805, Thos: Edmunds
    sec. Con. of Sarah Edmunds.
Harrison, Newton & Nancy Bradford, wid. Abel Bradford, 24 Apr.
    1837, Nathaniel J. Winder sec.
Harrison, Robert H. & Sally Dowty, 24 Nov. 1788, Seth Powell sec.
Harrison, Robert H. & Elizabeth Belote, dau. Levin Belote,dec.
    30 Sept. 1791, Laban Stott sec.
Harrison, Robert H. & Polly Ewing, 5 Sept. 1816, Charles West sec.
Harrison, Seth & Molly Anderson, 29 Mar. 1810, Thomas S. Brickhouse
    sec.
Harrison, William & Anne Green, 1 July 1776, William Nottingham sec.
Harrison, William G. & Susanna Dowty, 7 Feb. 1810, Peter M.Clegg
    sec.

**Harman, Edmund & Elishe Webb, ___ ____ 1791
Harman, George & Anne Elliott, dau. James Elliott, 15 Feb. 1775,
    James Elliott sec.
Harman, George & Peggy Smith, 9 Mar. 1797, Thomas Dixon sec.
Harman, Keley & Sarah Savage, ward of Calvin H. Read, 13 June,
    1821, Calvin H. Read sec.

45

Harman, Thomas & Bridget Bell, 23 Nov. 1811, Anthony Bell sec.

Harlow, David & Molly Cary, 3 Oct. 1806, William Rippin sec.

Haslop(Hyslop), Custis & Susanna Holland, 12 June, 1787, Benj:Griffith
sec.

*Hatton, William P. & Ann Eliza James, 4 June 1853

Hays, John & Nancy Christian, dau. Michael Christian, 6 Sept. 1777,
William Steele sec.

Hazard, Thomas, of the Province of Rhode Island, & Mary Bowdoin,
dau. Peter Bowdoin, Gent., 15 Nov. 1746, Peter Norley Ellegood
sec.

Heath(Heth), Augustus C.E. & Edith E.Fisher, wid. William R.Fisher,
17 July 1830, Isaac Andrews sec.
Heath, Carey & Sally Pratt, wid., 4 Mar. 1822, John Bull sec.
Heath, George & Peggy Savage, 4 Aug. 1800, James Heath sec.
Heath, James & Mary Guy, wid. 17 Mar. 1778, Major Wilkins sec.
Heath, James & Patience Tankard, 14 Nov. 1780, Jacob Abdell sec.
Heath, James & Sally Turner, dau. John Turner, dec. 18 Feb. 1794,
William Roberts, Jr. sec.
Heath, John S. & Mary Ames, 30 Apr. 1811, Thomas Nottingham sec.
Heath, Josiah & Mary Floyd, wid. John Floyd, 17 Dec. 1778, Mary
Bryon sec.
Heath, Rufus & Susan T.W.Brickhouse, 21 Sept. 1835, Isaac Andrews
sec. Con. of John N. Brickhouse, father of Susan.
Heath, Seth & Grace Elliott, 26 Nov. 1798, Zorobabel Jones sec.
Con. of John Elliott, father of Grace.
Heath, William, Sr. & Mary Carpenter, wid. 1 July 1769, Thomas
Dolby sec.
Heath, William & Henrietta Joyne, dau. Edmund Joyne, 21 Sept.
1770, Edmund Glanville sec.
Heath, William & Polly Dennis, 27 Dec. 1826, William Martin sec.
Heath, William & Patsy Dennis, dau. Reubin Dennis, 8 Dec. 1845,
William Dennis sec.

Henderson, James T. & Sally Ross, wid. John Ross, 11 Feb. 1840,
James Sturgis, of John, sec.
Henderson, John & Maria Sturgis, 23 Dec. 1816, Thomas E.Addison
sec.
Henderson, John T. & Rachel Scott, 24 Aug. 1829, Thomas O.Hunt sec.
Henderson, John M. & Louisa W. Addison, dau. John Addison, dec.,
11 Sept. 1837, Teackle W. Jacob sec.
Henderson, Robert & Nancy Jacob, 2 June 1795, John Gleason sec.
Henderson, Thomas & Rosey Fisher, 12 Feb. 1798, George Mehollams
sec.
Henderson, Thomas & Rosey Parramore, 29 Dec. 1812, Thomas W.
Badger sec.
Henderson, William & Susanna Stott, 20 Dec. 1821,Wm.Watson sec.

Henderson, Zorobabel & Edna Ward, 13 Dec. 1811, Joshua Garrison sec.
Con. of Golding Ward, father of Edna.

Henry, James & Susanna Harmanson, dau. John Harmanson, Esq., 25 Dec.
1786, Nathaniel Darby sec.

Herritage, Freshwater & Ann Eshon, 11 Apr. 1783, Obed Cary sec.

Heth(Heath),Luke & Bridget Dunton, dau. Elias Dunton, dec. 28 Sept.
1763, William Christian sec.

Hickman, Edward & Elishe Thompson, 21 July 1814, William Clarke sec.
Hickman, Nathaniel & Louisa Dawson, 22 June 1818, William E.
Nottingham sec.
Hickman, Nathaniel & Rachel Griffith, wid. 11 Mar. 1823, John S.
Spady sec.
Hickman, Nathaniel & Sally Elliott, wid. Thomas Elliott, 2 Sept.
1826, John N. Stratton sec.

Hill, Charles & Susan S. Wescoat, dau. Hezekiah P. Wescoat,Sr.,
11 Mar. 1850, John B. Maddox sec.
Hill, Joseph & Margaret Nottingham, 30 Oct. 1820, John Adams sec.

Hitchens(Hitchings), David R. & Margaret Dixon, 11 June 1821.
Hitchens, David & Rosey Kellam, 1 Jan. 1846, Luther W. Roberts sec.
Con. of Frances Hitchens, mother of David & of Margaret
Costin, mother of Rosey.

Hitchings(Hitchens),George & Frances Widgeon, 24 Jan. 1807, John
Williams sec.

*Holt, Albert G. & Emory S. Roberts, 3 Oct. 1853
Holt, George & Anne Custis, dau. Edmund Custis, dec. 31 Dec. 1757,
Addison Nottingham sec.
Holt, George & Elizabeth Ann Savage, ward of William Nottingham,
2 Sept. 1824, William Nottingham sec.
Holt, Martin & Adah Mapp, dau. Howson Mapp, 18 Feb. 1769, Howson
Mapp sec.
Holt, Martin M. M. & Esther W. Dixon, 19 Dec. 1820, Abram Costin
& Laban Godwin sec.
Holt, Stuart & Anne Johnson, 11 Jan. 1772, Stephen Tompson sec.
Con. of Benjamin Johnson, father of Anne
Holt, Stuart & Elizabeth Nelson, wid. Southy Nelson, 7 Feb. 1783,
John Lewis Fulwell sec.
Holt, Stuart & Susanna Moor, 28 Apr. 1784, John Savage sec. Con.
of Arcadia Moor, mother of Susanna.

Holbrooke, Samuel & Peggy Stott, 16 July 1763, Walter Hyslop sec.
Con. of Laban Stott, father of Peggy

Holmes, Edward & Elizabeth Parsons, dau. William Parsons, 25 July
1772, William Floyd sec.

Holland, John & Margaret Wilkins, dau. John Wilkins, blacksmith, 22
    Mar. 1775, John Wilkins B. sec.
Holland, Nathaniel & Susanna Bryan, 20 Dec. 1788, Walter Hyslop sec.

Hooks, Samuel & Nancy Justice, 11 Feb. 1795, Michael Matthews sec.

Hopkins, Maximilian & Elizabeth Armistead, 9 July 1799, Nathaniel
    Darby sec.
Hopkins, William W. & Ann W. Fisher, 28 Apr. 1810, George Fisher sec.

Horner, Benjamin & Margaret Hitchens, 19 June 1821, Thomas Williams
    sec.
Hornsby, William & Susanna Carpenter, wid. Charles Carpenter, 28
    Apr. 1787, Kendall Addison sec.

Hosier(Hozier), John & Nancy Kellum, 8 June 1819, William Matthews
    sec.
Hosier, John & Mahala Waterfield, 22 Dec. 1824, Major Bool sec.
    Con. of Meshack Waterfield, father of Mahala.

?House, William & Susanna Press, dau. Edmund Press, 27 Aug. 1788,
    Edmund Press sec.

?Howell, Custis & Rachel Beavans, dau. Molly Beavans, 2 Oct. 1837,
    Molly Beavans & Montcalm Oldham sec.
Howell, John & Margaret Pitts, dau. Jacob Pitts, 10 Sept. 1771,
    Jackson Rodgers sec.
Howell, John & Patsey Kelly, 16 Sept. 1806, John Waterfield sec.
Howell, Jesse & Margaret Maley, 9 Dec. 1780, Henry Guy sec.
Howell, William & Elizabeth White, 16 Nov. 1797, Hezekiah Pitts sec.

Howard, William & Rachel Dennis, 28 Mar. 1786, Whittington Stripe
    sec. Con. of Joseph Dennis.

Hozier(Hosier), Emanuel & Betsey Collins, 9 Nov. 1797, Preeson
    Abdil sec.
Hozier, Thomas & Adah Dunton, 26 Dec. 1804, Stephen Waistcoat sec.

Hubberd, Edmund & Anne Scott, 3 Oct. 1785, Abel Garrison sec.

Hughs, John & Mary Stockley, 16 Oct. 1779, Thomas Bullock sec.
Hughes, John & Mary McDonald, wid. Hugh McDonald, 6 Jan. 1781,

Hunt, Azariah & Frances Benthall, dau. Azel Benthall, 31 Jan.
    1759, Azel Benthall sec.
Hunt, Azariah & Sarah Bishop, wid. 3 Aug. 1771, Douglas Willett
    sec.
Hunt, Hillary & Delitha Lucre, 28 Jan. 1796, Obediah Hunt sec.
Hunt, John G. & Mary E. Nottingham, ward of L.B.Nottingham, 21
    May 1827, Leonard B. Nottingham sec.
Hunt, Obediah & Nancy Goffigon, 29 Nov. 1796, Benjamin Griffith
    sec. Con. of Nathaniel Goffigon, Gdn. of Nancy.
Hunt, Obediah & Nancy Mathews, 7 Oct. 1803, Michael Dunton sec.
    Con. of Mary Mathews, mother of Nancy.

Hunt, Obediah & Margaret M. Nottingham, 18 Dec. 1819, Southy
    Goffigon sec.
Hunt, Thomas & Frances Goffigon, 18 May 1791, Walter Hyslop sec.
    Con. of Nathaniel Goffigon, father of Frances.
Hunt, Thomas O. & Margaret B. Nelson, dau, Southy Nelson, dec., 26
    Nov. 1832, Smith Nottingham sec.

Hurtt, William M., of Kent County, Md., now living near Eastville
    in the State of Virginia, son of Elizabeth C. Hurtt, Born
    4 Apr. 1823, & Elizabeth Ward, dau. Stephen Ward, 11 July
    1846, Joshua P. Wescoat sec.
Hurtt, William M. & Peggy T. Savage, ward of Walter Raleigh, 10
    Apr. 1848, Walter Raleigh sec.

Hutson, Jesse & Margaret Holbrook, wid. Samuel Holbrook, 23 Oct.
    1767, John Mapp sec.

Hyslop(Haslop),Harvey & Nancy Pratt, 12 Sept. 1842, Thomas H.
    Dunton sec. Con. of Sarah Pratt, mother of Nancy.
Hyslop, John A. & Nancy Parsons, 13 May 1811, Custis Hyslop sec.
Hyslop, John C. & Nancy Whitehead, 22 Dec. 1814, Thomas Graves sec.
    Con. of John Whitehead, father of Nancy.
Hyslop, John C. & Anne Hayley, dau. Robert Hayley, 30 July 1823,
    Robert Hayley sec.
Hyslop, Littleton & Mary Travis, his ward, 11 July 1825, Thomas
    L. Evans sec.
Hyslop, Walter & Anne Bryan, wid. Hessey Bryan, 3 Oct. 1782,
    William Stith sec.

Inquest, Frederick & Lavenia Ann Speakman, dau. William S. Speak-
    man, 2 Dec. 1845, William S. Speakman sec.

Isdale(Esdel,Isdell,Isdel), John & Mary Bunting, wid. 22 Aug.
    1821, James Dennis sec.
Isdale, Matthew & Leah Jeffries, 3 Dec. 1807, John Jacob sec. Con.
    of Isaac Nottingham, Gdn. of Leah.
Isdale, Nathaniel & Betsey Luke, 10 Jan. 1799, Levin Belote sec.
Isdale, William & Nancy Dunton, wid. John Dunton, 10 June, 1822,
    William Roberts sec.

Isdel(Esdel,Isdale,Isdell), James & Lovey Mears, his ward, 9 Aug.
    1824, William R. Roberts, sec.

*Isdell(Esdel,Isdale,Isdel), William & Sally Savage, ward of
    Rosey M. Savage, 27 Jan. 1852.

Jackson, George W. & ___(no name)___ 3 July 1816, Edward H.C.
    Wilson sec.
Jackson, James & Sabra Kellum, dau. Stephen Kellum, 1 June 1793,
    Michael Matthews sec.
Jackson, James & Rose Kellum, 26 Dec. 1794, George Willis sec.

**Jackson, James & Louise Evans, 13 July 1816

Jacob, Arthur & Sally Thomas, 13 Feb. 1822, John K. Floyd sec.

Jacob, Edward & Susan Jacob, dau. William Jacob, 9 Nov. 1840,
Littleton Wilson sec.

Jacob, Esau & Betty Haggoman, 4 June, 1741, Thomas Gibbons & Jonathan Porter sec.

Jacob, Esau & Vianer Gray Pitts, dau. Major Pitts, dec., 12 Nov.
1762, Walter Hyslop sec.

Jacob, Esau, & Margaret Joyne, 21 Oct. 1789, Jacob Abdell sec.

Jacob, George T. ward of Devorax Godwin & orph. of Teackle Jacob,
dec., & Elizabeth S. Dunton, dau. Matthew Dunton, dec., 16
Sept. 1846, James Fitchett sec.

Jacob, Hancock, Jr. & Sarah Harmanson, 21 Dec. 1773, William
Harmanson sec.

Jacob, Hancock & Ann James, 20 June 1803, Hancock Dunton sec.

Jacob, Isaac & Anne Savage, wid. 31 Mar. 1750, Nehemiah Fitchett
sec.

?Jacob, James & Patience Only, 23 Dec. 1809, Cudjo Stephens sec.

Jacob, James, & Emeline Johnson, dau. James Johnson, Free Negroes,
19 Dec. 1838, Smith Nottingham & James Johnson sec.

Jacob, John & Peggy Turner dau. George Turner, dec. 20 Apr.
1767, William Major sec.

Jacob, John & Nancy Abdell, 15 Mar. 1804, William Lankford sec.

Jacob, John C., son of Thomas Jacob, & Emily Nottingham, orph.
of William Nottingham, & ward of Robert B. Nottingham, 4
Nov. 1828, Robert B. Nottingham sec.

Jacob, John & Polly Wilson, dau. Moses Wilson, dec., 19 Apr.
1830, Moses Wilson sec.

Jacob, John, widower, & Catharine Barcraft, spinster, 21 June,
1841, Smith S. Nottingham sec.

*Jacob, John C. & Tabitha R. Cutler, ward of Littleton W. Young,
8 Dec. 1852

Jacob, Richard & Adriana Mapp, wid. 17 Jan. 1749, John Flood sec.

**Jacob, Richard & Sally Whitehead, _____ 1816

Jacob, Richard & Mrs Harriet Rooks, wid. John Rooks, 11 Sept.
1837, Thomas Smith, Jr. sec.

Jacob, Robert & Anne Jacob, wid., 9 June 1764, John Stratton sec.

Jacob, Robert C. & Margaret C. Wilkins, ward of George F. Wilkins,
16 Dec. 1833, George F. Wilkins sec.

Jacob, Teackle & Margaret Addison, 27 Mar. 1783, Elisha Dowty sec.

Jacob, Teackle & Peggy Widgeon, 14 Apr. 1818, James Travis sec.

Jacob, Thomas & Nancy Abdell, wid. 20 Aug. 1788, Teackle Jacob sec.

Jacob, Thomas & Mary Gilden, wid. Charles Gilden, 25 Apr. 1790,
Teackle Jacob sec.

Jacob, Thomas & Sally Savage, 24 July 1795, Robins Mapp sec.

Jacob, Thomas, Jr. & Henrietta Parramore, 14 Dec. 1801, Thomas
Parramore, Sr. sec.

Jacob, Thomas, son of Teackle, & Sally White, 23 Apr. 1805, Thos:
Jacob, Jr. sec.

Jacob, Thomas & Elizabeth White, 28 July 1821, Calvin H. Head sec.

Jacob, Thomas L., ward of Edw. W. Nottingham & Elizabeth Ann
Wilkins, 25 Sept. 1838. Con. of William E. Wilkins,
father of Elizabeth Ann.

Jacob, William & Mary Jacob, dau. Hancock Jacob, 17 Dec. 1766, Edmund
    Glanville sec.
Jacob, William & Mary Bell, 10 Jan. 1775, William Waltham sec.
Jacob, William & Leah Gault, 27 Aug. 1784, Richard Dunton, Jr. sec.
Jacob, William & Peggy Henderson, 4 July 1795, Kendall Belote sec.
Jacob, William & Elizabeth Andrews, 22 Aug. 1816, William White sec.
Jacob, William W. & Sally Ann Godwin, dau. Edwin Godwin, 18 Nov. 1844,
    William T. Nottingham sec.

James, Abel, of Isle of Wight County, & Margaret Abdel, wid. 5 June
    1790, Thomas Jacob, Jr. sec.
James, Abel & Ann Craik, wid. William Craik, 13 Dec. 1824, Thomas E.
    Addison sec.
James, Andrew & Sally James, 23 Jan. 1800, John Ross sec.
James, Edmund P. & Sally Bird, dau. John Bird, dec., 7 June 1827,
    William Bird sec.
James, Hezekiah P. & Margaret Trower, dau. John Trower,Sr., 11 June
    1838, John T. Trower, Sr. sec.
James, John & Esther Dolby, 20 Oct. 1796, Henry Smaw sec.
James, John & Nancy Bell, 15 Mar. 1824, Edward Kellam sec.
James, John S. & Margaret C. James, 9 Oct. 1827, Arthur R. Savage,
    sec. Con. of Margaret Savage, Gdn. of Margaret C. James.
**James, John & Nervilla Belote, dau. Kendall Belote, 21 Jan. 1853
James, Levin T. & Lavenia C. Floyd, 14 Aug. 1848, William J. James
    sec.
James, Robert & Sarah Tilney, wid. 5 June 1751, Jacob Marshall sec.
James, Robert & Elizabeth Christian, 15 Dec. 1753, Esau Jacob sec.
James, Robert & Rosey Dowty, 18 Dec. 1820, Andrew James sec.
James, Thomas & Rebecca Mac_____, wid. 17 Nov. 1714, Fran:
    Wainhouse sec.
James, Thomas & Kessey Jacob, dau. Hancock Jacob, 6 Feb. 1764,
    Isaac Clegg sec.
James Thomas & Mary Heath, wid., 7 July 1764, Luke Heath sec.
James, Thomas & Elizabeth Dunton, dau. William Dunton, dec. 13
    Dec. 1774, William Jacob sec.
James, Thomas & Nancy Taylor, 13 July 1807, Robert Walker sec.
James, William & Sukey Smith, 25 Sept. 1798, Thomas James sec.
James, William & Margaret Major, 2 June 1806, John Simkins sec.
    Con. of Thomas James, Jr. Gdn. of Margaret.
James, William & Susan Ann Wilson, 25 Nov. 1828, Luther Ball sec.
    Con. of Arthur A. Wilson, father of Susan Ann.
James, William J. & Elizabeth A. Johnson, 12 Mar. 1834, Hezekiah P.
    James sec. Con. of Jeptha Johnson, father of Elizabeth A.
James, William & Fanny Tyson, wid. Samuel Tyson, 22 Apr. 1844,
    Joshua P. Wescoat sec.

Jamison, John & Adah Clegg, 13 Aug. 1751, Henry Tomlinson sec.
    Con. of Isaac Clegg, brother of Adah

Jarvis, George T. & Sally F. Goffigon, dau. Southy Goffigon, dec.
    8 Mar. 1847, Nathaniel S. Goffigon sec.
Jarvis, Jesse N. & Virginia A. Dalby, dau. Benjamin J. Dalby, 9
    Apr. 1848, Benjamin J. Dalby sec.

Jarvis, Thomas & Anne S. Bell, dau. Thomas Bell, 26 May 1789, William
    Jarvis sec.
Jarvis, William & Sarah Hunt, 26 Dec. 1780, William Rasco sec.
Jarvis, William & Fanny Hunt, 14 Dec. 1795, Hillary Hunt sec.
Jarvis, William, Jr. & Nancy Wilkins, 25 Aug. 1798, William Wilkins
    sec. Con. of Elizabeth Wilkins as to Nancy.
Jarvis, William & Elizabeth U. Robins, 14 May 1808, Arthur Simkins
    sec. Con. of John Robins, father of Elizabeth U.
Jarvis, William & Margaret Williams, 14 Sept. 1812, John Nelson,Sr.
    sec. Con. of Margaret Williams, mother of Margaret.
Jarvis, William W. & Leah Turpin, wid. Thomas H. Turpin, 13 Oct.
    1823, Smith Nottingham & William Jarvis sec. Con. of William
    Jarvis, Sr., father of William W.

?Jeffry(Jeffery,Jeffries,Jefferys),Littleton & Nancy Collins, 18 Sept.
    1810, James Jacob sec.
? Jeffery, Littleton & Lurany Collins, dau. Peggy Collins, 13 June,
    1827, Nathan Drighouse & Mack Collins sec.
? Jeffery, Solomon & Tinsey Jacob, 16 Jan. 1788, William Satchell,
    Jr. sec.
? Jeffery, Solomon & Nancy Collins, 3 Dec. 1817, Mack Collins sec.
? Jefferys, William & Sarah Bullock, dau. Thomas Bullock, 18 Sept.
    1781, William Wood sec.
?Jeffries, William & Polly Bingham, 26 Jan. 1803, Samuel Beavans sec.

Jefferson, Peter & Polly Freshwater, 18 Oct. 1813.
Jefferson, Silas & Polly Costin, 15 Mar. 1814, Lawrence Enholm sec.
    Con. of William Costin, Sr. father of Polly.

Jenkins, George & Charlotte Terrier, ward of William S. Floyd, 27
    Apr. 1838, William S. Floyd sec.

Jenne, William & Margaret Fisher, wid. Thomas Fisher, dec. 12 Feb.
    1782, John Darby sec.
Jenne, William & Betsy Ewing, 20 July 1787, David Jones sec.

Johnson, Abel B. & Susan Dalby, dau. Branson Dalby, 13 Feb. 1822,
    Charles B. Stockly sec.
Johnson, Benjamin & Rose Hunt, wid. 30 July 1773, John Smith sec.
Johnson, Christopher, of the State of Maryland, & Susanna Stith,
    dau. Griffin Stith, Sr., 10 May 1780, Thorowgood Smith sec.
Johnson, Edmund S. & Jane Dunton, dau. William Dunton, dec. 25
    Apr. 1774, John Blair sec.
Johnson, Edmund & Polly Dowty, dau. Hezekiah Dowty, 22 June 1781,
    Addison Dowty sec.
Johnson, Edmund & Anna Smaw, 5 Nov. 1807, Henry Smaw sec.
Johnson, Edmund & Mary Savage, 27 Oct. 1818, Preeson Savage sec.
Johnson, Edward N. & Mahala Waterfield, 12 Mar. 1827, Harrison T.
    Rayfield sec.
Johnson, Edward & Sally Bull, 2 Nov. 1840, Jacob Spady sec.
Johnson, Esme & Rachel Darby, wid. 1 Aug. 1761, James Perkins sec.
Johnson, George R. & Elizabeth S. Johnson, dau. John J. Johnson,
    dec., 23 Mar. 1842, Nathan R. Fletcher sec.

Johnson, Isaac & Matilda Stuart, 9 Jan. 1812, James Johnson sec.

Johnson, James & Betsey Stott, 2 Oct. 1794, George Lewis sec.

Johnson, James & Elizabeth Giddens, 22 July 1806, Wm.R.Finney sec.

Johnson, James & Mary Baker, 16 Jan. 1809, Edward Ironmonger sec.

Johnson, James & Ann Godwin, 8 May 1810, Henry Scarborough sec.

Johnson, James,Sr. & Susanna Elligood, 25 May 1813, Thomas S. Satchell sec.

Johnson, Jeptha & Rosanna James, 18 Aug. 1807, Revel Watson sec.

*Johnson, Jeptha & Polly Bishop, 7 Nov. 1851

Johnson, Johannes & Ansly Savage, 12 July 1785, Hezekiah Pitts sec.

Johnson, Johannes & Elizabeth Stripe, 13 Aug. 1821, Charles West sec.

Johnson, John & Margaret Jacob, wid. 11 Oct. 1774, Alexander McLaughlin sec.

Johnson, John & Rose Shores, 13 Mar. 1797, George Nehollows sec.

Johnson, John P. & Catharine Ames, 11 Jan. 1798, John Milby sec.

Johnson, John & Eliza Downes, ward of Nathaniel Dalby, 21 Feb. 1827, Nathaniel Dalby sec.

Johnson, John Y. & Louisiana W. Trower, ward of William Costin, 24 Dec. 1833, William Costin sec.

Johnson, John T. & Susan Fitchett, dau. William Fitchett, Sr. dec., 29 May 1842

Johnson, John & Elizabeth Belote, dau. Susan Belote, 17 Apr. 1843, William Dennis sec.

Johnson, Joshua & Esther Savage 12 Aug. 1788, John Robins sec.

Johnson, Laban & Anne Gascoigne, wid. 14 Feb. 1775, William Harmanson sec. Johnson, Laban S. & Elizabeth Waples, 18 Feb. 1820, Thomas West sec.

Johnson, Laban S. & Elizabeth W. Stott, 11 Feb. 1839, John W. Leatherbury sec.

Johnson, Moses & Sarah Nottingham, dau. Isaac Nottingham, 12 Nov. 1767, William Major sec.

Johnson, Moses & Sarah Powell, dau. George Powell dec. 24 July 1770, Jonathan Johnson sec.

Johnson, Obadiah & Leah Abdell, ward of William P. Johnson, 30 Nov. 1824, William P. Johnson sec.

Johnson, Obedience & Elishe Godwin, 8 Feb. 1772, Robert Polk sec. Con. of Devorax Godwin, father of Elishe.

Johnson, Obedience R. & Mary A. Young, wid. James Young, 18 Dec. 1836, Robert B. Savage sec.

Johnson, Powell & Elizabeth Goffigon, dau. James Goffigon, 22 Dec. 1768, Thomas Underhill sec. Con. of Southy Goffigon, Gdn. of Elizabeth.

Johnson, Richard & Polly B. Bloxom, 29 Aug. 1812, Nath'l.West sec.

Johnson, Robinson & Mary Johnson, wid. Edmund Johnson, 3 Aug. 1786, William Jenne sec.

Johnson, Samuel & Agatha Gilden, 12 Sept. 1723, Matthew Harmanson & John Waterson sec.

Johnson, Solomon & Adah Johnson, dau. Obedience Johnson, dec., 4 June, 1770, Moses Johnson sec.

Johnson, Thomas & Sally Savage, 31 Aug. 1795, Joseph Hanby sec.

Johnson, Thomas & Peggy Wheelor, 24 Mar. 1796, William Hanby sec.

Johnson, Thomas & Sarah Nelson, spinster, 29 Nov. 1802, John Goffigon sec.

Johnson, Thomas & Feriba Dalby, 13 June 1807, David Harlow sec.

Johnson, Thomas & Frances Wescot, 7 Mar. 1814, William Westcot sec. Con. of William Westcot, father of Frances.

Johnson, Thomas E., ward of John Simkins, & Mary A. Knight, dau. William Knight, 10 Aug. 1840, John Simkins & Smith Nottingham sec.

Johnson, William & Elishe Haggoman, dau. Silvanus Haggoman, 15 Mar. 1757, Esau Jacob sec.

Johnson, William & Hannah Andrews, 6 Sept. 1778, Nathaniel Powell sec.

Johnson, William & Hannah Carter, 26 Apr. 1794, George Savage sec.

Johnson, William R. & Margaret D. Brickhouse, dau. Thomas S. Brickhouse, 17 Dec. 1842, Smith L. Brickhouse sec.

**Joliff, Richard & Eskey Ames, _____ 1800.

Jones, Cave, of Accomack, & Margaret Upshur, 14 Jan. 1794, John Upshur, Jr. sec.

Jones, David & Sarah Ellegood, dau. John Ellegood, dec. 24 Aug. 1759

Jones, David & Esther Mapp, wid. William Mapp, 2 Dec. 1788, John Dennis sec.

Jones, Isaac & Smart Waterfield, 25 June, 1790, Peter Warren sec.

Jones, James & Lucy Dowty, 13 Feb. 1815, Sheppard Floyd sec. Con. of Archibald Dowty, father of Lucy.

Jones, John & Nancy Stripe, 28 Aug. 1801, John Scott sec.

Jones, John W. & Catherine S. Floyd, dau. John K. Floyd, 25 June 1823, John K. Floyd sec.

Jones, John & Tabitha M. Godwin, dau. Littleton Godwin, dec. 26 July 1837, Thomas Smith, Jr. sec.

Jones, Littleton & Margaret Graves, 30 Apr. 1791, Moses Wilson sec. Con. of Peter Graves, father of Margaret.

Jones, Major & Esther Waterfield, 10 July 1787, Thomas Jones sec.

Jones, Nathaniel & Sally Griffith, 5 June 1797, Littleton Jones sec.

Jones, Obediah & Elizabeth Caple, 12 July 1798, Matthias Jones sec. Con. of Catharine Caple, mother of Elizabeth.

Jones, Richard & Margaret Clegg, 6 Mar. 1812, Stuart Saunders sec.

Jones, Richard & Sally Whitehead, 11 Dec. 1815, John Warrington sec.

Jones, Thomas & Sarah Parkerson, 10 June, 1787, Major Jones, sec.

Jones, Thomas & Sally Caple, 8 June 1793, Littleton Jones sec.

Jones, Thomas & Elisa Simkins, 13 Jan. 1823, John Simkins sec.

Jones, William & Elishe Joynes, 11 Dec. 1779, Jacob Warren sec.

Jones, William & Anne Graves, wid. 24 Dec. 1791, Thomas Jones sec.

Jones, William & Nancy McCrady, 5 Mar. 1803, James Fisher sec.

Jones, Zorobabel & Susanna Mapp, 16 June, 1790, David Jones sec.

Jones, Zorobabel & Adah Heath, 28 Sept. 1798, David Topping sec. Con. of Bridget Heath, mother & Gdn. of Adah.

Jourden, George & Susanna Caul, dau. Daniel Caul, 10 Apr. 1765, Henry Jourden sec.

Jourden, Thomas & Elizabeth Warren, wid. 18 June, 1765, John Luke sec.

Joyne(Joynes), Edmund, Mariner, & Esland Rogers, 23 Nov. 1752,

Edward Holbrook sec.

Joyne, Edmund & Mary Scott, 22 Dec. 1787, Hancock Jacob sec.

Joyne, Harmanson & Sarah Carpenter, dau. Stephen Carpenter, dec. 2
Jan. 1756, Patrick Harmanson sec.

Joyne, John & Rachel Andrews, 14 Dec. 1756, Littleton Andrews sec.

Joyne, Watkins & Rachel Brickhouse, dau. Major Brickhouse, 17 Dec.
1764, Charles Floyd sec.

Joyne, William & Mary Parsons, dau. John Parsons, 31 Dec. 1779,
Walter Hyslop sec.

Joyne, William & Margaret Tankard, 3 June 1789, Jacob Roberts sec.

Joynes(Joyne), Edmund & Peggy Michael, dau. John Michael,Jr.19 Sept.
1792 Arthur Rodgers sec.

Joynes, Edward & Nancy Kendall, 31 Oct. 1809, Seth Warren sec.

Joynes, Edward J. son of Robert A. Joynes, & Sally Wescoat, ward
of Robert A. Joynes, 12 Dec. 1831, Robert A. Joynes sec.

Joynes, George & Betsey Purnal Major, 19 Dec. 1799, Arthur Roberts
sec.

Joynes, John & Susanar Kellum, 29 Sept. 1778, Smith Kellam sec.

Joynes, John & Peggy Floyd, 29 Dec. 1796, William Joynes sec.

Joynes, John & Elishe Willis, 28 Aug. 1820, Daniel Smaw sec.

*Joynes, John L. & Catharine S. Floyd, ward of Lavenia Floyd, 30
Dec. 1851

Joynes, Kendall & Sally Milby, 6 Mar. 1797, John Milby sec.

Joynes, Levin S. & Maria S. Baptist, 29 Jan. 1824, Edward R.
Boisnard sec.

**Joynes, Nathaniel & Sally Griffith _____ 1798

Joynes, Robert A. & Elizabeth Widgeon, wid. Thomas Widgeon, 1 Nov.
1821, Thomas Lehollams sec.

Joynes, Robert A. & Margaret Matthews, wid. Levin Matthews, 9 Sept.
1835, John Lecato sec.

Joynes, Sheppard A. & Peggy S. C. Walter, dau. Solomon Walter, 8
Aug. 1825, Solomon Walter sec.

Joynes, Thomas M. & Leah Wise, 9 Nov. 1818, Stephen S. Gunter sec.

Joynes, Tully W. A. & Sabra P. Fitchett, 24 June, 1844, James H.
Stewart sec.

Joynes, William & Sukey Floyd, 1 Jan. 1827, Nathaniel B. Hickman
sec.

Joynes, William & Margaret Tankard - Con. of John Tankard, Gdn.
of Margaret Tankard, dated 1 June, 1789 (see mar. bond of
William Joyne & Margaret Tankard)

? Judah, Mark & Adah Pool, his ward, 14 July 1823, George Pool &
Isaac Thompson sec.

Justice, Ralph & Sarah Marshall, 13 Mar. 1738, John Marshall &
Thomas Marshall sec.

Kellam(Kellum), Augustus J. F. & Mary E. Goffigon, 12 Nov. 1838,
Major D.Colonna sec. Con. of Wm.Goffigon,Gdn. of Mary E.

Kellum, Charles & Sally Howell, 11 Apr. 1796, William Howell sec.

Kellam, Charles & Rosey Ann Wingate, dau. James Wingate, 5 Jan.

1836, James Wingate sec.

Kellam, Custis & Margaret Dunton, 9 Sept. 1817, Levin Lewis sec.

Kellum, Edmund & Mary Pearson, 3 Apr. 1825, George F. Outten sec.

Kellum, Edward & Sally Nottingham, 5 Dec. 1814, Thomas Jacob sec. Con. of William Nottingham, father of Sally.

Kellam, Edward & Sarah Wilkins, wid. John, son of John, 4 Apr. 1838, Edmund R. Custis sec.

Kellam, Edward & Virginia Underhill, dau. William Underhill, dec., 5 Sept. 1842, Calvin H. Savage sec.

Kellum, Evans & Elizabeth Costin, 13 July 1820, Thomas Peed sec.

Kellam, James & Peggy Dorman, 10 Oct. 1801, John Dunton sec.

Kellam, James & Rose Costin, 3 Feb. 1819, Silas Jefferson sec. Con. of William Costin, father of Rose.

Kellam, James L. & Susan Ann Goffigon, 28 Feb. 1837, Thomas A. Coleburn sec.

Kellam, Jesse & Mary J. Mears, 16 Jan. 1830, Egbert G. Bayly sec. Con. of Richard Mears, of William, father of Mary.

Kellam, John & Eliza Harrison, an illegitimate dau. of Peggy Clegg, 10 Dec. 1832, Peggy Clegg sec.

*Kellam, John H. & Mary A. Evans, ward of Alfred Parker, 20 Jan. 1852

Kellam, Lewis & Nancy Nortrip, wid. Daniel Nortrip, 30 Aug. 1830, John Robins   sec.

Kellam, Lewis & Lovey Collins, Free Negroes, 13 May 1850, John W. Leatherbury sec.

Kellum, Nathaniel & Rosey Addison, 11 Jan. 1786, Abel Kellum sec.

Kellum, Robert & Sally Stott, 22 Sept. 1798, William Stratton sec.

Kellum, Samuel & Elizabeth Downing, 4 Mar. 1816, Thomas Scarborough sec. Con. of Edmund Downing, Gdn. of Elizabeth.

Kellam, Samuel E.D. & Louisa Kendall, 11 Sept. 1848, Alex.W.F.Mears sec. Con. of Catharine H.G.Kendall, mother of Louisa.

Kellam, Shadrack & Leah Mapp, 12 Oct. 1779, Howson Mapp sec.

Kellum, Shepherd & Polly Ashby, 25 Mar. 1819, Robert Ashby sec.

Kellum, Stephan & Elizabeth Belote, wid. Benjamin Belote, 10 May 1845, Edward Rayfield sec.

Kellum, Teackle & Betsey Floyd Smith, 22 Apr. 1801, Zerobable Jones sec.

Kellum, Thomas H. & Elizabeth B. Dorsey, 22 Jan. 1819, Peter Bowdoin sec.

Kellam, Thomas H. & Mrs Harriet B. D. Parramore, 24 Feb. 1837, William H. Parker sec.

Kellam, Thomas & Mary L. Tyler, dau. Benjamin Tyler, 22 Jan. 1850, Benjamin Tyler sec.

Kellam, Walter & Sarah Turpin, 27 Jan. 1801, Ismay Johnson sec.

Kellam, William H. & Catherine West, ward of Abel Bradford, 28 Dec. 1825, Abel Bradford sec.

Kellam, William H. & Mahala F. Mears, dau. Richard Mears, 8 Nov. 1830, Richard Mears sec.

*Kellam, William T. & Emily S. Willis, ward of Custis Willis, 26 Apr. 1853.

*Kelly, Abel & Rosey Savage, dau. Caleb Savage, dec.27 Aug. 1850.

Kelly, Alexander & Henrietta Stott, 25 Oct. 1780, William Waterfield sec.

Kelly, Charles & Elizabeth Roberts, 8 June 1826, William Isdell sec.
    Con. of Nancy Isdell, mother of Elizabeth Roberts.
Kelly, Charles & Eliza Ann Brown, dau. Allen Brown, 11 July 1836,
    Charles Dillion & Allen Brown sec.
Kelly, James & Peggy Joynes, 20 Dec. 1808, William Savage sec.
Kelly, James & Mary Taylor, dau. John Taylor, 18 Dec. 1849, John Taylor
    sec.
Kelly, John & Sally Churn, dau. John Churn, late dec., 29 Dec. 1840,
    William M. Savage sec.
Kelly, Laban & Ann Goffigon, 28 Nov. 1814, Abraham Costin sec.
**Kelly, Stephen & Elizabeth Belote, 10 May 1845.
Kelly, Sylvester M. & Elizabeth B. Fitchett, wid. Thomas Fitchett,
    Jr. 30 Dec. 1846, John S. Turpin sec.
Kelly, Thomas B. & Sophia Savage, wid. John Savage, dec. 26 Sept.
    1836, Samuel G. Carpenter sec.
Kelly, Thomas, son of Jesse Kelly, dec. & Margaret J. Kelly, dau.
    Stephen Kelly, dec. 28 Mar. 1842, Arthur E. Roberts sec.
Kelly, Thomas & Margaret Ann Savage, 24 Mar. 1845, Alex. W. F.
    Mears sec. Con. of Mary Savage.
Kelly, Timothy & Elizabeth Bradford, 14 Mar. 1825, William Mears
    sec.
Kelly, Timothy & Elizabeth Taylor, dau. George Taylor sec. 7 May
    1842, Thomas Kelly sec.
Kelly, William T. & Kiturah Churn, dau. William Churn, 19 Dec. 1848,
    Thomas N. B. Roberts sec.

Kemp, John & Adah Dunton, dau. Stephen Dunton, 11 Mar. 1769,
    Stephen Dunton sec.

Kendall, Custis & Elizabeth W. Jarvis, 20 Feb. 1816, William Jarvis,
    Sr. sec.
Kendall, Custis & Elizabeth Bowdoin, 9 Apr. 1746, Isaac Nottingham
    sec.
Kendall, George Mason & Elishe Harmanson, 17 Mar. 1740, John
    Marshall sec. Con. of Elizabeth Harmanson, mother of Elishe.
Kendall, Henry B. & Catherine Dalby, 4 Oct. 1814, Custis Kendall
    sec.
Kendall, John & Elizabeth Harmanson, 15 Sept. 1741, Littleton Eyre
    & George Kendall sec. Con. of Elizabeth Harmanson, mother
    of Elizabeth.
Kendall, John & Sarah Satchell, dau. Southy Satchell, dec. 22 Jan.
    1768, William Satchell sec.
Kendall, John, Jr. & Lucretia Guy, dau. Henry Guy, dec. 3 Nov.
    1779, Edm: Glanville sec. Con. of Henry Guy, brother & Gdn.
    of Lucretia.
Kendall, John W. & Susanna Harmanson, 5 Feb. 1802, John R. Waddy
    sec. Con. of Henry Harmanson, father of Susanna.
Kendall, John & Sally Simkins, 3 July 1802, John Simkins sec.
    Con. of Lucretia Kendall, mother of John
Kendall, John C. & Juliet J. Andrews, wid. Isaac Andrews, 24
    Sept. 1845, Alex. W. F. Mears, sec.
Kendall, Lemuel & Susanna Robins, 10 May 1738, Thomas Cable sec.
Kendall, Littleton & Sally Dixon, 21 July 1807, Thomas V. Custis
    sec.

Kendall, Littleton, Jr. & Maria Robins, 28 Feb. 1809, George Kendall
   sec. Con. of John Robins, father of Maria.
Kendall, Littleton & Mary Holt, dau. George Holt,dec.,1 Dec. 1755,,
   John Harmanson sec.
Kendall, Thomas & Anne Wilkins, dau. John Wilkins (O.P.), Gent., 27
   Nov. 1776, John Respess sec.
Kendall, Thomas & Elizabeth Matthews, 11 Sept. 1793, George Savage
   sec.
Kendall, Thomas L. & Mrs Susan W. Heath, wid. Rufus Heath, 2 Apr.
   1849, William J. Bowdoin sec.
Kendall, William & Nancy Parsons, 17 Oct. 1771, Henry Bryant sec.
Kendall, William J. & Mary Waggoman, 13 Apr. 1774, Obedience Johnson
   sec.
Kendall, William & Jane Parks, 16 Oct. 1706, Samuel Palmer sec.
   William Kendall son of Capt. William Kendall, dec.
Kendall, William & Susan Dalby, 21 Jan. 1818, Edward Kellam sec.

Kennard, William & Anne W. Stratton, 5 Mar. 1827, Henry Tazewell sec.
Kennard, William B. & Margaret Nottingham, dau. Thomas Nottingham,
   dec. 29 Oct. 1844, Tully A. T. Joynes sec.

*Ker, Edward & Caroline T. Rutter, 16 Oct. 1850
Ker, George & Sarah C. Winder, dau. Sarah U. Winder, 2 Oct. 1849,
   Sarah U. Winder sec.
Ker, John & Mary Waddey, 15 May 1822, John E. Nottingham sec.

Kerby, Robert & Elizabeth Marshall, 18 June 1744, John Custis sec.

Kerwin, Andrew & Anne Luke, 4 Aug. 1783, Charles Satchell sec.
Kerwin, Andrew & Susanna Grice, 2 Dec. 1783, John Dalby sec.

Kilmon, Charles & Rosey Ann Wingate, 7 May 1836

Kincaid, John & Margaret Preeson, 1 May 1738, Thomas Cable sec.

Kinney, Benson & Elizabeth C. Bedell, wid. James Bedell, 15 Mar.
   1838, Christopher D. Fitchett sec.
Kinney, Benson & Eliza Elliott, wid. James Elliott, 28 Mar. 1844,
   Samuel W. Williams sec.

Knight, Henry & Hamutal Knight, 22 Oct. 1756, John Moor sec.
Knight, John & Molly Floyd, dau. Charles Floyd, 24 Feb. 1790,
   Charles Floyd sec.
Knight, John & Betsey Wheelor, 2 Feb. 1808, Michael Dunton sec.
Knight, Kendall & Leah Nelson, dau. John Nelson,Sr., 10 Nov.
   1834, Thomas J. Nottingham sec.
Knight, Thomas & Susanna Fisher, 19 Aug. 1751, Tilney Michael sec.
**Knight, Thomas & Margaret Belote _____ 1794
Knight, Thomas & Eliza Trower, dau. John Trower, 1 Jan. 1828, John
   Trower sec.
Knight, William & Mary Benthall, dau. William Benthall dec. 28 May
   1777, William Jarvis sec.

Knight, William & Sally Kendall, 28 Dec. 1808, Nath'l. Widgeon sec.

Knower, John & Ann Fitzhugh, 5 Mar. 1835

Lankford, Killiam & Eleanor Cable, 2 Dec. 1803, John Jacob sec.

Lane, Ezekiel, of Worcester County, Md., & Hannah Harmanson, wid. 12
    Nov. 1763, William Christian sec.
Lane, William, of Gloster, & Margaret Fulwell, dau. John Lewis Fulwell
    7 Oct. 1789, John Lewis Fulwell sec.

Lawrence, Levin & Susanna Eshon, 18 Feb. 1780, James Williams sec.

Leatherbury, James M. & Elizabeth Powell, wid. Thomas Powell, 13
    Aug. 1838, Thomas K. Dunton sec.
Leatherbury, John W. & Sally C. West, 30 Nov. 1818, Jacob Notting-
    ham, Jr. sec. Con. of Charles West, father of Sally C.
Leatherbury, Perry & Agnes Roberts, wid. 9 Jan. 1770, Edmund
    Leatherbury sec.
Leatherbury, William J., son of John W. Leatherbury,& Virginia S.
    Harmanson, dau. William Harmanson, 13 July 1846, John W.
    Leatherbury & William Harmanson sec.

Lecato, John & Sally Dennis, ward of John W. Leatherbury, 27 Nov.
    1833, John W. Leatherbury sec.
Lecato, John & Elizabeth S. Wyatt, dau. John Wyatt, dec. 8 Feb.
    1848, William K. Matthews sec.

Lemount, Hardes & Elizabeth Pigot, wid., 6 Dec. 1758, Southy
    Goffigon sec.

Lewis, George & Margaret Nottingham, 10 Nov. 1789, Thomas Notting-
    ham sec.
Lewis, Issackar & Hannah Tankard, 17 Apr. 1811, John Tankard sec.
Lewis, Thomas & Sarah Williams 25 Jan. 1800, John Frost sec.

Lilliston, Edmund & Sukey Costin, dau. Samuel Costin dec. 2 Feb.
    1811, Arthur Simkins sec.
Lilliston, Jacob D. & Elizabeth Turpin, 19 Apr. 1837, Henry P.
    Lilliston & Elizabeth Turpin sec.
Lilliston, Robert C. & Nancy Cox, 19 Nov. 1806, William P. Harman-
    son sec. Con. of George Belote, Gdn. of Nancy.

? Liverpool, Daniell & Elishe Drighouse, 25 June 1799, Josias
    Liverpool sec.
? Liverpool, Henry & Kesiah Becket, 17 Mar. 1789, Solomon Liverpool
    sec.

Lockwood, Amos & Joice Twiford, 8 July 1794, Isaac Rose sec.

Luke, Daniel & Mary Walter, dau. John Walter, 25 June 1772, John
    Dalby sec.

Luke, Daniel & Molly McCrady, 25 May 1796, Eson Jacob sec.
Luke, Daniel & Sally Bell, 17 Apr. 1799, Littleton Dennis sec.
Luke, George & Catharine Lingo, 14 Mar. 1811, John Rayfield sec.
    Con. of Margaret Lingo, mother of Catharine.
Luke, Isaac & Elizabeth Wilson, 5 Jan. 1780, William Cable sec.
**Luke, John & Patience Lawrence _____ June, 1792

Luker, John & Elizabeth Mapp, 31 Dec. 1763, John Dolby sec.
Luker, John W. & Elizabeth N. Scott, 18 Nov. 1826, Levin Nottingham
    sec.
Luker, Walter & Sukey Hunt, orph., 24 Dec. 1791, John Goffigon sec.
    Con. of Nathaniel Goffigon, Gdn. of Sukey.
Luker, Walter & Sally Dunton, 18 Aug. 1812, Edmund Joynes sec.
Luker, Walter M. & Margaret S. Moore, dau. Matthew D. Moore, 24
    Dec. 1838, Matthew D. Moore sec.

Lunn, John & Sally Roberts, 11 May 1807, Levi Richardson sec.

Lyon, George A. & Anna G. Savage, 12 June 1815, Severn E.Parker sec.
Lyon, James & Sarah Eyre, 16 July 1799, John Eyre sec.

McCready, Ezekiel & Mary Gladston, dau. William Gladston, 13
    May 1786, Daniel Benthall sec.   Jr. sec.
McCroskey,Samuel Smith & Elizabeth Bowdoin,24 Nov.1780,Griffin Stith/
McCown(McCowan,McKown,Meccown),John & Esther Downs, 28 Sept. 1791,
    William Smith sec.
McCown, John & Nancy Griffeth, 21 Dec. 1802, Peter Wilkins sec.
**McCowan,John & Grace Jones, 25 June 1818
McCowan, William & Elizabeth Ann Costin, wid. Patrick F.Costin,
    9 Aug. 1828, James Sanford sec.

McDaniel, Charles & Molly Hickman, 3 Apr. 1802, Robert Haggoman
    sec.

McDonald, William Gibb & Sarah Michael, dau. Tilney Michael,dec.
    21 Sept. 1771, William Kendall,Jr. sec.
McDonald, William Gibb & Hannah Bell, 1 July 1773, Samuel
    Atchison sec.

McGreger, James & Sally Jacob 23 June 1795, Abel Savage sec.

McKown(McCown,McCowan,Meccown),Edward & Susan Ann Biggs, dau.
    John W. Biggs, dec., 4 Apr. 1843, Severn Wilkins sec.
McKown, Edward & Sarah Ann Heath, dau. John S. Heath,dec., 18
    Nov. 1857, William W. Scott sec.
McKown, John Thomas & Sally S. Joynes, 16 Jan. 1843, Severn
    Wilkins sec. Con. of Elisha Joynes, mother of Sally S.
McKown, William C. & Margaret Ann Wilkins, ward of William C.
    McKown, 11 Jan. 1847, John W. Williams sec.

Macky, Willock & Desdemona Jackson, 19 Sept. 1752, William
    Sargeant Kittridge sec.

Mahier, Richard & Mary Savage, 20 Apr. 1719, James Forse & Thomas
  Savage,Jr. sec.

Mail, George & Betsy Lewis, 21 Mar. 1848, Robert Bell sec.

Major, John & Anne Johnson, dau. Obedience Johnson, dec. 11 Oct.1791,
  Caleb Savage sec.
Major, Littleton & Sarah Dunton, dau. Jacob Dunton,dec. 5 Sept.1790,
  William Dixon sec.
Major, Littleton & Louisa Morris, dau. Levin Morris, 10 June, 1829,
  Levin Morris sec.
Major, Smith & Betsey Crippen, 14 Mar. 1796, John Turner sec.
Major, William & Rachel Underhill, 25 June, 1798, Arthur Roberts sec.
Major, William L., orph. of William Major & ward of James Kellam,
  of A., & Elizabeth Costin, dau. William Costin, 9 Feb. 1829,
  Joseph Kellam, of A.(Accomack?) & William Costin,Sr. sec.

Mann, William & Margaret Kellum, 23 Apr. 1790, John T. Turner sec.
Mann, William & Eulalie Dan_____, 13 Nov. 1800, John Brickhouse,Jr. sec.

*Mapp, Alfred N. H. & Laura S. Savage, ward of John C. Mapp,Jr.
  3 Sept. 1851
Mapp, Howson & Bridget Westerhouse, 25 Sept. 1759, Thomas Luker sec.
Mapp, John & Betty Haggoman, 16 Feb. 1765, Thomas Burk sec.
Mapp, John C. & Cassandra James, 21 Dec. 1813, Levin J.Thomas sec.
Mapp, John C. & Polly Jefferson,wid. Silas Jefferson, 11 Oct. 1838,
  Thomas Nottingham sec.
Mapp, John C.,Jr. & Mrs Malana Savage, wid. Severn Savage, 6 June
  1849, Alfred N. H. Mapp sec.
Mapp, Laban, ward of John R. Fisher, & Elizabeth J. Kellam, 13
  July 1835, George T. Belote sec.
Mapp, Laban & Phebe Robertson, ward of Joseph E. Bell, 10 Dec.
  1838, Joseph E. Bell sec.
**Mapp, Robert W. W. & Harriet Fitchett, dau. Mrs Leah Thurston,
  28 Dec. 1852
Mapp, Robins & Jane Holbrooke, dau. Rev. John Holbrooke, dec.
  12 Nov. 1755, John Harmanson sec.
Mapp, Robins & Margaret Matthews, 14 Jan. 1789, Edward Robins sec.
  Con. of Benjamin Dunton.
Mapp, Robins & Margaret C. Leatherbury, sister of Col. John W.
  Leatherbury, 21 May 1838, John W. Leatherbury sec.
Mapp, Samuel & Jane Baker,wid. 1 July 1776, Richard Nottingham
  sec.
Mapp, Samuel & Susanna Godwin, 26 Jan. 1786, Seth Powell sec.
Mapp, Victor A. & Hannah E. Scott, ward of George F. Wilkins,
  20 Dec. 1830, George F. Wilkins sec.
Mapp, Victor A. & Eliza Ann Scott, ward of George F. Wilkins, 3
  July 1832, George F. Wilkins sec.
Mapp, William & Esther Moor, wid. 28 Sept. 1770, Howson Mapp sec.
Mapp, William M. & Elizabeth Hallet, 30 Nov. 1821, Isaac W.
  Avery sec.
Mapp, William W. & Margaret A.Hallett, dau. John Hallett, 21

Jan. 1843, John Hallett sec.

*Mapp, William & Nancy Hall, dau. John Hall, dec. 5 Aug. 1852

Martin, James & Sukey Richardson, ward of Severn Martin, 31 Dec.1822,
    Luke Martin sec

Martin, John & Parmer Satchell, 7 Sept. 1785, Peter Bowdoin sec.

*Martin, John S. & Susan Dunton, dau. William M. Dunton, 1 Sept.1851

Martin, Louis & Polly Harrison, 17 Sept. 1778, Stephen Ward sec.

Martin, Luke & Elishe Freshwater, 8 June, 1786, Thomas Wilson sec.
    Con. of Mary Greenaway, mother of Elishe, con. also signed
    by Robert Greenaway.

Martin, Luke & Molly Barret, dau. David Barret, 6 Jan. 1789, William
    Phabin sec.

Martin, Luke & Mary Dalby, 12 June 1792, Nath'l. Powell sec.

Martin, Severn & Mary Dunton, ward of Seldon S. Ridley, 12 Aug.1822

Martin, Thomas & Mary Bell, 20 Dec. 1817, James Dalby sec.

Martin, Thomas, of Onancock, & Sally Craick, 20 July 1821, David
    Ross sec.

Martin, Thomas & Mahala Fletcher, 10 Sept. 1831, James R. B.Martin
    sec.

Martin, William & Rosey Clegg, dau. Major Clegg, dec. 22 Dec. 1827,
    Hezekiah Dalby sec.

Martin, William B. & Betsy Bloodsworth, 1 Feb. 1837, Pitt Price
    Bloodsworth sec.

Marshall, Jacob, of the County of Worcester,Md., & Margaret Roberts,
    wid. 29 Dec. 1749, John Marshall sec.

Marshall, Thomas John & Sarah Darby, 12 Feb. 175__,Henry Barlow sec.

Mason, George & Susanna Wilkins, 17 Aug. 1805, Johannes Wise sec.

Mason, John & Susan Matthews, 15 July 1813, Charles Mason & Sam'l.
    Matthews sec. Con. of Sally Mathews, mother of Susan.

Mason, William H. & Elizabeth Ann Moore, dau. Matthew D. Moore, 12
    Dec. 1848, Matthew Moore sec.

Mason, Zorobabel A. & Ann E.S.Addison, 19 Dec. 1837, Edward C.
    Thomas & Michael R.Matthews sec. Con. of William Addison,
    father of Ann E.

Masling(Mazlin),Thomas & Elizabeth Pigot, wid. 10 July 1773, John
    Lewis Fulwell sec.

Maslin, Thomas & Susanna Scott, 27 Apr. 1787, Smith Griffeth sec.

Maslin, Thomas & Betty Wheeler, 19 July 1792, James Weir sec.

Matthews(Mathews),Custis & Sarah Dixon, dau. John Dixon, dec. 8
    Dec. 1772, Charles Gilden sec.

Matthews, Custis & Sarah Andrews, 11 June 1777, Richard Smith sec.

Matthews, Isaiah & Juliet Becket, Free Negroes, 24 Dec. 1838,
    George F. Wilkins sec.

Matthews, Jacob & Susan Upshur, Free Negroes, 13 Jan. 1840,
    William J. Fitchett sec.

Matthews, John Custis & Elizabeth Barlow, 5 Nov. 1789, Michael
    Matthews, sec.

Matthews, Jonathan & Margaret Johnson, wid. 1 Aug. 1775, Obed
    Cary sec.

Matthews, Jonathan & Sarah Turner,wid. Samuel Turner, 13 Apr. 1790,
    Obed Cary sec.
Matthews, Levin & Mary Nottingham, 11 Jan. 1779, William Waterfield
    sec.
Matthews, Levin & Margaret Ann Godwin, ward of Robert A. Joynes, 20
    Dec. 1825, Robert A. Joynes sec.
Matthews, Lewis R. & Adah Dunton, 1 Mar. 1820, John Whitehead sec.
Matthews, Lewis R. & Harriet P. Hadlock, 5 Apr. 1830, John T.Wilson
    sec. Con. of Robert Hadlock, father of Harriet.
Matthews, Michael & Sally Barlow, 13 July 1790, Teackle Turner sec.
    Con. of Littleton Upshur, Gdn. of Sally.
Matthews, Michael & Lovy Roberts, wid. Arthur Roberts, 29 July 1833
Matthews, Michael R. & Elizabeth Mister, dau. William Mister,dec.
    26 Apr. 1847, Thomas Smith sec.
Matthews, Samuel H. & Vienna Westcot, 27 Nov. 1816, George C. Wescoat
    sec.
Matthews, Samuel & Henrietta Coleburn, 6 May 1818, Richard Coleburn
    sec.
Matthews, Samuel & Margaret Jackson, 1 Jan. 1819, Samuel Dennis sec.
Matthews, Samuel & Penda Read, 16 Oct. 1819, Isaac Read sec.
Matthews, Teackle & Betsey Wheelor, 17 Dec. 1811, James Dalby sec.
Matthews, Teackle & Betsey Johnson, sister of John Johnson, 28 June
    1824, John Johnson sec.
Matthews, William & Violetta Boole, 25 Apr. 1798, Meshack Water-
    field sec.
Mathews, William & Sally Wright, 8 Aug, 1803, Major Andrews sec.
Matthews, William K. & Elizabeth Ann Savage, 23 Sept. 1845, Lewis
    N. Matthews sec. Con. of Major Savage.

Mayo, Peter P. & Leah C. Upshur, 7 July 1824, A. P. Upshur sec.
Mayo, Peter P. & Anne E. Upshur,dau. Col. Littleton Upshur,dec.,
    27 Mar. 1841, John L. Upshur sec.

Mazlin(Masling,Maslin),Thomas & Nancy Pearson, wid. Thomas Pear-
    son, 24 Dec. 1827, William James sec.
Mazlin, William & Elizabeth B. Young, dau. Richard Young, 23
    Sept. 1834, Benjamin J. Dalby sec.

Mears, Alexander W. F. & Susan F. Hopkins, 17 Nov. 1840, James
    L. Kellam sec.
Mears, Elisha & Ann N. Powell, dau. George Powell, dec., 25 Jan.
    1833, Joshua B. Turner sec.
Mears, George T. & Pamela Richardson, dau. William Richardson,
    dec., 10 Dec. 1840
Mears, George W. & Adah Andrews, 24 May 1841, Arthur T. Roberts
    sec. Con. of Shepherd Andrews, father of Adah.
Mears, George M., ward of Nathan F. Cobb, & Elizabeth Ann Savage,
    dau. John M. Savage, 10 Dec. 1849, Nathan F. Cobb & John M.
    Savage sec.
Mears, James G. & Esther Carpenter, 17 June 1829, Eli Dowty sec.
    Con. of John Carpenter (Hog Island), father of Esther.
Mears, James & Anne Floyd, orph. of Shepherd B. Floyd & ward of
    William L. Eyre, 2 June 1834, William L. Eyre sec.

Mears, James W. & Caroline Bishop, dau. William Bishop,dec., 6 Dec.
  1848, John Mears sec.
Mears, John & Emeline Johnson,alias Emeline Bingham, dau. Lucretia
  Bingham, Free Negroes, 15 Jan. 1838, Joshua K.Roberts sec.
Mears, John & Rosey Abdell, dau. Peggy Abdell, 13 Dec. 1841, Major
  Dowty sec.
*Mears, Littleton & Edna Garrett, his ward, 10 Oct. 1853
Mears, Reuben & Sophia Scott, 21 Feb. 1825, Levin Beach sec.
Mears, Robert & Adah Stott, wid. Jonathan Stott, 25 Dec. 1829, Wm.
  Wyatt,Jr. sec.
Mears, Shadrack & Sally Fletcher, 26 Sept. 1807, Charles Floyd sec.
Mears, Shadrack & Jemima Westcoat, 9 Oct. 1811, George Westcoat sec.
Mears, Thomas C. & Frances L. Johnson, wid. Thomas Johnson,Jr.,3
  Apr. 1837, Smith Nottingham sec.
Mears, William & Betsey Watson, 20 Apr. 1816, Isackar Lewis sec.
Mears, William & Rosey Nottingham,wid. Severn Nottingham, 17 Apr.
  1837, Benjamin J. Dalby sec.

Meccown(McCown,McCowan,McKown),John & Grace Jones, 22 June 1818,
  Thomas Speakman sec.

Mehollams, George & Esther Core, 26 Oct. 1791, Jacob Robins sec.
Mehollams, George & Nancy Hampleton, 28 Mar. 1807, Arthur Cobb sec.
Mehollams, Stringer & Bridget Edmunds, 9 May 1781, John Mehollams
  sec. Con. of David Edmunds, father of Bridget, & Thomas
  Upshur, Gdn. of Stringer.
Mehollams, Thomas & Nancy Joynes, 19 Aug. 1801, John Bird sec.
Mehollomes, William W. & Margaret Stockley, dau. Charles B.
  Stockley, 28 May 1840, John Stockley sec.

Melvin, George & Agnes Clegg, 24 Dec. 1794, James Dolby sec.

Melvil, Hezekiah & Bridget Morris, 2 Jan. 1786, Reuben Reid sec.

Melson, Caleb & Miss Catherine B. Vaughn, 13 Dec. 1824, William
  S. Smith sec.
*Melson, James T. & Susan E. Maslin, 7 Mar. 1853
Melson, Smith & Esther Bell, 4 Feb. 1804, John Stratton sec.
*Melson, Thomas J. & Mary J. Mazline, 26 Feb. 1852

Michael, Joachim & Mary Blaikley Stith, dau. Griffin Stith, 12
  Apr. 1770, Robert Polk sec.
Michael, John, son of Joachim & Peggy Michael, born 3 Feb.
  1745/6, & Margaret Christian, 16 Feb. 1767, John Blair
  sec. Con. of William Christian, father of Margaret.
Michael, John, Jr. & Rose Wainhouse, 23 Jan. 1771, John
  Michael Sr. sec.
Michael, Thomas & Comfort Waterson, 30 Dec. 1747, Levi Moor sec.
Michael, Tilney & Mary Rascoe, wid., 28 May 1760, James
  Peterkin sec.
Michael, William Wainhouse & Margaret Downing,dau.Zerobabell
  Downing, 11 Feb, 1772, Teackle Robins sec.
Milliner, Smith & Jenney Dunton, 8 June 1808, James Travis sec.

Milman, Ephraim, of Accomack, _ Rachel Dowty, 17 Sept. 1791, Wm.
Bloxom sec.

Milbourn, John C. & Mary Williams, 12 May 1823, Ezekiel De La
Statius, sec.

Milby, Adill & Elizabeth Christian, dau. William Christian, 8 Jan.
1770, John Michael sec.
Millby, John & Sarah Turner, wid. 13 Aug. 1754, Gilbert Milby sec.
Milby, John & Leah Coward, wid. 18 Sept. 1756, John Stratton sec.
Milby, John & Nancy Aimes, 27 Aug. 1793, Coventon Simkins sec.
Con. of William Christian, Gdn. of John Milby.

Miles, Richard & Eliza: Richardson, 3 July 1838, John W.Leatherbury
sec. Con. of Elizabeth Richardson, mother of Eliza:
Miles, William & Sally Read, wid. 28 Jan. 1834, William Joynes sec.
Miles, William & Nancy Haley, wid. Robert Haley, 3 Dec. 1835,
Jeremiah Griffith sec.

Mills, Edmund & Susanna Fitchett, dau. Nehemiah Fitchett, 23 Feb.
1761, Savage Cowdrey sec.
Mills, Jacob & Agnes Graves, 17 Sept. 1795, John Graves sec.

Miller, Dr. Mathias H. & Catharine F. Jones, 6 Nov. 1848, Thomas
B. Rowe sec. Con. of Catharine S.Weisiger,mother of
Catharine F.Jones.

Minter, John P. & Harriet Wilkins, dau. John Wilkins,Sr. 24
June 1847, William H, Kendall sec.
Minter, William B. & Polly Elliott, ward of Nath'l. Hickman,
18 June 1838, Nathaniel Hickman sec.

Minson, John G. & Emeline J, Sanford, 14 May 1838, Teackle W.
Jacob sec. Con. of Robert Sanford,father of Emeline.
Minson, John G. & Margaret S. Brickhouse, wid. Albert Brick-
house, dec, 29 July 1846, William P. Nottingham sec.

Mingo, Ewell & Sukey Church, dau, Isaac Church, Free Negroes,
11 Jan, 1828, William Stephens sec.
? Mingo, John & Adah Collins, 14 Dec. 1816, Isaac Stephens sec.

*Mister, John & Nancy Horner, dau. Susan Horner, 5 Oct. 1853

Mitchell, William D. & Elizabeth Fitzhugh,. dau. Henry Fitzhugh,
26 Nov. 1823, Henry Fitzhugh sec.

Moore(Moor), Abraham & Betsey Hanby, 8 Feb. 1800, Thomas Lewis
sec.
Moore, Abram & Lavinia Isdell, ward of William Welsh, 18 Sept.
1828, William Welsh sec.
Moore, Abraham & Betsey Taylor, 24 July 1812, Thomas Lewis sec.
Moore, Abram & Elisha Williams, dau. Peter Williams, dec. 1
Jan. 1842, Benjamin Nottingham sec.
Moore, George W., son of Matthew D. Moore, & Emily S. Rooks,
dau. John Rooks, dec. 22 Dec. 1842, Matthew D.Moore sec.

Moore, Jacob & Agnes Odear, 17 Jan. 1780, Ralph Dixon sec.

Moor, Jacob & Elizabeth Wilkins, wid. Joachim Michael Wilkins, 7 Feb. 1789, Nathaniel Powell sec.

Moore, Jacob & Peggy Robins, wid. Mark Robins, 2 Nov. 1792, Henry Snaw sec.

Moor, John, of James City County, 8 Feb. 1780, Golding Ward sec.

Moore, John & Susey Pratt, 11 Nov. 1800, William Wilson sec.

Moore, John & Peggy Roberts, 16 Mar. 1802, William Havard sec. Con. of Samuel Costin, Gdn. of Peggy.

Moore, John & Nancy Collins, wid. John Collins, 4 Jan. 1825, James Willis sec.

Moore, John C. & Angeline Griffith, 12 Jan. 1841, Elias Roberts sec. Con. of Mary Pettit, mother of Angeline Griffith.

Moore, John D. & Fanny Copes, dau. Levin Copes, dec. 15 Jan. 1844, Matthew D. Moore sec.

*Moore, John & Eliza Willis, dau. William Willis, dec. 18 Dec. 1850

Moore, Levi & Sarah Waterson, 25 Sept. 1744, George Kendall sec.

Moore, Lewis, Ellen Dalby, wid. Nathaniel Dalby, 19 Aug. 1848, Lloyd Q. Moore sec.

Moore, Lloyd, son of Matthew D. Moore, & Emory Casey, ward of William G. Costin, 13 Nov. 1848, William G. Costin & Matthew D. Moore sec.

Moore, Mack & Sally Dalby, dau. Peggy Dalby, 30 Dec. 1836, Wm. Welch sec.

Moor, Matthew, Jr. & Peggy Wilkins, 14 Apr. 1752, John Stratton sec.

Moor, Matthew & Esther Joyne, dau. Edmund Joyne, dec., 20 Jan. 1764, Con. of Douglas Willett as to Esther.

Moore, Matthew & Nancy Freshwater, 13 Jan. 1798, Jacob Moore, sec.

Moore, Matthew & Betsey Downs, 22 Nov. 1809, Robert Fitchett sec.

Moore, Peter & Mary Ann Bonwell, ward of Charles Bonwell, 13 July 1824, Charles Bonwell sec. Con. of Matthew Moore as to Peter.

Moore, Richard & Polly Cullin, 27 Feb. 1796, William Hanby sec.

Moore, Richard & Lavenia Spady, dau. Westerhouse Spady, 8 Dec. 1843, Westerhouse Spady sec.

Moore, Socrates & Arinthia Melborne, dau. John Melborne dec. 13 Feb. 1849, Samuel Savage sec.

Moore, Thomas & Sally Stripe, 6 Jan. 1802, Charles Dillon sec.

Moore, Thomas & Elishe Scott, 6 Apr. 1812, Nath'l. Bishop sec.

Moore, Thomas & Catharine Spady, 27 June 1827, Thomas Kellam sec.

Moore, Thomas D. & Drusilla Groten, 6 Jan. 1841, Thomas E. Evans sec.

Moore, Thomas, of John, & Sarah Ann Bool, dau. Spencer Bool, 14 Sept. 1846, William Kennard & William G. Costin sec.

*Moore, Thomas & Rosey E. Spady, dau. Westerhouse Spady, 29 Dec. 1852

Moor, William & Peggy Dixon, 6 Mar. 1780, Nathaniel Wilkins, Jr. sec.

Moor, William & Margaret Wood, 5 Jan. 1782, Stuart Holt, sec. Con. of William Wood, father of Margaret.

Moor, William & Santica Dixon, 29 Aug. 1783, Christopher Dixon sec.

Moore, William D. & Angeline B. Brickhouse, dau. Thomas S. Brickhouse, 7 Dec. 1831, Thomas S. Brickhouse sec.

Moore, William H. & Mary Isdell, dau. James Isdell, 11 Feb. 1850,
James Dennis sec.

**Morris, Dennard & Rebecca Costin _____ 1808
?Morris, George & Mary Stevens, 19 Oct. 1785, David Jones sec.
*Morris, Henry & Adah Pool, Free Negroes, 24 Dec. 1851
Morris, Isaac & Juno Read, ward of Isaac Morris, Free Negroes, 24
Oct. 1823, William Stephens, F.N., sec.
? Morris, Jacob & Phillis Only, 23 Aug. 1802, York Stepney sec.
? Morris, Revel & Dilly Drighouse, 7 Sept. 1801, James Smith sec.
Morris, Stockley & Chilametha Read, Free Negroes, 21 May 1831,
Jacob Thompson, Jr. sec.

?Moses, Daniel & Rachel Teague, 25 Sept. 1802, Levin Morris sec.
?Moses, Ezekiel & Diana Becket, ward of Mark Becket, 22 Aug. 1791
William Stith sec.
? Moses, George, son of Jenny, & Sarah Pool, ward of Peggy Ames, 13
Mar. 1848, Jenny Moses & Peggy Ames sec.
? Moses, Mark & Mary Becket, 13 Dec. 1785, Isaac Becket sec.

**Moulton, E. L. & Mary Gadd, 5 Feb. 1852

Murray, James, of the Province of Md., County of Dorchester, &
Hannah Savage, dau. Thomas Savage, Gent., dec. 16 May
1764 Edward Noel, of Maryland, sec.

Neale, Presley & Susanna Satchell, dau. Charles Satchell, 12 Sept.
1780, Robert Brickhouse sec.

? Nedab, Abraham & Lusey Bingham, 29 Dec. 1813, Stephen Nedab sec.
Con. of Tinsey Weeks, mother of Lusey.

Nelson, Charles & Sally Fisher, 14 Mar. 1821, John Nelson sec. Con.
of W. R. Fisher, Gdn. of Sally
Nelson, James & Mary Hamilton, 11 July 1780, William Abdell sec.
*Nelson, James F. & Sallie E. Wilson, dau. James B. Wilson, 22 Dec.
1851
Nelson, John & Sarah Goffigon, dau. James Goffigon, dec. 17 Oct.
1772, Southy Goffigon sec.
Nelson, John & Adah Carpenter, 6 July 1790, William Carpenter sec.
Nelson, John & Lear Wilkins, 20 June 1800, James Goffigon sec.
Nelson, John, Jr. & Jenney Wilkins, 12 Jan. 1805, John R. Waddey
sec.
**Nelson, John & Rosey Goffigon _____ 1813
Nelson, John, Jr. & Catherine S. Teackle, 18 June, 1827, William
S. Floyd sec.
Nelson, John, Sr. & Elizabeth Biggs, 9 Dec. 1833, John W. Biggs sec.
Nelson, Southy & Elizabeth Willett, dau. Thomas Willett, dec. 5
May 1770, Samuel Williams sec.
Nelson, Southy & Sally Joynes Brickhouse, 14 Nov. 1803, George
Brickhouse sec.

Nicholson, James M. & Arinthia D. Parker, 21 June, 1838, John Eyre
 sec.

Nicholson, John W. & Elizabeth Stewart, dau. James Stewart, 11 Oct.
 1841, James Stewart sec.

Nicholson, William J. & Elizabeth A. Martin, wid. Peter Martin, 27
 Nov. 1849

Nivison, John & Sarah Stratton, dau. John Stratton,Sr., Esq., 6
 Dec. 1781, William Stith sec.

Nolen, Lewis & Molly Warren, 8 Dec, 1789, Daniel Benthall sec.

Nottingham, Addison & Barbary Powell, wid. 15 July 1763, Walter
 Hyslop sec.

Nottingham, Addison & Peggy White, 25 Apr. 1826, Elias Dunton sec.
 Con. of Susannah White, mother of Peggy.

Nottingham, Benjamin & Frances Williams, dau. Peter Williams,Sr.,
 26 May, 1828, Peter Williams,Sr. sec. Con. of Elisha
 Nottingham, mother of Benjamin.

Nottingham, Cornelius & Mary Rooks, ward of William J.Fatherly,
 8 Dec. 1845, William J. Fatherly sec.

Nottingham, Edward W. & Henrietta P. Jacob, 9 Nov. 1830, Richard
 Cutler sec. Con. of Thomas Jacob, father of Henrietta.

Nottingham, Edward T. & Maria Godwin, dau. William Godwin,dec., 2
 Apr. 1839, Obadiah Goffigon sec.

Nottingham, Edward W. & Harriet Spady, 18 Sept. 1844, Piner W.
 Clark sec.

Nottingham, Elijah, Jr. & Virginia S. Nottingham, dau. Sally R.
 Nottingham, 31 Dec. 1840, Sally R. Nottingham sec.

Nottingham, Ellison S., ward of Jacob Nottingham, & Margaret S.
 Brickhouse, dau. Elam L. Brickhouse, 10 Dec. 1849
 Elam L. Brickhouse sec.

Nottingham, Harrison & Elizabeth Andrews, 8 Sept. 1817, Thomas
 Smith sec.

Nottingham, Harrison & Patsey Hickman, 9 Sept. 1822, John Warren
 sec.

Nottingham, Isaac & Sarah Freshwater, 31 Aug. 1748, James
 Westwood, of Elizabeth City County, sec. Con. of Mark
 Freshwater, father of Sarah.

Nottingham, Isaac & Mary Kendall, wid. 23 Nov. 1763, John Gleson
 sec.

Nottingham, Isaac & Sophia Dixon, 12 Sept. 1792, William Hallett
 sec.

Nottingham, Jacob, Jr. & Sarah Bell, 14 July 1804, William
 Nottingham, Sr. sec.

Nottingham, Jacob, Jr. & Rosey G. Wescoat, ward of George C.
 Wescoat, 14 June 1824, George C. Wescoat sec.

Nottingham, Jacob E. & Ann Spady, 21 Jan. 1828, Thomas Powell
 sec. Con. of Southy Spady, father of Ann.

Nottingham, James & Ann Costin, ward of Thomas Downes, 18 Sept.
 1827, Thomas Downes sec.

Nottingham, John & Peggy Nottingham, 27 Dec. 1788, Isaac Bratten
 sec. Con. of Severn Nottingham, father of Peggy.

Nottingham, John & Betsy Taylor, 8 Dec. 1789, James Dolby sec. Con.
        of Thomas Teackle Taylor, father of Betsy.

Nottingham, John & Nancy James, 28 Dec. 1802, Major Taylor sec.

Nottingham, John E. & Elizabeth P. Upshur, 30 Dec. 1820, Littleton
        Upshur sec.

Nottingham, John E.m of Severn E., & Caroline S. F. Luker, dau.
        Walter Luker, dec., 4 June, 1831, James Saunders sec.
        Con. of Thomas Young, Gdn. of Caroline.

Nottingham, John E. & Mary Ann Burris, 26 Oct. 1839, James D.
        Williams sec.

Nottingham, John R., son of Jacob Nottingham, & Susan Ann Cutler,
        late ward of Edwin J. Fisher & dau. of William W.Cutler,
        dec., 3 Dec. 1849, Jacob Nottingham sec.

*Nottingham, John E. & Sally S. Kennard, 20 Oct. 1851.

Nottingham, Joshua & Mary Bearcraft, 16 Jan. 1817, Joseph
        Nottingham sec.

Nottingham, Joshua & Margaret Parkerson, dau. George Parkerson,
        28 Feb. 1829, Thomas Brickhouse & George Parkerson sec.

Nottingham, Joseph & Amelia Roberts, 14 May 1793, Severn Widgeon
        sec.

Nottingham, Joseph & Anne Jacob, 1 Jan. 1794, George Lewis sec.

Nottingham, Joseph D., son of Joseph Nottingham, & Polly Widgeon,
        orph. of Severn Widgeon & ward of Nathaniel Widgeon, 17
        Jan. 1823, Nathaniel Widgeon sec.

Nottingham, Joseph & Polly Dixon, 12 May 1828, Joshua Nottingham
        sec.

Nottingham, Joseph W. & Sarah Ann Griffith, dau. William Griffith,
        25 Nov. 1845, Joshua P. Wescoat & Thomas K. Dunton sec.
        Con. of Thomas Griffith, Gdn. of Sarah Ann.

Nottingham, Joseph W. & Miss Frances Griffith, 14 May 1849, Thos.
        M. Wilkins sec. Con. of Thomas Griffith, father of
        Frances.

Nottingham, Leonard B. & Emeline Waddey, ward of John Ker, 20
        Nov. 1827, John Ker sec.

*Nottingham, Leonard J. & Ellen S. Floyd, ward of John S. Parker,
        1 Mar. 1853

Nottingham, Levin & Sally Hubbard, 11 Mar. 1811, Peter Williams
        sec.

*Nottingham,Lloyd C. & Virginia S.W.Roberts, dau. Sally A.
        Roberts, 3 Oct. 1853

Nottingham, Luther & Emeline Nottingham, ward of George P.
        Fitchett, 25 Dec. 1837, Severn E. Bowdoin sec. Con. of
        Jesse J. Simkins, Gdn. of Luther.

Nottingham, Luther & Catharine E. Dalby, dau. Hezekiah Dalby,
        1 Oct. 1849, William L. Dalby sec.

Nottingham, Nathaniel & Mary Jacob, 17 Aug. 1799, Nath'l.Bryan,
        sec. Con. of Joseph W. Nottingham, Gdn. of Mary.

Nottingham, Richard & Mary Evans, dau. Arthur Evans, 18 Dec.
        1776, Edmund Glanville sec.

Nottingham, Richard & Anne Harrison, dau. Salathiel Harrison,
        dec. 18 Jan. 1785, Branson Dalby sec.

Nottingham, Richard & Nancy Bullock, 28 Dec. 1805, Joseph
        Nottingham sec.

Nottingham, Richard & Susanna Cox, 30 Aug. 1806, William Harrison sec.

Nottingham, Richard & Mary B. Fisher, 28 July 1811, Thomas Johnson, Jr. sec. Con. of Sally G. Fisher, mother of Mary.

Nottingham, Richard & Mary Steäd Pinckney Gardiner, 19 July 1814, Nathaniel Widgeon sec. Con. of W. C. Gardiner, father of Mary S.P.

Nottingham, Capt. Robert & Elishe Stringer, wid. 15 Nov. 1741, George Mason Kendall sec.

Nottingham, Robert & Anne Johnson, 12 Apr. 1785, Hezekiah James sec.

Nottingham, Robert B. & Mary Jacob, 1 Oct. 1828, Robins Mapp sec. Con. of Thomas Jacob, father of Mary.

Nottingham, Samuel Y. & Leah F. Carpenter, 5 June, 1826, William Nottingham sec. Con. of Samuel G. Carpenter, brother of Leah.

Nottingham, Severn & Elizabeth Evans, dau. Arthur Evans, 10 Feb. 1769, Jacob Nottingham sec.

Nottingham, Severn & Nancy Waterfield, 5 Oct. 1790, John Williams, Jr. sec.

Nottingham, Severn & Betsey Bell, 6 Dec. 1802, John Nottingham sec.

Nottingham, Severn & Rosy Smith, dau. Thomas Smith, Sr. dec. 6 May 1828, John Ker sec.

Nottingham, Severn E. & Bridget Goffigon, orph. of William Goffigon, 20 Mar. 1830, James Saunders sec. Con. of John Goffigon, Gdn. of Bridget.

Nottingham, Smith & Sally Williams, 3 Mar. 1810, William Williams sec.

Nottingham, Smith, B. & Polly Elliott, ward of Daniel G. Smaw, 4 Apr. 1826, Daniel G. Smaw sec.

Nottingham, Smith & Esther S.B.Nottingham, dau. William Nottingham, 23 June 1830, Leonard B. Nottingham sec.

Nottingham, Thomas, Jr. & Peggy Johnson, dau. William Johnson, dec., 8 Nov. 1776, Richard Nottingham sec. Con. of M. Christian, Gdn. of Peggy.

Nottingham, Thomas & Patsey Costin, 18 Apr. 1801, Westerhouse Widgeon sec. Con. of Francis Costin, father of Patsey.

Nottingham, Thomas & Ann Davis, 27 Dec. 1802, John Taylor sec.

Nottingham, Thomas & Nancy Floyd, 8 May 1809, James Floyd sec.

Nottingham, Thomas & Peggy Turner, 13 Oct. 1812, Littleton Kendall, Sr. sec.

Nottingham, Thomas & Susan Biggs, 21 Dec. 1815, Jacob Watson sec. Con. of Nancy Biggs, mother of Susan.

Nottingham, Thomas & Peggy Frost, ward of Obed Hunt, 23 July 1822, Obed Hunt sec.

Nottingham, Thomas & Harriet Addison, 23 Feb. 1828, Thomas B. Fisher sec. Con. of William Addison, father of Harriet.

Nottingham, Thomas J. & Catherine E. Nottingham, ward of John W. Biggs, 24 Dec. 1828, John W. Biggs sec.

Nottingham, Thomas J. L. L. & Tabitha S. West, dau. Charles West, 28 Nov. 1831, Smith Nottingham sec.

Nottingham, Thomas W. & Elizabeth Snead, wid., 20 Dec. 1836, William Spady sec.

Nottingham, Thomas H. & Jenny Nottingham, dau. Nathaniel Nottingham, dec. 11 Dec. 1849, Joseph E. Bell sec.

Nottingham, Victor A. & Edith S. Nottingham, 23 May 1842,

Leonard B. Nottingham sec.

Nottingham, William & Leah Walter, dau. John Walter, 16 Nov. 1768,
    Edmund Glanville sec.

Nottingham, William & Peggy Fitchett, 6 July 1795, William Eyre sec.

Nottingham, William & Elishe Parks, 21 Apr. 1797, William Wingate sec.

Nottingham, William & Molly Bell, 6 Feb. 1798, Thomas Jarvis sec.

Nottingham, William, Jr. & Margaret Turner, 27 Aug. 1802, Nath'l.
    Bryan sec.

Nottingham, William E. & Margaret S. Wilson, 6 May, 1814, William
    Savage sec. Con. of Anne Wilson, mother of Margaret.

Nottingham, William, of Robert, & Susan Hyslop, 5 July 1817, James
    Travis sec. Con. of Susanna Hyslop, mother of Susanna.

Nottingham, William, brother of Thomas W. Nottingham, & Sally Jones,
    sister of Teackle Jones, 8 Nov. 1823, Teackle Jones & Thomas
    W. Nottingham sec.

Nottingham, William P. & Charlotte L. Winder, dau. John H. Winder,
    28 Nov. 1837, Leonard B. Nottingham sec.

Nottingham, William J. & Margaret M. Upshur, dau. William M. Upshur,
    dec. 19 Dec. 1837, Edwin J. Fisher sec.

Nottingham, William & Elizabeth Snead, ward of Thomas J. Nottingham,
    10 Sept. 1838, Thomas J. Nottingham sec.

Nottingham, William T. & Margaret S. Williams, 19 Nov. 1844, Robert
    J. Nottingham sec. Con. of Ann J. Williams, mother of
    Margaret S.

Nottingham, William C., son of Benjamin Nottingham, & Elizabeth S.
    Wilkins, ward of Thomas M. Wilkins, 4 Dec. 1848, Benjamin
    Nottingham & Thomas M. Wilkins sec.

*Nottingham, William T. & Lucy Ann Carpenter, dau. Samuel G.
    Carpenter, dec. 31 Aug. 1852

?Nutts, Edmund & Mary Bibbins, 18 June 1800, Southy Collins sec.
    Con. of Nanny Bibbins.

Nutall, Charles & Ansley Mathews, 18 Sept. 1804, Major Pettit sec.

Oast, William & Margaret Campbell, ward of William J. Campbell,
    13 Apr. 1829, William J. Campbell sec.

Odear, George & Elizabeth Smith, dau. George Smith, dec., 8 Sept.
    1834, Thomas Griffith sec.

Odear, George & Lilly Griffith, 1 Sept. 1838, Robert F. Williams
    sec. Con. of Moses Griffith, father of Lilly.

Odear, John & Esther Phaben, 2 July 1788, William Phaben sec.

O'Dear, John & Patsey Whaley, 1 Jan. 1810, Robert Fitchett sec.

O'Dear, Joseph & Molly Nagle, 24 Dec. 1799, John Floyd sec.

Odear, Stephen & Susan Parsons, ward of William Whitehead, 9
    Apr. 1832, William Whitehead sec.

Odear, William & Susey Williams, 9 Jan. 1804, Nath'l.Benthall sec.

Oldham, Leroy & Jenney Wheelor, 1 Oct. 1806, William Andrews sec.

Oldham, Montcalm, ward of John Ker, & Maria A. Harmanson, ward
    of William W. West, 3 Dec. 1835, John Ker & Wm.W.West sec.

Oliver, Joseph & Elizabeth Watson, 23 Aug. 1806, Branson C. Dalby sec.

*Only, John Wesley & Ailsey Guy, dau. Mary Guy,Free Negroes,10 Nov.1851
Only, William & Catharine Benson, 1 Dec. 1803, William Parramore sec.

Osburn, Nehemiah & Polly Willis, 6 Apr. 1821, George Hitchens sec.

Outten, George F. & Ann S. Williams, 27 Mar. 1827, Leonard B. Nott-
      ingham sec.
Outten, Isaac, son of Jacob Outten, & Sally Wingate, dau. William
      Wingate, 1 Jan. 1844, Benjamin Nottingham sec.
Outen, Jacob & Susan Saunders, 14 July 1817, Michael Savage sec.
Outten, John & Susan Mears, 30 Dec. 1833, Thomas Smith,Jr. sec.
      Con. of Susan Mears, mother of Susan.
Outten, Timothy & Betsey Moore, 13 Feb. 1796, Joseph Odear sec.
Outten, Timothy & Kesiah Mathews, 23 June 1810, James Williams sec.

Owen, Thomas, of Somerset County, Md., & Elishe Wilson, 21 July
      1774, Richard Nottingham sec.

Page, Robert & Esther Turner, dau. John Furbush Turner, 28 Nov.
      1778, John Tomkins sec.

*Paine, Daniel & Peggy Poole, 13 Feb. 1815, Charles Pool sec.

Parker, Clement & Elizabeth Core, 23 Oct. 1798, Richard Nottingham
      sec.
Parker, George & Amie Major, 18 Dec. 1721, William Major sec.
Parker, George, of Accomack, & Margaret Eyre, dau. Severn Eyre,
      Esq., dec., 12 Oct. 1786, Con. of Littleton Eyre, Gdn. of
      Margaret - Thomas Lytt: Savage sec.
Parker, George & Elizabeth Stith, 25 May 1802, Thomas Lytt:
      Savage sec.
Parker, Jacob G. & Ann Gertrude Stratton, 29 Jan. 1811, John B.
      Taylor sec.
Parker, James & Nancy Vermillon, 29 Nov. 1806, Labon Godwin sec.
Parker, John A. & Harriet Darby, 29 May 1802, Nath'l. Darby sec.
Parker, John S. & Anne E. Floyd, dau. Anne S. Floyd, 16 Dec.1839,
      Anne S. Floyd sec.
Parker, Severn Eyre & Maria Teackle Savage, 13 July 1811, George
      Parker sec.
**Parker, Thomas J. & Anne M. Gault, 23 Dec. 1817.
Parker, Tully W. & Peggy T. Evans, 22 Jan. 1840, James B. Poulson
      & Edward R. Waddey sec.
Parker, William A. & Margaret A. Parramore, 2 Dec. 1811, Abel P.
      Upshur sec.

Parkinson(Parkerson), James & Nancy Johnson, 5 Feb. 1815, Levin
      Beach sec.
Parkinson, William & Peggy Dowty, 13 Dec. 1813, Thomas Henderson
      sec.
Parkinson, William & Betsey Stott, 23 May 1817, Arthur Cobb sec.

Parkerson(Parkinson), George & Mary Jacob, 19 Aug. 1806, John Wescoat, Jr. sec.

Parkerson, George & Mary Tylor, 4 Oct. 1820, Samuel Mathews sec.

Parkerson, George & Mary Harrison, 18 Jan. 1825, Samuel H. Matthews sec.

*Parkerson, George & Margaret Spady, dau. Margaret Spady, 3 Feb. 1752

Parkerson, James & Elizabeth Holland, wid. John Holland, 1 Aug. 1787, James Hawkins sec.

Parkerson, Joseph & Lydia Smith, wid., 13 Dec. 1754, Thomas Dolby sec.

Parkerson, Levin & Hannah Brown, dau. Nathaniel Brown, dec., 26 Dec. 1834, George Charnock sec.

Parkerson, William & Peggy Fletcher, 21 May 1804, Robert Peak sec.

Parkhurst, William C. & Mary Jarvis, orph. of William B. Jarvis, 4 Jan. 1834, John Kendall sec. Con. of Margaret Jarvis, mother of Mary.

Parsons, Archibald & Margaret Floyd, wid. William Floyd (of Major), dec., 24 July 1838, William Miles sec.

Parsons, Carvey & Rosey Collins, 23 Dec. 1824, William Parsons sec. Con. of John Parsons, father of Carvey.

Parsons, Francis W. & Rosy Ann Elliott, 17 Oct. 1843, Elias Roberts sec. Con. of Rachel Elliott, mother of Rosy.

Parsons, John & Susanna Costin, 27 Sept. 1803, Francis Costis sec.

Parsons, John & Sally Warren, dau. Joseph Warren, 7 Nov. 1836, Joseph Warren sec.

Parsons, Marriot & Elizabeth Homes, 4 Oct. 1803, George Smith sec. Con. of William Parsons, Gdn. of Elizabeth.

Parsons, Thomas & Nancy Hyslop, 11 Mar. 1805, Custis Hyslop sec.

Parsons, Thomas & Anne Wise, dau. Col. John Wise,dec., 26 May, 1772, William Kendall sec. Con. of Sarah Parsons, mother of Thomas & of Isaac Avery, Gdn. of Anne.

Parsons, William, of Elizabeth City County, & Sarah Cable, 13 Feb. 1749, Thomas Preeson sec. Con. of Margaret Cable, mother of Sarah.

Parsons, William & Mary Costin, 11 Mar. 1783, Laban O'Dear sec. Con. of Francis Costin.

Parsons, William & Susan Elliott, dau. Jeremiah Elliott, 8 Nov. 1830, Jeremiah Evans sec.

Parramore, Thomas & Esther Burton, dau. John Burton dec. 22 Dec. 1787, John Guy sec.

Parramore, Thomas, Jr. & Mary Darby, 22 Apr. 1797, Nath'l.Darby sec.

Parramore, William, of Accomack, Gent., & Sarah Seymour, dau. Digby Seymour, of Northampton, Gent., dec., 22 Oct. 1763, Michael Christian sec.

Parrott, George & Adah Evans, 3 Apr. 1804, Michael Dunton sec.

*Paulin, Joseph W. & Elizabeth Rush, wid. Thomas Rush, 30 Oct. 1851

Peak, Robert & Elishe Smith, 8 Mar. 1800, David Harlow sec.
Peak, Robert & Seymour Dowty, 13 Nov. 1800, Thomas Dunton sec.
Peak, Robert & Molly Campbell, 10 Dec. 1805, David Harlow sec.
Peak, Robert & Sukey Jarvis Flood, 25 July 1807, Richard Young sec.
Peak, Thomas & Sally McCrady, 10 Mar. 1797, Richard Nottingham sec.

Pearson(Pierson), Joseph J. & Latitia M. Jones, wid. John Jones,
 1 Jan. 1850, Joseph B. Brittingham sec.
Pearson, Patrick & Polly Craik, 11 June 1821, Thomas E. Addison sec.
Pearson, Patrick & Elizabeth Lewis, ward of Thomas E. Addison, 9
 Aug. 1824, Thomas E. Addison sec.
Pearson, Thomas & Nancy McGregor, 18 Jan. 1814, Major Pettitt sec.
 Con. of Sally McGregor, mother of Nancy.
Pearson, Thomas & Sally Belote, dau. Kendall Belote, dec. 27 Dec.
 1838, William H. Floyd sec.
Pearson, Thomas J. & Emeline Pearson, dau. Patrick Pearson, dec.,
 18 Jan. 1848, John Belote sec. Con. of Elizabeth Pearson,
 mother of Emeline.

*Peck, William Noble & Nancy Warren, wid. John P. Warren, 24 June
 1852

Peed, Thomas & Susan Trower, wid. 28 June 1821, Silas Jefferson
 sec.
Peed, William J. F. , ward of William Costin, & Virginia T.
 Costin, ward of James H. Costin, 21 Dec. 1841, Con. of
 William Costin.

Phaben, Paul & Mary Wilson, wid., 31 May 1779, Littleton Wilson
 sec.

Philips, Zerobabel & Margaret Nottingham, dau. Benj. Nottingham,
 26 Dec. 1848, Benj. Nottingham sec.

Pierson(Pearson), George & Sally Dolby, 6 Apr. 1797, John James
 sec.

Pigot, John & Peggy Nottingham, 7 Sept. 1787, Abel Nottingham
 sec.
Pigot, Ralph & Mary Bullock, 21 Oct. 1724, Godfrey Pole &
 Abraham Bowker sec.

Pettitt, Bartholomew, of Norfolk County, & Leah Pitts, wid.
 4 Feb. 1765, William Pettitt sec.
Pettit, Jacob & Nancy Pettit, 15 Dec. 1810, Abel Harrison sec.
Pettitt, John & Adah Pettitt, dau. John Pettitt, Sr., 11 Jan.
 1780, Levin Matthews sec.
Pettit, Laban & Joanna Wilkins, 29 July 1768, Walter Hyslop sec.
Pettit, Major & Susanna Bradford, 17 Sept. 1795, Esau Smith sec.
Pettitt, Stuart & Peggy Dustin, 9 Oct. 1787, Isaac Bell sec.
Pettitt, Stewart B. & Mary Griffith, 19 Aug. 1829, William
 Martin sec.

Pettitt, Thomas & Anne Custis, dau. Robinson Custis, dec., 24 Sept.
1767, Henry Bryan sec.

Pettit, Thomas & Polly Stakes, 23 Oct. 1797, Soloman Richardson sec.

Pettitt, William & Mary Custis, wid., 17 June 1754, William Westerhouse sec.

Pettitt, William Major & Sarah Frances Cooper Tankard, age 17 years,
7 months & 13 days, 15 Nov. 1823, William P. Johnson sec. Con.
of John Tankard, father of Sarah

Peterkin, John & Anne Holt, wid. 20 Jan. 1758, John Harmanson sec.

Pitts, George & Elizabeth Dewey, born 1761, 14 July 1783, Maddox
Fisher sec.

Pitts, Jacob & Rachel Kelly, 27 Dec. 1742, Robert Kerby sec.

Pitts, John & Nancy Major, 10 Dec. 1798, Maxamilian Hopkins sec.

Pitts, John & Peggy Stewart, Free Negroes, 11 Jan. 1838, Smith S.
Nottingham sec.

Pitts, Purnal & Elizabeth Gilden, dau. Charles Gilden, dec., 13
Sept. 1791

? Pool, Anderson & Catharine Drighouse, 23 June 1800, Jacob
Holland sec.

? Pool, Charles & Anne Driggus, 1 Jan. 1820, Cudjo Stephens sec.

? Pool, George & Comfort Weeks, 10 May 1793, Abraham Lang sec.

? George Pool & Patience Stephens, 27 Sept. 1819, Daniel Pool sec.

? Pool, Isaac & Sophia Morris, 17 Dec. 1811, John Upshur, sec.

? Pool, Littleton & Sinah Clayton, 27 Apr. 1818, Abel Stokeley sec.

? Pool, Marshall & Margaret Weeks, 27 Dec. 1817, John Weeks sec.
Con. of James Weeks, father of Margaret.

** ? Pool, Seth & Nancy Cutlor _____ Jan. 1794

? Pool, Solomon, son of George, & Nancy Anthony, dau. Abel, 10
Dec. 1827, George Pool & Abel Anthony sec.

? Pool, William, son of Charles, & Rosey Baker, dau. Thomas, 24
July 1827, Thomas Baker & Charles Pool sec.

Potter, Edmund, of Accomack, & Mary Floyd, 30 May 1752, John
Floyd sec.

*Poulson, George & Rachel Church, Free Negroes, 17 Jan. 1853

Poulson, James & Elizabeth Guy, 8 Mar. 1798, Robert James sec.

Poulson, James B. & Elizabeth P. Williams, dau. Margaret
Williams, 20 May 1829, Margaret Williams sec.

Poulson, John, of Accomack, orph. of John Poulson, & Elizabeth
Cutler, (John Young appointed her Gdn.), 20 Nov. 1810,
Henry Scarborough sec. Con. of Erastus Poulson, brother
of John.

Poulson, Samuel & Jenny Bradford, 28 Oct. 1814, Abraham Smith sec.

Powell, Abel & Margaret Savage, 2 Nov. 1812, Littleton Savage sec.

Powell, George & Molly Nottingham, dau. Jacob Nottingham, 22
June, 1776, Richard Nottingham sec.

Powell, George & Mary P. Nottingham, 29 Dec. 1818, Abram Costin
sec.

Powell, James & Sukey Fitchett, 24 Feb. 1800, Robert Rogers sec. Con.
    of Joshua Fitchett, father of Sukey.
Powell, James & Sukey Trower, 9 Sept. 1805, James Johnson sec.
Powell, Nathaniel & Susanna Milby, dau. John Milby dec. 11 Aug. 1772,
    William Taylor sec.
Powell, Nathaniel & Rose Dunton, 7 Oct. 1784, Joseph Milhan sec.
Powell, Robert & Betsey Collins, 24 Jan. 1820, James Jacob sec.
Powell, Seth & Elizabeth Dowty, 18 Mar. 1791, John Kendall sec.
Powell, Seth & Elizabeth Powell, 15 Oct. 1810, George Powell sec.
Powell, Thomas & Elizabeth Costin, ward of Jesse Simkins & dau. of
    Abraham Costin, dec., 18 Feb. 1832, Jesse J. Simkins sec.

Pratt, James & Margaret Bull, ward of Joshua K. Roberts, 13 Feb.
    1826, Joshua K. Roberts sec.
Pratt, John & Nancy Williams, 7 May 1796, Moses Griffith sec.
Pratt, John & Miss Sarah Hanaford, 14 Sept. 1824, Christopher
    Fitchett sec. Sarah Hannaford niece of Patsy Fitchett.
Pratt, Scarborough & Sally Johnson, 25 Mar. 1799, William Rippin sec.
Pratt, William & Anne Rippin, dau. William Rippin, 9 Mar. 1779,
    William Rippin sec.
Pratt, Zorobabel & Elishe Widgeon, 6 Jan. 1814, Nath'l. Widgeon sec.

Preeson, Thomas & Esther Cable, 12 Mar. 1738, George Kendall sec.

? Press, Edmund, Old Town, ward of Samuél Bevans, Sr. & Nancy
    Collins, dau. Peggy Collins, 14 Feb. 1832, William Francis
    sec.
? Press, George & Mary Baker, wid. Thomas Baker, 15 Nov. 1831,
    John Bevans sec.
? Press, Littleton & Molly Fisherman, 14 Dec. 17__, Reubin Reed sec.

Prentis, Joseph & Margaret Bowdoin, dau. John Bowdoin, dec., 11
    Dec. 1778, con. of Grace Bowdoin, mother of Margaret -
    Samuel Smith McCroskey sec.

*Price, Alfred G. & Esther M. Kellam, dau. Edmund Kellam, dec.,
    25 Dec. 1850

Pritchard, John H. & Caroline James, dau. Thomas James, 3 Sept.
    1832, James Charnock sec.

Pugh, Francis & Farabee Savage, 8 Sept. 1722, James Forse sec.
Pugh, Theophilus, of Nansemond County, & Esther Robins, 9 Feb.
    1738 - Con. of John Robins, father of Esther.   Edward
    Robins sec.

Rabyshaw, William & Grace Harmanson, wid. 19 Mar. 1709/10, John
    Mapp sec.
Rafield(Rayfield,Reafield), Charles & Susanna Jones, dau. Isaac
    Jones, 5 Aug. 1791, Edmund Aimes sec.

Rascoe, James & Joanna Stott, dau. Jonathan Scott, 12 June 1770,
    Levin Widgeon sec.

Rascoe, William & Anne Hunt, dau. Thomas Hunt, 5 Nov. 1779, Samuel
    Johnson sec.
Rasco, William & Sally Dunton, 19 Nov. 1799, Dickie Dunton sec.

Rasin, Thomas Savage, of Kent County, Md., & Susanna Reynolds, 16
    Apr. 1770, Nathaniel Littleton Savage sec.

Rayfield(Reafield, Rafield), Dennard & Mary Brickhouse, dau. Thomas
    S. Brickhouse, 4 Sept. 1832, Thomas Smith, Jr. sec.
Rayfield, Harrison T. & Janette H. Stott, 28 Apr. 1820, Laban Stott
    sec.
Rayfield, Harrison & Margaret Ann Johnson, ward of H. Rayfield, 28
    Feb. 1825, Spencer Boole sec.
Rayfield, John & Peggy Luke, 28 Sept. 1801, Thomas Dixon sec. Con.
    of John Raifield, Gdn. of Peggy.
Rayfield, John H. & Eliza Fitchett, 30 Dec. 1837, William J. Fitchett
    sec. Con. of Susan Fitchett, mother of Eliza.
Rayfield, John H. & Mary S. Rayfield, wid. Dennard Rayfield, 17 Feb.
    1847, James Fitchett sec.
Rayfield, Thomas W. & Margaret Waterfield, dau. Thomas Waterfield,
    22 Aug. 1839, William Savage sec.
Rayfield, Wisly & Miss Letta Lewis, 1 Aug. 1849, John H. Rayfield sec.
    Con. of William Lewis, father of Letta.

Reafield(Rayfield, Rafield), Thomas & Nancy Thomas, 6 Apr. 1798, Wm.
    Thomas sec.

Read(Reed, Reid), Calvin & Margaret L. Powell, 20 Jan. 1817, Thomas
    Jacob sec.
Read, Edmund & Nancy Ward, 9 Feb. 1818, William Scarborough sec.
Read, John & Sally Parsons, 25 Sept. 1810, William Parsons sec.
Read, John W. & Adah S. Mears, wid. George Mears, 7 Jan. 1845,
    Walter Raleigh sec.
Read, Littleton S. & Mary W. Fisher, ward of Thomas B. Fisher, 10
    Jan. 1844, Alex. W. F. Mears & Leonard B. Nottingham sec.
    Con. of Mary L. Read, mother of Littleton S.
Read, Luther & Mary Simkins, 14 Nov. 1808, John Simkins sec.
Read, Richard H. & Margaret D. Jacob, dau. Hancock Jacob, dec., 10
    Feb. 1835, George Brittingham sec.
Read, Richard P. & Sally C. Henderson, wid. William Henderson,
    29 Apr. 1839, William Goffigon sec.
Read, Richard H. & Margaret S. Read, dau. Calvin H. Read, dec.,
    12 Feb. 1844, Peter B. Savage sec.
?Read, Spencer, alias Weeks, & Priscilla Custis, alias Becket, dau.
    Sarah Becket, 17 Dec. 1832, Sarah Becket sec.
*Thomas Read & Mary Satchell, Free Negroes, 19 Apr. 1851

?Reed(Read, Reid), Isaac & Betty Stevens, 2 July 1793, Ralph Collins
    sec.

*Reid(Read, Reed), Victor F. & Ann W. Smith, dau. Capt. George Smith,
    dec., 20 Nov. 1852

Respess, John & Elizabeth Kendall, wid. 30 Apr. 1766, John Guy sec.

Respess, John & Susanna Luker, 9 July 1791, Elijah Baker sec.

Respass, Matthew & Sophia Harmanson, 23 July 1790, Nathaniel
 Goffigon sec.

Respess, Thomas & Esther Burton, wid. 16 Dec. 1746, William Scott
 sec.

Revel, John B. & Rosey D. Seymour, 16 Sept. 1816, William A. Christian sec.

Revell, John B. & Ann W. Hopkins, 9 Dec. 1820, William A. Christian
 sec.

Rew, Southy & Elizabeth G. Smaw, wid. John Smaw, 24 Dec. 1828,
 Luther Ball sec.

Richardson, Albert & Rebecca Bell, ward of Jacob Nottingham, 11
 Dec. 1843, Jacob Nottingham sec.

Richardson, Charles A. & Nancy Costin, wid. William Costin, 13
 May 1844, James M. Savage sec.

Richardson, Edward J. & Margaret Evans, ward of Edmund S. Godwin,
 11 Nov. 1837, Edmund S. Godwin sec.

Richardson, Eli & Polly Currie, 23 Mar. 1799, Solomon Richardson
 sec.

Richardson, George & Eliza J. Bell, dau. Anthony Bell, 22 Jan.
 1828, Anthony Bell sec.

Richardson, John & Kesiah Dalby, 19 Feb. 1802, Severn Dalby sec.

Richardson, John & Rosey Pratt, - Con. of Elishe Pratt, mother &
 Gdn. of Rosey, dated 12 Dec. 1831, witnessed by John Tyson
 & John Widgeon.

Richardson, John & Sarah Ann Evans, orph. of William Evans, 14
 Aug. 1843, John W. Elliott sec.

Richardson, Jonathan & Fanny Johnson, 5 Jan. 1818, John Sturgis
 sec.

Richardson, Levi & Susey Russel, 9 Aug. 1805, Moses Roberts sec.

Richardson, Levi & Rachel Ward, 11 July 1814, William Roberts sec.

Richardson, Major & Sally Maggoman, 9 Jan. 1827, Jenry B. Kendall
 sec.

Richardson, Smith B. & Ann Ames, dau. James Ames, dec. 23 July
 1835, Nathaniel Ames sec.

Richardson, Solomon & Esther Roberts, 2 Nov. 1797, Moses Roberts
 sec.

Richardson, Thomas & Sally Wyatt, dau. Susan Wyatt, 25 Dec. 1837,
 William Beach sec.

Richardson, William & Peggy Dalby, 24 Dec. 1812, James Dalby sec.

Richardson, William & Elizabeth Dunton, 7 Aug. 1815, Allen Brown
 sec.

Ridley, Shelton & Ann Rodgers, 1 Feb. 1819, John Widgeon sec.

Ridley, Seldon S. & Susanna Beloate, Born Oct. 1800, 21 Nov. 1821,
 Benjamin Dunton sec. Con of Laban Belote, father of
 Susanna.

Ridley, William R. & Sally Powell, 10 Dec. 1811, George Powell sec.

Ridley, William W. & Elizabeth Savage, 27 Jan. 1817, Treson Savage,
 Jr. sec.

Ridley, William P. & Esther Belote, 14 Oct. 1844, Thomas J.Smith,Jr.,
    sec.

*Riley, George T., of Accomack, & Catherine Horner, 24 Aug. 1853
Riley, William G., of Accomack, & Elizabeth J. Leatherbury, dau. John
    W. Leatherbury, 9 June, 1845, John W. Leatherbury sec.

Ringgold, Thomas L. & Susan P. B. Upshur, dau. Judge A. P. Upshur,dec.,
    & ward of Lieut. George P. Upshur, 27 July 1846, George P.
    Upshur sec.

Rippin(Rippon), David & Adah Downs, 13 June 1805, Littleton Jones
    sec.
Rippin, James & Nancy Stoit, dau. John Stoit, 14 Dec. 1829, George
    N. Bool sec.
Rippin, John & Betty Elliot, 22 May 1756, Robins Mapp sec. Con. of
    Thomas Elliot, father of Betty.
Rippin, Thomas & Anne Wilkins, 13 Nov. 1792, William Scott sec.
    Con. of Major Wilkins, father of Anne.
Rippin, Thomas & Susanna Willis, 18 Aug. 1807, Marriott Willis sec.
Rippin, Thomas & Margaret Williams, dau. Peter Williams, Sr.,dec.,
    31 Dec. 1839, John Spady sec.
Rippin, Thomas & Ursula B. Brickhouse, dau. Thomas S. Brickhouse,
    26 Dec. 1843, Victor A. Nottingham sec.
Rippon, Thomas & Sarah E. Tyler, dau. Benjamin Tyler, 2 June, 1846,
    Benjamin Tyler sec.
**Rippin, William & Peggy Wilkins, 17 Mar. 1790.
Rippin, William & Susanna Russel, 17 Mar. 1790, William Bain sec.

Roberts, Arthur, of Accomack, & Margaret Bagwell, 3 Nov. 1724,
    Abel Upshur, of Accomack, sec.
Roberts, Arthur & Elizabeth Major, 2 Mar. 1793, John Major sec.
Roberts, Arthur & Betsey Underhill, 11 May 1795, Thomas Underhill
    sec.
Roberts, Arthur & Nancy Stott, 16 Dec. 1809, George Fisher sec.
    Con. of Coventon Stott, father of Nancy.
Roberts, Arthur & Lovey Clegg, wid. Peter Clegg, 8 Mar. 1824,
    Thomas J. Wescoat sec.
Roberts, Arthur & Catherine Bell, 23 Dec. 1829, Thomas Smith,Jr.
    sec. Con. of Jesse Bell, father of Catherine.
Roberts, Arthur E., ward of Joshua K. Roberts, & Elizabeth S.
    Pearson, dau. William Pearson, 9 June 1834, Joshua K.
    Roberts & William Pearson sec.
Roberts, Arthur T. & Eliza Andrews, ward of Major Dowty, 26 Mar.
    1839, Major Dowty sec.
Roberts, Arthur E. & Margaret A. S. Smith, dau. John C. Smith,
    18 Apr. 1842, John C. Smith sec.
Roberts, Arthur B. & Miss Lavenia Andrews, 5 Mar. 1849, William
    J. Leatherbury sec. Con. of Shephard Andrews, father
    of Lavenia.
Roberts, Edmund & Sarah Mapp, 20 Dec. 1814, William White,Jr.
    sec. Con. of Margaret Mapp, mother of Sarah.

Roberts, Edward P. & Elizabeth A. Fitchett, wid. William P.C.Fitchett, dec. 1 Nov. 1843, John T. Wilkins sec.

Roberts, Elias & Ann Collins, 17 May 1836, James Hampleton sec. Con. of Mary Collins, mother of Ann & wid. of Nathaniel Collins.

Roberts, Emanuel & Rachel Powell, dau. Abel Powell, dec. 12 Feb. 1760, Laban Stott sec.

Roberts, Humphrey & Anne Mifflin, wid., 23 Jan. 1759, James Peterkin sec. Humphrey Roberts of the County of Norfolk, Merchant.

Roberts, Jacob & Sarah Taylor, 25 Apr. 1793, John Nottingham sec.

Roberts, Jacob & Lucy Gale, 6 Mar. 1797, John Milby sec.

Roberts, John & Rachel Harrison, 24 Feb. 1787, William Roberts sec.

Roberts, John & Sarah A. Smith, dau. Thomas Smith,Sr. 10 Nov. 1823, Thomas Smith sec.

?Roberts, Legustis & Eliza Collins, dau. Mary Collins, 11 Feb. 1833, Douglas Trower sec.

*Roberts, Leonard W. & Laura M. Savage, dau. Mahala Savage, 13 Jan. 1851

Roberts, Luther W. & Elizabeth Wilson, 10 June 1845, William T. Nottingham sec. Con. of James B. Wilson, father of Elizabeth.

Roberts, Moses & Susanna Dowty, 12 Oct. 1784, Hezekiah Dowty sec.

Roberts, Moses & Milly Dalby, 22 Feb. 1787, Major Brickhouse sec.

Roberts, Moses & Olive Snails, 12 Aug. 1791, John Widgeon sec.

Roberts, Moses & Nancy Richardson, 21 July 1802, Levi Richardson sec.

Roberts, Moses & Sarah Harrison, dau. Robert Harrison, 24 Nov. 1825, William Roberts sec.

Roberts, Obedience & Peggy Dalby, 30 Apr. 1785, Benjamin Dalby sec.

Roberts, Teackle & Frances Courser, 19 June 1794, Major Pettit sec.

Roberts, Teackle & Peggy Hutson, 7 Nov. 1801, James Johnson sec.

Roberts, Teackle & Sally Broughton, 19 Nov. 1825, Edward Joynes sec.

Roberts, Thomas & Elizabeth Willis, 1 Jan. 1787, Jacob Spady sec.

Roberts, Thomas & Mary Walker, 29 Mar. 1794, Edward Williams sec.

Roberts, Thomas & Sally Griffin, 17 Aug. 1807, James Travis sec.

Roberts, Thomas, Jr. & Charlotte Bell, dau. Tinney Bell, 23 Mar. 1833, Thomas Roberts, Sr. sec.

Roberts, William & Elizabeth Haughton, wid. Jacob Haughton, 15 Aug. 1778, Thomas Bullock sec.

Roberts, William & Abigal Carpenter, 9 July 1795, Stuart Pettitt sec.

Roberts, William & Peggy Miller, 18 Dec. 1804, Johannes Wise sec.

Roberts, William & Sukey Dunton, 22 Dec. 1810, James Travis sec.

**Roberts, William & Mary Abdell, 30 Jan. 1838

Roberts, Zorobabel & Peggy Trower, 20 Dec. 1806, John Francis,Jr. sec.

Robins, Abraham J. & Sally B. Mears, dau. Thomas C. Mears, 20 Apr. 1849, Thomas C. Mears sec.

Robins, Arthur & Zillah Braiser, 6 Jan. 1783, John Sturgis sec.

Robins, Arthur & Bekah Abdell, orph. of Jacob Abdell, 16 Oct. 1800, David Topping sec. Con. of Jehugh Johnson,Gdn. of Bekaj.

Robins, Arthur & Julia Ashby, 12 June 1820, William Mears, of William, sec.

Robins, Edward T. & Anne S. Jacob, dau. Robert Jacob, dec. 2 June
    1829, William W. Wilkins sec.

Robins, George M. & Margaret Jane Bell, 12 Nov. 1838, Hugh G.Smith
    sec. Con. of Tabitha Bell, mother of Margaret Jane.

Robins, George W. & Mary Susan Bell, 1 Aug. 1838, Samuel G. Carpenter
    sec. Con. of Tabitha Bell, mother of Mary Susan.

*Robins, Isaac D. & Eliza E. Ward, 29 Apr. 1853

Robins, James T. & Sarah M. Ketcham, 12 May 1842, Kendall F. Addison
    sec. Con. of Oliver Ketcham, father of Sarah M.

Robins, John, Jr. & Sarah Harmanson, 8 Oct. 1729, John Harmanson sec.

Robins, John, Jr. & Susanna Godwin, 17 June 1734, Thomas Wable sec.

Robins, John & Sarah Harmanson, 13 Mar. 1749, Edward Robins sec.
    Con. of Katharine Robins as to John.

Robins, John & Jane Core, 10 Dec. 1810, John Core sec. Con. of
    Thomas Robins, father of John.

Robins, John & Margaret Tignor, 24 Mar. 1824, Isaac Andrews sec.

Robins, John Edward & Margaret Abdell, 31 Dec. 1835, John S.Robins
    sec. Con of Edmund W.P.Downing, Gdn. of Margaret.

Robins, John & Betsy Teagner, 11 Mar. 1839, John Stockley sec.

Robins, John A. & Sally Giddens, wid. Henry Giddens, 27 May 1841,
    Devorax Warren sec.

Robins, Joshua & Sarah Green, dau. William Green, 12 July 1768,
    William Green sec.

Robins, Louis S. & Miss Sarah Ann Roberts, dau. Frank Roberts,
    3 Oct. 1849, William Beach sec.

Robins, Teackle & Elizabeth Stott, dau. William Stott, dec. 29
    Apr. 1772, William Wainhouse Michael sec. Con. of Francis
    Andrews, father in law of Elizabeth.

**Robins, Teackle & Frances Cursey, _____1794

Robins, Temple N. & Maria Smith, 10 May 1819, Isaac Smith sec.

Robins, Thomas & Rachel Graves, 22 Aug. 1805, Johannes Wise sec.

Robins, William & Sally Burris 10 Oct. 1814, Thomas S. Brickhouse
    & William Dixon, Jr. sec.

Robinson, George W. & Polly Bell, dau. Edmund Bell, 1 Apr. 1839,
    Smith Bell sec.

Robinson, George L. W. & Margaret Bell, dau. Edward Bell dec.
    10 Apr. 1841, John H. Powell sec.

Robinson, John Lilly & Peggy Roberts, 24 Aug. 1802, Thomas
    Lewis sec. Con. of Moses Roberts "to wed my nease
    Margaret Roberts"

Robertson & Mary Abdell, 30 Jan. 1838, Laban S. Johnson sec.

Rodgers(Rogers),John W. & Mary M. Thomas, 2 Feb. 1820, Anthony
    Bell sec.

Rodgers, Richard, of Accomack, & Sarah Kendall, 5 Jan. 1808,
    John Brickhouse sec.

Rodgers, Robert & Susanna Walter, 1 Dec. 1784, Walter Hyslop
    sec.

Rodgers, Robert, of Accomack, & Anne Ash, 6 Jan. 1736,William
    Waterfield sec.

Roe, William & Rosey Tatem, dau. James Tatem,dec., 30 Dec. 1845,

William Dennis sec.

Rogers(Rodgers), James W. & Maria Scott, dau. Hillery Scott, dec.
    29 Jan. 1845, James Douty sec.
Rogers, John & Ann Bell, 9 Mar. 1807, Kendall Richardson sec.
Rogers, Major & Margarett Roberts, 8 May. 1753, Watkins Joyne sec.
    Con. of Arthur Roberts as to Margarett.
Rogers, Michael E. & Elizabeth Isabella Carpenter, dau. John Car-
    penter, 15 Oct. 1841, Robert N. Rogers sec.
Rogers, Nath'l. & Mary Johnson, dau. Moses Johnson, 12 Aug. 1755.
Rogers, Nathaniel & Ann Ritter Savage, 22 Oct. 1807, Nathaniel
    Savage sec.
Rogers, Richard & Esther Floyd, 11 Oct. 1813, John Joynes sec.
    Con. of John Joynes, Gdn. of Esther.

Ronald, William & Elizabeth Kendall, dau. George Kendall, dec.
    10 Oct. 1769, John Kendall sec.

Rooks, Arthur & Ann Williams, his ward, 8 Jan. 1827, John Rooks sec.
Rooks, John & Harriot Bull, 14 Apr. 1817, Samuel West sec.
Rooks, Oliver & Elizabeth Ann Nottingham, dau. Joseph D. Nottingham,
    28 Dec. 1846, Joseph D. Nottingham sec.
Rooks, Patrick & Sally Wheeler, 1 Jan. 1820, John Warren sec.
Rooks, William & Bridget Dalby, 8 Jan. 1788, John Dalby
Rooks, William, Sr. & Sally Godwin, wid. Deveraux Godwin, 17 Nov.
    1823, Johannis Johnson sec.
Rooks, William D. & Mary A. Welche, 18 Oct. 1847, John W. Leather-
    bury sec. Con. of William Welche, father of Mary A.

Rose, Isaac & Rosey Rose, wid. 15 Apr. 1793, William Stith sec.
Rose, Isaac & Polly Joynes, 13 July 1795, George Fisher sec.
Rose, Jacob & Rosanna Addison, wid. Littleton Addison, 14 Feb.
    1792, Samuel Cox sec.
Rose, John & Polly Turner, 11 Dec. 1787, Isaac Smith sec.
Rose, Samuel & Adah Pettit, 22 Jan. 1795, Andrew Stewart sec.

Ross, David & Susanna Andrews, 2 Mar. 1808, Jesse Ross sec.
Ross, David & Nancy White, 10 Feb. 1817, George D. White sec.
*Ross, Jesse & Betsey Henderson, dau. John T. Henderson, 30 Dec.
    1852
Ross, John & Nancy Hutson, 8 Feb. 1802, George Turner sec.
Ross, John, Jr., son of John Ross, Sr., & Sally Roberts, ward of
    Alexander W. Ward, 9 Feb. 1824, John Ross, Sr. & Alexander
    W. Ward sec.

Rush, Thomas J. & Elizabeth W. Kellam, dau. Edmund Kellam, 1
    Sept. 1842, Edmund Kellam sec.

Russel, Ignatius & Joanna Roberts, 4 Mar. 1784, William Roberts
    sec.
Russel, Ignatius & Susanna Odear, 19 June 1787, Edw. Williams sec.
Russell, John & Mary Annis, 1 July 1814, George Eshon sec.

Russell, Thomas & Delia Ball, 5 Nov. 1832, William James sec.

Salisbury, William & Elizabeth Costin, 4 Feb. 1796, Abraham Costin
       sec.

Salts, John & Clara Knight, 27 Dec. 1797, John Knight sec.
Salts, William & Peggy Luke, dau. Daniel Luke, 3 June 1765, Joseph
       Dalby sec.

?Sample, Billy & Christina Weeks, 26 Nov. 1817, Frank Sample sec.
? Sample, Edmund & Nancy Beavans, 14 Jan. 1812, Abraham Lang sec.
? Sample, John & Sally Drighouse, alias Sally Morris, 5 Mar. 1822,
       Con. of Dilly Drighouse, mother of Sally - Harold L. Wilson
       sec.
? Sample, John & Kesiah Beavans, 13 Feb. 1810, Isaiah Carter sec.
? Sample, Littleton & Sukey Drighouse, 22 June 1824, Arthur Evans
       sec. Con. of Dilly Drighouse, mother of Sukey.

Sampson, John & Anne Holt, wid. 28 Oct. 1758, Savage Cowdry sec.
Sampson, Stephen & Anne Holt, dau. George Holt, 7 Mar. 1761,
       Thomas Luker sec.
Sampson, Stephen & Anne Pettitt, wid. Thomas Pettitt, 9 June,
       1799, John Mapp sec.

Sanford, James & Sarah Bell, 27 Nov. 1797, Teackle Turner sec.
Sanford, James H. & Sally Dalby, dau. Henry Dalby, 13 Jan. 1825,
       Robert Sanford sec.   Jr.
Sanford, Robert & Rachel Dalby, 22 Nov. 1814, William White/sec.

Saunders, James & Maria Nottingham, 24 July 1820, Thomas S.
       Satchell sec. Con. of Thomas Downs, Gdn. of Maria.
Saunders, John & Elizabeth Campbell, 9 Mar. 1786, John Welch sec.
Saunders, John & Kesiah Abdeel, wid. 12 July 1788, William Rooks
       sec.
Saunders, John & Mary Scott, 24 Dec. 1793, Michael Dixon sec.
Saunders, John, ward of Thomas Milbourn, & Grace Wilson, ward of
       Thomas Milbourn, 14 Jan. 1822, Thomas Milbourn sec.
**Saunders, Macneal & Esther Odear_____1797
Saunders, Samuel & Molly Hampleton, wid. William Hampleton, 24
       Dec. 1833, Severn W. Wilkins sec.
Saunders, Robert & Sarah Bowdoin, 11 Feb. 1795, John Eyre sec.
Saunders, Stuart & Sally Clegg, 17 Jan. 1792, Hillary Clegg sec.

Savage, Abel & Elizabeth Dunton, 27 Nov. 1776, John Lewis Fulwell
       sec.
Savage, Abel & Susanna Clegg, wid. 8 Sept. 1789, Thomas Bell sec.
Savage, Albert & Emeline Trower, 8 Nov. 1841, Obediah Goffigon,
       sec. Con. of Delitha Trower, mother of Emeline & wid.
       of John Trower.
Savage, Arthur & Elizabeth Smith, 18 June 1794, Major Pettit,
       sec. Con. of Caleb Smith, father of Elizabeth.
Savage, Arthur & Ann Dunton, 8 June 1800, Dickie Dunton sec.

Savage, Arthur R. & Sarah Rasco, 9 June 1806, Obed Cary sec.

Savage, Arthur R. & Catharine George, 1 July 1812, Obedience White
    sec. Con. of Major Pettit "to marry my niece"

Savage, Capt. Calvin H. & Emily Read, 14 Nov. 1837, Albert G. Wyatt
    sec. Con. of William Wyatt, Gdn. of Emily.

Savage, Caleb & Elishe Johnson, 10 Dec. 1784, John Major sec.

Savage, Caleb & Elizabeth Jesse, 2 Dec. 1794, Major Pettit sec.

Savage, Caleb & Sally Clegg, 26 Nov. 1816, Richard Johnson sec.

Savage, Caleb & Rosy M. Johnson, dau. John Johnson, 23 Feb. 1828,
    Robert B. Savage sec.

*Savage, Edward C. & Ann P. Wescoat, dau. John Wescoat, dec. 10
    Dec. 1851

Savage, George & Elizabeth Harmanson, orph. Kendall Harmanson, 11
    Jan. 1774, John S. Harmanson sec.

Savage, George & Sarah Stith, 19 May 1795, John Stratton sec.

Savage, George, Jr. & Nancy Bool, 24 Dec. 1800, Thomas Jacob sec.

Savage, George J. & Sally T. Dowty, 25 May 1814, William White, Sr.
    sec.

Savage, George L. & Rosey Dowty, ward of James Dowty, 27 May 1839,
    James Dowty sec.

Savage, James M. & Mary Ann Underhill, dau. James Underhill, 8
    Nov. 1830, Thomas B. Fisher sec.

Savage, James & Elizabeth Savage, ward of Robert B. Savage, 17
    Jan. 1832, Robert B. Savage sec.

Savage, James M. & Mary W. Upshur, dau. William M. Upshur, dec.,
    12 Sept. 1836, William H. Core sec.

Savage, John & Mary Godwin, 14 Apr. 1738, Gawton Hunt sec.

Savage, John & Rachel Belote, dau. John Belote, 31 Jan. 1763,
    Josiah Dowty sec.

Savage, John & Tabitha Belote, 11 May 1764, Edward Belote sec.

Savage, John & Susanna James, dau. Robert James, 11 June 1776,
    Solomon Bunting sec.

Savage, John M. & Ann Smith, ward of Benjamin Dunton, 21 Dec.
    1825, Benjamin Dunton sec.

Savage, John W. & Susan Ann Bull, dau. Susan Bull, 16 Han. 1850,
    John W. Gunter sec.

*Savage, Kiah, alias Hezekiah, & Peggy Anthony, dau. Mary Anthony,
    Free Negroes, 10 Jan. 1853

Savage, Littleton & Margaret Burton, dau. William Burton, 14 Jan.
    1768, William Kendall sec.

Savage, Littleton & Elizabeth Jacob, 11 Dec. 1792, George Lewis
    sec.

Savage, Michael & Betsey Mapp, 7 Oct. 1794, John Nottingham sec.

Savage, Michael & Margaret Johnson, 10 Mar. 1817, Jeptha Johnson,
    sec.

Savage, Nathaniel & Margaret James, 19 Dec. 1812, William D.
    James sec.

Savage, Peter B. & Elizabeth Jane Read, 21 Feb. 1835, John D.
    Upshur, sec. Con. of Margaret L. Read, mother of
    Elizabeth Jane.

Savage, Preeson & Esther Jenney, 11 June 1810, Hancock Dunton sec.

Savage, Preeson & Mahala Warren, 1 Feb. 1819, William W. Ridley
    sec. Con. of Adah Warren, mother & Gdn. of Mahala.

Savage, Revel & Nancy Turner, 10 June, 1794, John Poggs sec.

Con. of John Furbush Turner, father of Nancy.

Savage, Robert B. & Rosey W. Addison, wid. Thomas E. Addison, 16 Feb. 1827, Isaac Andrews sec.

Savage, Robert B. & Margaret S. Matthews, 16 Aug. 1848, Obedience R. Johnson sec. Con. of Margaret Ann Joynes, mother of Margaret.

Savage, Robins M. & Rosey Ann Fisher, dau. John Fisher, 30 July 1849, George Waterfield sec.

Savage, Samuel G. & Elizabeth J. M. Mears, ward of Heley D. Bagwell, 9 Oct. 1837, Heley D. Bagwell sec.

Savage, Severn & Betsey Trower, 23 Sept. 1800, Lewis Nolen sec.

Savage, Severn & Malana James, ward of John Simkins, 12 Dec. 1831, John Simkins sec.

Savage, Southy Littleton & Harriot Reynolds, 25 Apr. 1805, Edward Evans sec. Con. of Susanna Taylor "to marry my neice Harriot Reynolds".

Savage, Thomas,Jr. & Esther Littleton, 27 Nov. 1722, James Forse & Edward Mifflin sec.

Savage, Thomas Littleton & Mary Burton Savage, 21 May 1789, Walter Hyslop sec. Con. of Littleton Savage, father of Mary Burton.

Savage, Thomas Lyttleton & Margaret Teackle, 7 Jan. 1796, James Lyon sec. Con. of John Teackle,Jr. of Craddock, brother of Margaret.

Savage, Thomas L. & Louisa M. Mayo, 28 June 1831, George J. Yerby sec.

Savage, Thomas D. & Polly Wescoat, dau. Patty Wescoat, 24 Dec. 1832, John Roberts sec.

Savage, William & Peggy Savage, 29 June, 1779, William Satchell sec.

Savage, William B. & Susanna Smith, 12 May 1795, William Eyre sec. Con. of Littleton Savage as to William B. "to marry Billy Savage".

Savage, William & Comfort Michael, 7 Nov. 1797, John Milby sec. Con. of Edmund Joynes, Gdn. of Comfort.

Savage, William & Susey Joynes, 23 Dec. 1806, William Dixon sec.

Savage, William K. & Mary Savage, 14 Dec. 1812, Reavel Savage sec.

Savage, William & Betsey Knight, 22 June, 1817, Benjamin Scott sec.

Savage, William & Margaret Nottingham, wid. William E.Nottingham, 16 June, 1821, Peter Wilkins sec.

Savage, William & Miss Ritta Bool, 27 Sept. 1824, Isaac Andrews sec.

Savage, William T. & Elizabeth P. Young, 16 May 1825, Isaac Andrews sec. Con. of Thomas Young, father of Elizabeth P.

Savage, William L. & Ann Bunting, dau. Jonathan Bunting,dec. 2 July 1833, John S. Bunting sec.

Savage, William M. & Nancey S. Addison, ward of Robert B.Savage, 10 Mar. 1834, Robert B. Savage sec.

Savage, William & Margaret Henderson, dau. John T. Henderson, 5 Dec. 1841, William Ridley sec.

Savage, William T., ward of Levin N. Matthews, & Miss Mary J. Lewis, 9 July 1849, Teackle W. Jacob sec. Con. of William Lewis, father of Mary J.

Satchell, Charles & Margaret Green , 4 Feb. 1778, William Harrison sec.

Satchell, John & Elizabeth Green, 13 Jan. 1787, William Harrison sec.

Satchell, John & Sally Barrett, wid. William Barrett, 17 May 1821,
Warren H. Pool sec.

*Satchell, Peter & Mary Jane Satchell, Free Negroes, 24 May 1852

Satchell, Thomas S. & Mary Satchell, 22 Dec. 1813, John R. Waddey
sec.

Satchell, William & Elizabeth Stringer, 30 May 1796, John Mac
Gowan sec.

Scarburgh, Charles & Bridget Robins, 20 Aug. 1794, Carvey Dunton sec.

Scarborough, Edmond & Elizabeth Parker, 2 Oct. 1810, William Clark
sec. Con. of Elizabeth Parker as to Elizabeth.

*Scarborough, Francis M. & Susan B. Fisher, wid. Samuel P. Fisher,
22 Jan. 1852

Scarburgh, John, of Worcester County, Md., & Anne Kendall, 26
June 1759, William Wood sec. Con. of John Kendall, father
of Anne.

Scarbrough, Capt. John & Mary Jacob, 14 June 1784, Maddox Andrew
sec. Con. of Hezekiah Pitts, Gdn. of Mary.

Scarburgh, Samuel, of Worcester County, Md., & Peggy Kendall, dau.
John Kendall, 10 Apr. 1759, John Kendall sec.

Scarburgh, William, of Accomack, & Margaret Jacob, dau. Abraham
Jacob, dec. 23 Apr. 1776, Con. of Isaac Cleg, father in
law of Margaret. John Wilkins, Occohannock, sec.

Schroeder, Henry B. & Elizabeth W. Wilkins, dau. William Wilkins,
Sr. dec., 7 Aug. 1846, Thomas Tyson sec.

*Scott, Rev. A. Francis & Margaret E. Holt, dau. George Holt, dec.,
31 May 1852

Scott, Benjamin & Sally Nottingham, 23 Sept. 1796, John Nottingham sec.

Scott, Benjamin, Jr. & Elizabeth Waterfield, 13 Jan. 1818,
Rickards Dunton, Jr. sec.

Scott, Benjamin N. & Mary Ann Goffigon, 19 June, 1824, James
Goffigon sec.

Scott, Daniel & Esther Warren, dau. Hillery Warren, 13 Feb.
1788, Isaac Bell sec.

Scott, Daniel & Susan Warrington, dau. George Warrington, 14
Feb. 1834, Edward Kellam sec.

Scott, George & Sarah Kemp, 22 Dec. 1790, Arthur Evans sec.

Scott, George & Nancy T. Kellum, 15 July 1826, Shep[d] B. Floyd
sec.

Scott, George T. & Virginia S. Tyson, dau. William Tyson, 26
June 1839, Thomas L. Kendall sec. Con. of George F.
Wilkins, Gdn. of George T. Scott.

Scott, Hillary & Susan Hamby, 20 Jan. 1817, Samuel S. Stott
sec.

Scott, Hillary & Maria James, 1 June 1818, Andrew James sec.

Scott, James & Nancy Groten, 20 Dec. 1821, Thomas Groten sec.
Con. of Thomas Groten, father of Nancy.

Scott, James B. , ward of Nathaniel L. Goffigon, & Emily S.
Williams, ward of John W. Williams, 2 Mar. 1847,

John W. Williams & Nathaniel L. Goffigon sec.

Scott, John & Susanna Hart, wid. Stephen Hart, 17 May --(not dated-
Bundle marked 1780-82) Abel Nottingham sec.

Scott, John & Betsey Churn, 4 Feb. 1797, William Barecraft sec.

Scott, John & Peggy Salts, 18 Aug. 1801, Henry Smaw sec.

Scott, John & Sally Chance, 17 June 1806, John Trower sec.

Scott, John, Sr. & Jenney Rogers, 1 May 1810, William Powell sec.

Scott, John N. & Sally Powell, 24 June 1820, Isaiah W. Baker sec.

Scott, John T. ward of Thomas Smith, Jr., & Mary Ann Nottingham,
dau. Thomas Nottingham, 13 Apr. 1835, Thomas Nottingham sec.

Scott, John T. & Elizabeth S. Harmanson, 25 May 1840, Edward P.
Roberts sec.

Scott, John T. P., ward of Joshua B. Trower, & Virginia A. J.
Nottingham, dau. Jacob Nottingham, 11 July 1842, Jacob
Nottingham sec.

Scott, Levin & Nancy Peaton, 26 Jan. 1818, Thomas G. Scott sec.

Scott, Levin T. & Sarah Spady, dau. William Spady, 26 Dec. 1843,
William Spady sec.

Scott, Michael & Nancy Whitehead, 25 June 1790, William B. Wilson
sec.

Scott, Obadiah & Elizabeth Heath, dau. John S. Heath, 10 Sept.
1838, Edward Kellam sec.

Scott, Thomas & Sarah Johnson, dau. Thomas Johnson, dec. 9 May
1772, Amos Underhill sec.

Scott, Thomas & Nancy Kendall, 8 Apr. 1805, George Scott sec.

Scott, Thomas & Sukey Hunt, 8 Apr. 1816, Walter Luker sec.

Scott, Thomas W. & Sally Holmes, 14 Feb. 1818, S. Jefferson sec.

Scott, Thomas & Ann Mary Scott, dau. John W. Scott, dec. 26
June 1830, William Whitehead sec.

*Scott, Thomas & Rebecca Knight, ward of Jesse N. Jarvis, 28
Dec. 1852

Scott, William, Sr. & Ann Davis, wid. 2 July 1709, William
Scott, Jr. & Gawton Hunt sec.

Scott, William & Betty White, dau. William White, dec. 4 Apr.
1764, Thomas Pettit sec.

Scott, William & Betsy Hunt, 20 Dec. 1783, Southey Goffigon sec.

Scott, William W. & Nancy Scott, 1 July 1819, Sarah Scott sec.

Scott, William W. & Henny Mason, dau. Arroda Mason, 8 Oct. 1832,
Levin Beach sec.

*Scott, Dr. William J. & Martha E. Dixon, dau. William Dixon,
2 Nov. 1852

Scott, Zorobabel & Mary Bell, 16 Nov. 1781, Edmund Glanvill sec.

Seaton, Thomas & _____ _____, 31 May 1787, William Warren sec.

Segar, John & Sarah Fitchett, wid. William Fitchett, 21 July
1828, Luther H. Read sec.

Seymour, Digby & Rose Christian, 10 Feb. 1736, Neech Eyre sec.

Seymour, William D. & Miss Anne W. Bayly, 4 Oct. 1826, Richard
D. Bayly sec.

Shepherd, Hezekiah & Ibby Baker, 28 Nov. 1787, John Moore sec.

Shea, William & Ann Burnham, 13 Nov. 1844, Nathan R. Fletcher sec.

Showers, William & Nancy Langdon, dau. Michael Langdon, 29 June 1835,
    Zorobabel Showers sec.

*Sidelinger, Jeremiah & Margaret S. Wilkins, dau. James C. Wilkins,
    13 Apr. 1852

Simkins, Arthur & Peggy Dolby, 19 Aug. 1761, John Mathews sec.
Simkins, Arthur & Sally Jarvis, 22 Apr. 1801, William Jarvis sec.
Simkins, Coventon & Bridget Westerhouse, dau. William Westerhouse,
    30 May 1781, Con. of Henry Harmanson, Gdn. of Bridget.
    James Taylor sec.
Simkins, Coventon & Margaret Satchell, 21 Feb. 1788, William
    Simkins, Jr. sec.
?Simkins, George & Leah Stephens, dau. Amy Stephens, 29 Dec. 1832,
    Edward W. Nottingham sec.
Simkins, George & Leah Becket, dau. Joshua Becket, dec. Free
    Negroes, 25 Aug. 1837, Montcalm Oldham sec.
Simkins, Jesse J. & Frances D. Goffigon, dau. James Goffigon, 13
    Aug. 1830, James Goffigon sec.
Simkins, Jesse J. & Esther W. Goffigon, 29 Oct. 1832, John Segar
    sec. Con. of John Goffigon, father of Esther.
Simkins, Jesse J. & Laura Jarvis, dau. William Jarvis, Sr. sec.,
    13 Feb. 1838, Thomas R. Jarvis sec.
Simkins, John & Anne W. Powell, 22 Apr. 1800, Maximilian Hopkins
    sec.
Simkins, John & Sally James, dau. Hezekiah James, 27 Feb. 1786,
    William Simkins sec.
Simkins, John & Peggy Harmanson, 22 Dec. 1802, William Bain sec.
Simkins, John & Sarah Satchell, 20 Dec. 1808, Jacob G. Parker sec.
Simkins, John A. & Elizabeth S. Spady, 1 Jan. 1839, Edwin Goffigon
    sec. Con. of Southy Spady.
Simkins, John A. & Margaret S. Fitchett, 22 June 1846, Robert B.
    Nottingham sec.
Simkins, Thomas D. & Susan Brickhouse, 17 Nov. 1810, John White-
    head sec. Con. of John Brickhouse, Gdn. of Susan.
Simkins, William & Anne Dunton, dau. William Dunton, 24 May 1769,
    Elias Dunton, Sr. sec.
Simkins, William & Sally Dunton, 22 Sept. 1783, Christopher
    Dixon sec.
Simkins, William & Peggy Dunton, 17 Apr. 1793, John Simkins sec.
    Con. of Betty Dunton, mother of Peggy.

Simpson, John & Elizabeth Bird, 2 Feb. 1823, Custis Trehearn sec.
Simpson, John & Fanny Waterford, 18 Jan. 1830, Peter Williams sec.

? Sisco, Daniel & Betsey Weeks, 9 Dec. 1794, William Roberts, Jr.
    sec.
Sisco, Henry, son of Betsy, & Maria Becket, Free Negroes, 11 Jan.
    1837, Betsy Sisco & John S. Parker sec.
Sisco, Samuel & Adah Collins, Free Negroes, 3 Jan. 1835, George
    Perkins sec.

Smaw, Daniel & Ann W. Elliott, 22 Dec. 1820, Thomas W. Scott sec.
Smaw, George & Peggy Evans, dau. William Evans, dec. 19 Jan. 1785,
        John Nelson sec.
Smaw, George & Nancy Smaw, 22 June, 1795, John Nelson sec.
Smaw, Henry & Elizabeth Holland, 17 Oct. 1783, John Nelson sec.
Smaw, John & Mary Griffith, 15 July 1766, Eyres Stockley sec.
        Con. of Daniel Griffith as to Mary.
Smaw, John & Elizabeth Odear, dau. Mary Odear, 10 Dec. 1823,
        Thomas Knight sec.
Smaw, John & Elizabeth Dalby, dau. James Dalby, 26 Dec. 1825,
        James Dalby sec.
Smaw, John G. & Elmira Simkins, dau. Thomas Simkins, dec. 7 Jan.
        1835, Thomas J. Nottingham sec.

Smith, Caleb & Sarah Johnson, wid. 8 June, 1779, Thomas James sec.
Smith, Charles & Catherine Teackle, 21 Mar. 1786, Griffin Stith,
        sec. Con. of Litt: Savage as to Catherine.
Smith, Charles, of Accomack County, & Hannah Powell, 6 Nov. 1802,
        Charles S. Satchell sec. Con. of John Simkins, as to
        Hannah & of George Smith, Sr., father of Charles.
Smith, George & Rebecca Sickles, 14 Dec. 1778, Solomon Bunting sec.
Smith, George & Esther Parsons, 26 Dec. 1787, William Parsons sec.
Smith, George & Nancy Parsons, 1 June 1802, William Parsons sec.
Smith, George & Sukey Costin, 14 Apr. 1806, John Griffith sec.
Smith, George & Patsy S. Widgeon, 24 Nov. 1828, Leonard B.
        Nottingham sec. Con. of Nancy Widgeon, mother of Patsy S.
Smith, Henry & Mary Ann Williams, 13 Jan. 1840, Edwin Goffigon sec.
Smith, Isaac & Elizabeth Goffigon, 24 Apr. 1790, George Scott sec.
**Smith, Isaac & Ann Teackle, 6 Apr. 1814.
Smith, James & Anne Anderson, 15 Aug. 1789, William Trower sec.
        Con. of Matthew Anderson, father of Anne.
Smith, James & Nancy Meholloms, 4 Jan. 1799, Joseph Hanby sec.
Smith, John & Sarah Johnson, 9 Jan. 1765, Francis Darby, of Acco-
        mack, sec. Con. of Benjamin Johnson, father of Sarah.
Smith, John & Elizabeth Johnson, dau. Isaac Johnson, 8 Dec. 1789,
        William Smith, Jr. sec.
Smith, John & Nancy Stott, 5 June, 1802, James Johnson, son of
        Isaac, sec.
Smith, John & Drusilla Dowty, ward of said John Smith, 12 Jan.
        1824, Arthur Roberts sec.
Smith, John B. & Sarah Ann Kellam, 3 Dec. 1838, George F.
        Wilkins sec.
Smith, John & Mrs Ann S. Briggs, 23 July 1839, Leonard B. Nott-
        ingham & William S. Parsons sec. Con. of George Smith,
        Gdn. of John.
Smith, John C. & Elizabeth Mears, dau. William Mears, dec. 12
        Dec. 1845, William B. Upshur sec.
Smith, Jonathan & Anne Westerhouse, wid. 21 Dec. 1772, John
        Dalby sec.
Smith, Jonathan & Nancy Joynes, 26 Jan. 1798, Thomas Costin sec.
Smith, Jonathan & Esther Savage, 29 Aug. 1799, Michael Dixon sec.
Smith, Joshua & Margaret Floyd, ward of John Hallet, 18 Apr. 1825,
        John Hallet sec.

Smith, Joshua J. & Nicey H. Stott, 25 Dec. 1827, Spencer Bool sec.
 Con. of Laban Stott, father of Nicey.

Smith, Richard & Susanna Dixon, 17 Jan. 1761, Benjamin Dixon sec.

Smith, Richard & Peggy Dixon, dau. Tilney Dixon, 4 Apr. 1792, Thomas
 Dixon sec.

Smith, Richard & Juliet E. Heath, 28 Mar. 1819, William Satchell
 sec. Con. of William Satchell, Gdn. of Juliet Heath.

Smith, Thorowgood, of Accomack, & Mary Blaikley Michael, 28 June
 1775, John Lewis Fulwell sec.

Smith, Thomas & Susanna Jacob, dau. Esau Jacob, 11 Sept. 1770; John
 Floyd sec.

Smith, Thomas & Susanna Johnson, dau. Obediah Johnson, 9 Feb. 1778,
 Thomas Fisher sec.

Smith, Thomas & Anne Pitts, dau. John Pitts, 27 June 1778, Archibald
 Godwin sec.

Smith, Thomas & Esther Andrews, 24 Dec. 1790, John Smith sec.

Smith, Thomas & Lucy Rispass, 14 Oct. 1817, Sophia Rispass sec.

Smith, Thomas, Sr. & Peggy Sturgis, wid. Jacob Sturgis, 14 Jan.
 1828, Edward R. Turner sec.

Smith, William & Peggy Addison, 28 Dec. 1784, William Abdeel sec.

Smith, William & Mary Scott, 23 Apr. 1791, Isaac Johnson sec.

Smith, William & Fanny Parsons, 6 Sept. 1813, William Parsons sec.
 Con. of William Parsons.

Smith, William G. & Elizabeth U. Bowdoin, dau. Peter Bowdoin, 19
 Nov. 1825, Peter Bowdoin sec.

Smith, William & Fanny Haley, 21 Dec. 1825, Benjamin & William
 Griffith sec. Con. of Benjamin Haley, father of Fanny.

Snead, Smith & Rosetta Christian, 12 Feb. 1783, Thomas Parker, of
 Accomack sec.

Snead, Thomas & Nancy Waddy, 26 Feb. 1800, Michael Christian sec.

Snead, Thomas & Sarah Meholloms, 12 June 1804, John Core sec.

*Snead, Tully S. & Frances S. Costin, dau. William G. Costin, 3
 Mar. 1852

Snead, William & Adah Satchell, dau. William Satchell, Sr., 16
 Jan. 1788, William Satchell, Jr. sec.

Snead, William B. & Emma E. Gardner, ward of John Simkins, 1 Oct.
 1823, George F. Wilkins sec.

Snead, William H. & Salley Smith, 13 June 1831, Zorobabel Chandler
 sec.

Snead, William & Susan Parsons, wid. William Parsons, Jr. 21 Sept.
 1833, Edmund R. Custis sec.

Somers, George S. & Mary Milbourn, wid. John C. Milbourn, 5 Jan.
 1833, Jeremiah Griffith sec.

*Soper, Capt. William & Nancy Carpenter, 7 July 1851.

Sorsby, Samuel & Kessy Richardson, 14 Oct. 1824, Jesse Bell sec.

Spady, Benjamin & Adah Spady, 10 Mar. 1798, James Spady sec.

Spady, Benjamin & Polly Hamby, 6 Nov. 1827, Thomas Hamby sec.

Spady, Benjamin & Ann Scott, wid. Thos. Scott, 26 Dec. 1845,

Joseph Warren sec.

Spady, Jacob & Sarah Roberts, 18 Dec. 1788, Westerhouse Widgeon sec.

Spady, Jacob & Anne Barnes, dau. Preeson Barnes, dec. 21 July 1830, William Dennis, Jr. sec.

Spady, Jacob & Elizabeth Fox, 25 Sept. 1848, James S. Webb sec.

Spady, James & Catherine Dalby, 28 Mar. 1785, John Dolby sec.

Spady, James & Mary Hughes, 3 June 1796, William Carpenter sec.

Spady, James & Lear Evans, 17 Apr. 1802, Robinson Custis sec.

Spady, James & Amelia Goffigon, 16 Aug. 1803, John Spady sec.

Spady, James & Peggy Willis, 13 Dec. 1828, James Williams sec. Con. of Thomas Willis, father of Peggy.

Spady, James & Rosy Ann Becket, Free Negroes, 4 May 1839, John W. Leatherbury sec.

Spady, John, Jr., son of John, Sr., & Leah Williams, 8 Jan. 1827, John Spady, Sr. sec.

Spady, John H., son of Thomas S. Spady, & Margaret A. Jarvis, 24 Sept. 1832, Thomas S. Spady sec. Con. of Margaret Jarvis, mother of Margaret A.

Spady, Samuel & Polly Moore, dau. Abram Moore, 15 Jan. 1834, James Spady, of John, sec.

Spady, Samuel & Esther Welch, dau. William Welch, 11 Aug. 1845, Benjamin Nottingham sec.

Spady, Southy & Susanna Mills, 21 Jan. 1783, Jacob Spady sec.

Spady, Southy & Mary Joynes, 10 Jan. 1786, William Nelson sec.

Spady, Southy & Nancy Trower, 11 May 1790, Robert Trower sec.

Spady, Southy & Rosa Trower, ward of William E. Wilkins, 18 May 1822, Christopher Fitchett sec.

Spady, Thomas & Mary Wheeler, 8 Mar. 1780, John Wheeler, Sr. sec.

Spady, Thomas & Sarah Green Williams, 5 Dec. 1809, William Wilson sec. Con. of Ann Williams as to Sarah G.

Spady, Thomas & Sally Fitchett, 23 June, 1810, William Wilson sec. Con. of Joshua Fitchett, Sr., father of Sally.

Spady, Thomas & Betsy McCowan, 8 May 1821, Moses Griffith sec.

Spady, Thomas S. & Elizabeth Williams, 22 Nov. 1823, Thomas Knight sec. Con. of Margaret Williams, mother of Elizabeth.

Spady, Thomas F. & Maria Ann Jarvis, 27 Mar. 1843, Nath'l. S. Goffigon sec. Con. of Elizabeth U. Jarvis.

Spady, Westerhouse & Elizabeth Nottingham, 30 Sept. 1829, Benj: Nottingham sec. Con. of Elisha Nottingham, mother of Elizabeth.

Spady, William & Susanna Caple, 9 June, 1796, John R. Floyd sec.

Spady, William & Margaret Nottingham, ward of William Floyd, 14 July 1823, William Floyd sec.

Speakman, John & Elizabeth Wilkins, 12 Sept. 1796, Thomas Tyler sec. Con. of Elizabeth Wilkins, mother of Elizabeth & of Stephen Wilkins, Gdn. of Elizabeth.

Speakman, Thomas & Betsey Tylor, 13 June 1796, Stephen Wilkins sec.

Speakman, William & Caty Griffeth, 31 May 1803, Thomas Speakman sec.

Speakman, William & Charlotte Jones, 21 Dec. 1820, Severn

Wingate sec. Con. of Littleton Jones, father of Charlotte.
Speakman, William & Mary Ann Brown, dau. Allen Brown, 13 Nov. 1826,
    Allen Brown sec.

Spencer, Moses & Anne Arnold, 31 May 1769, John Burton sec.

? Stepney, York & Peggy Lewis, 6 June 1807, Jacob Morris sec.

Sterling, John & Elizabeth Seaton, dau. Mrs Jenny Seaton, 15 May,
    1846, James Bunting sec.
Sterling, Levi & Mary Ann Gunter, ward of Smith Belote, 3 Oct. 1838,
    John G. Minson sec.
Sterling, Severn H., born 21 Oct. 1817, & Cinthia Ann Ward, dau.
    Alex: W. Ward, 11 July 1843, Alex: W. Ward sec.

? Stevens(Stephens) Cugis & Betsey Pool, 20 Dec. 1806, Charles
    Pool sec.
? Stevens, George & Mary Francis, ward of Sam'l. Beavans, 18 Oct.
    1828, Samuel Beavans sec.
? Stevens, George & Elizabeth Collins, dau. Ritta Collins, 11 May
    1838, Smith S. Nottingham & Ritta Collins sec.
? Stevens, Isaac & Rachel Thomson, 22 Jan. 1791, Coventon Simkins
    sec.
? Stevens, Isaac & Sabra Nutts, 16 Aug. 1809, Isaac Stevens,Sr.sec.
? Stevens, John & Betsey Thompson, 7 Aug.1798, Ben Lewis sec.
? Stevens, Samuel & Nancy Lang, 16 July 1779, Abraham Lang sec.
? Stevens, Toby & Bridget Nutts, 7 Sept. 1804, Ben. Dunton sec.

? Stephens(Stevens), Ephraim & Leah, alias Leah Read, 11 Dec.
    1832, Peter S. Bowdoin sec.
Stephens, George & Caty Stephens, Free Negroes, 16 Jan. 1823,
    Major Scisco sec.
*Stephens, George & Louisa Collins, Free Negroes, 24 Sept. 1852.
Stephens, Isaac & Eliza Johnson, Free Negroes, 31 Dec. 1838,
    Sabra Stephens sec.
Stephens, William & Elizabeth Dixon, dau. John Dixon, 29 Oct.
    1773, John Dixon sec.
? Stephens, William, of J., & Caroline Press, ward of William
    Stephens, of Jinny, 13 July 1829, William Stephens, of
    A., sec.
Stephens, William, son of George Stephens, & Sally Pool, Free
    Negroes, 28 Dec. 1848, John S. Turpin sec.

**Stewart, George & Elizabeth Collins, 13 May 1838.
Stewart, John & Scarbrough Burton, 27 Apr. 1780, Nathanèel Tyson
    sec.
Stewart, John L., born 1818, & Susan Bool, dau. Ezekiel Bool,
    dec., & ward of Joshua K. Roberts, 15 Mar. 1841, Joshua
    K. Roberts sec.
Stewart, Joshua G. & Margaret Savage, dau. Praeson Savage, 9
    Nov. 1847, John W. Nicholson sec.

Stith, Griffin, Jr. & Anne Stratton, 24 June 1778, Edward

Robins, Jr. sec.

Stott, Abel & Sarah Watson, 10 Feb. 1789, Jacob Rose sec.
Stott, Abel & Barbara White, ward of Harrison Rayfield, 8 May 1826,
    Harrison Rayfield sec.
Stott, Abel & Margaret E. Tyson, ward of Thomas Tyson & dau. of
    John Tyson, dec. 17 Jan. 1831, Thomas Tyson sec.
Stott, Abel & Margaret H. Wise, dau. Peter Wise, dec. 19 Feb. 1844,
    James Window sec.
Stott, Bennet & Eliza Godwin, ward of William Rooks, Sr., 13 Feb.
    1826, William R. Savage sec.
*Stott, Charles & Jenny Collins, Free Negroes, 31 May 1852.
Stott, Coventon & Kesiah Fisher, dau. Daniel Fisher, dec. 17 Dec.
    1788, Abel Savage sec.
Stott, David & Elishe Hanby, 14 Feb. 1775, Custis Matthews sec.
Stott, Keley & Susanna Willis, born 3 June 1802, dau. Josiah Willis,
    dec., 23 June 1823, Nathaniel Benson sec.
Stott, Isaac & Betsey Hughes, 28 Nov. 1804, John Rayfield sec.
Stott, John & Mary Dewey, 4 July 1759, James Peterkin sec.
Stott, John & Susanna Smith, wid. 17 Aug. 1759, John Bowdoin sec.
Stott, John, Sr. & Anne James, 2 July 1763, Hezekiah James sec.
    Con. of Thomas James, father of Anne.
Stott, John & Sarah Wise, wid. John Wise, 16 Sept. 1775, Francis
    Andrews sec.
Stott, John & Polly Waterfield, 27 July 1787, George Willis sec.
Stott, John & Molly Giddens, 5 July 1788, Jacob Waterfield sec.
    Con. of John Giddens, father of Molly.
Stott, John & Hannah Warren, 18 Feb. 1796, Thomas Johnson sec.
Stott, Jonathan & Susanna Hays, wid. 12 May, 1761, John Harmanson
    sec.
Stott, Jonathan & Anne Walter, dau. John Walter, 21 Feb. 1772,
    Elias Waterfield sec.
Stott, Jonathan & Adah Pearson 24 Mar. 1802, Patrick Carpenter sec.
Stott, Laban & Sarah Roberts, 27 July 1752, Henry Tomlinson sec.
Stott, Laban & Susanna Belote, 17 May 1793, Isme Heath sec.
Stott, Laban & Betsey Heath, 11 June 1795, William Dorman sec.
Stott, Laban, Sr. & Peggy Waterfield, 15 Nov. 1808, Zorobabel
    Jones sec.
Stott, Laban W. & Susan Roberts, 3 July 1819, Jacob Nottingham
    sec.
Stott, Samuel & Ann Griffith, dau. Charles & Sally Griffith,
    dec. 30 June 1846, John Kendall sec.
Stott, Timothy B. & Lahala Sturgis, ward of Patrick Pearson,
    9 Feb. 1824, Patrick Pearson sec.

?Stockley(Stockly,Stoakley), Abel & Kesiah Pool, 27 Jan. 1802,
    William Hanby sec.
Stockly, Charles B. & Drusilla Andrews, 1 Dec. 1813, Leroy
    Oldham sec.
Stockley, Charles B. & Sarah Tatem, dau. Polly Tatem, dec.,
    23 Dec. 1843, Branson Dalby sec.
Stockly, John, Sr. & Isabell Moore, 14 Feb. 1798/9, William
    Willett sec.

Stockly, John & Peggy Scott, 9 Dec. 1816, Samuel Stott sec.

Stockley, John, son of Charles B. Stockley, & Polly Joynes, dau. Robt. A. Joynes, 30 July 1839, Charles B. Stockley & Robert A. Joynes sec.

Stockly, John, Sr. & Rachel Dennis, wid. Archibald Dennis, 22 Sept. 1846, William W. Mehollams sec.

Stockley, Thomas & Hannah Scott, 31 July 1798, William Scott sec.

**Stockley, Thomas & Mrs Freshwater, _____ July 1800.

Stockley, Thomas S. & Sarah Ann Scott, dau. Thomas G. Scott & ward of George F. Wilkins, 24 Nov. 1829, George F. Wilkins sec.

Stockley, Thomas G. & Sally Booth, orph. of John Booth, dec. & ward of John Smith, 14 Mar. 1831, John Smith sec.

Stockley, William & Adah Stratton, dau. Benjamin Stratton, 21 Jan. 1774, John Wilkins, Blacksmith, sec. Con. of W. M. Scott as to William Stockley.

Stockley, William & Elizabeth Jarvis, 30 Aug. 1775, William Scott sec.

**Stockley, William & Nancy Freshwater, _____ July 1800.

Stockley, William & Betsey Mills, 1 July 1808, John Dunton sec.

Stoit(Stoyt), Luther, & Sally Jacob, dau. John Jacob, dec. 3 Apr. 1843, Benjamin Tyler sec.

*Stoit, Walter & Margaret E. Spady, dau. William Spady, dec. 8 Dec. 1851

Stoyt(Stoit), Benjamin & Mary Speakman, 27 Dec. 1820, William Thomas sec. Con. of Thomas Speakman, father of Mary.

Stratton, Benjamin & Susanna Henry, wid. 1 Jan. 1789, Matthew Guy sec.

Stratton, Benjamin & Margaret Mapp Harmanson, 5 June, 1794, William Harmanson sec.

Stratton, Benjamin & Esther Parsons, 4 Sept. 1799, John Stratton sec.

Stratton, Edward & Mary Ann F. Wilson, 13 Oct. 1819, Jacob G. Parker sec.

Stratton, John & Gertrude Tazewell, 19 Feb. 1754, John Harmanson sec.

Stratton, John & Peggy Wilkins, 25 Jan. 1780, Daniel Roles Hall sec. Con. of John Wilkins of Old Plantation.

Stratton, Nathaniel & Elisha Hunt, dau. Azariah Hunt, 28 Sept. 1757, Isaac Jacob sec.

Stratton, William & Esther Guy, 28 Apr. 1787, Thomas Kendall sec.

Stratton, William & Adah Snead, 11 Dec. 1809, Littleton Kendall sec.

Stringer, Hillary & Alicia Harmanson 23 Jan. 1722, Argall Harmanson sec.

Stringer, Hillary & Margaret Kendall, 12 Oct. 1779, John Bowdoin sec.

Stringer, Hilary B. & Sally B. Parker, 14 Apr. 1814, Peter Bowdoin sec.

Stringer, John & Rachel Wilkins, dau. Jonathan Wilkins dec. 11

Nov. 1760, Savage Cowdry sec.

Stringer, John & Elizabeth Buckner Stith, dau. Griffin Stith, 7 Feb. 1767, Walter Hyslop sec.

Stringer, John & Susanna Dalby, wid. John Dalby, 12 Nov. 1777, Edmund Glanville sec.

Stringer, John & Mary Godwin, dau. Archibald Godwin, 23 Feb. 1785, Archibald Godwin sec.

Stringer, Thomas & Frances Willis, dau. Marriot Willis, dec. 24 Nov. 1827, Elizabeth Young sec.

Stringer, Thomas & Mary S. Nottingham, 5 May 1838, Edmund R. Custis, sec.

Stringer, Walter & Caty McCowan, dau. John McCowan, 28 Dec. 1830, John McCowan sec.

Stringer, William & Nancy Wilkins, 8 Apr. 1811, Marriott Willis sec.

Stripe, Littleton & Betsey Outten, 20 Feb. 1796, William Hanby sec.

Stripe, Peter & Kessey Dunton, 15 Feb. 1820, Charles Dillion sec.

Stripe, Whittington & Mary Cox, 25 Feb. 1790, William Bain sec.

Sturgis, Jacob & Sarah Scott, dau. Bartholemy Scott, 10 Aug. 1779, John Dowty sec.

Sturgis, Jacob & Margaret Nottingham 10 Feb. 1817, Thomas Scarborough sec.

Sturgis, James & Vianna Wescoat, dau. John Wescoat, dec., 22 Nov. 1831, William Wyatt sec.

Sturgis, Richard & Margaret Dolby, 21 Jan. 1787, Edmund Joynes sec.

Sturgis, Samuel Y. & Mary Ann Lawson, 13 June, 1836, George D. White sec.

Sturgis, Thomas & Esther W. Holt, wid. Martin M. M. Holt, 22 July 1830, George Holt sec.

Sturgis, William & Peggy Gascoyne, dau. Henry Gascoyne, 18 Feb. 1764, Ezekiel Bell sec.

Sturgis, William & Sally Andrews, 12 Apr. 1824, Levin J. Thomas sec.

Style, John & Nancy Rutherford, 11 Sept. 1812, Southy Wingate sec.

Tabb, Thomas & Elizabeth Teackle, 27 Dec. 1790, John Stratton, Jr. sec.

Tankard, Azariah & Rachel Pettitt, dau. William Pettitt, dec. 3 Feb. 1764, Howson Mapp sec.

Tankard, George L. E. & Anne K. J. Dunton, 10 Apr. 1826, Smith Nottingham sec.

Tankard, John & Sarah Andrews, 12 Feb. 1778, John Thomas sec.

Tankard, Dr. John & Zilla Downing 10 Jan. 1791, John Eyre sec.

Tatum, James & Polly Brickhouse, 18 Sept. 1805, Thomas Jacob sec.

Tatem, William T. & Alichia Biggs, dau. Christopher Biggs, dec., 12 Dec. 1838, Daniel Scott sec.

Taylor, Bartholomew & Polly Evans, dau. Richard Evans, dec., 9

Apr. 1805, Joshua Garrison sec.

Taylor, Bartholomew & Mrs Nancy Rooks, 8 Apr. 1839, William Fitchett
    sec.

Taylor, David C. & Margaret S. Dalby, 24 June, 1824, John N.Stratton
    & James Young sec. Con. of John B. Thomas, Gdn. of Margaret.
    David Taylor son of Crippen Taylor.

Taylor, George & Elizabeth Garris, orph. of Thomas "Garrott" - 28
    Jan. 1791, Thomas Jacob sec. Con. of Robert Brickhouse as to
    Elizabeth.

Taylor, George & Sarah Dalby, 20 Aug. 1799, William Teackle Taylor sec.

Taylor, George & Elizabeth Evans, 2 May 1812, Bartholomew Taylor sec.

Taylor, George & Sukey Scott, wid. Thomas Scott, 30 July 1821,
    Thomas Peed sec.

Taylor, James & Susanna Rasin, 16 Jan. 1774, William Harmanson sec.

Taylor, James & Nancy Jacob, 28 Dec. 1808, Edward Joynes sec.

Taylor, James & Esther Bryan 13 Jan. 1816, John Taylor sec.

Taylor, John & Nancy Addison, 25 Feb. 1800, Con. of Thomas Addison
    as to Nancy. Major Andrews sec.

Taylor, John & Polly Davis, 17 Aug. 1802, John Dalby sec.

Taylor, John & Caty Savage, 10 Apr. 1809, John Turner sec.

Taylor, John & Elizabeth Dowty, 9 Mar. 1818, Thomas Dowty sec.

**Taylor, John & Peggy Spady, 17 Dec. 1818

Taylor, John & Nancy Harrison, dau. Abel Harrison, 14 June, 1826,
    Abel Harrison sec. John Taylor"son in law"of William

Taylor, John E. & Eliza J. Matthews, orph. Lewis Matthews, dec.,
    20 June 1843, John G. Nelson sec. Con. of Margaret
    Joynes, mother of Elizabeth Matthews.

Taylor, John & Lucy Mazlin, 27 Mar. 1844, William T. Nottingham
    sec.

Taylor, Joshua, of Accomack, & Martha Sturgis, dau. William
    Sturgis, 11 May 1775, Thomas Hurst sec.

Taylor, Major & Sally Luke, 2 Oct. 1802, Jacob Roberts sec.

Taylor, Shadrack & Polly Richardson 7 Jan. 1823, Custis Kellam
    sec. Con. of Shadrack Taylor, father of Shadrack.

**Taylor, Thomas & Anne Bishop, _____1799

Taylor, Thorowgood & Susanna Rodgers, 10 Jan. 1816, John N.
    Fitchett sec.

Taylor, William & Henrietta Dunton, dau. Stephen Dunton dec.
    11 Feb. 1773, William White sec.

Taylor, William & Sarah Wheeler, 2 Nov. 1780, Levin Laurence
    sec.

Taylor, William E. & Margaret A. Lyon, dau. Dr. James Lyon,dec.,
    21 Feb. 1831, John Eyre sec.

Taylor, William J. & Virginia A. Hunt, 1 May 1848, David A.
    Dunton sec. Con. of Mary E. Hunt, mother of Virginia.

Tazewell, William & Sophia Harmanson, 10 June 1723, Thomas Cable
    sec.

** ? Teague, Abraham & Martha _____ July 1791

Teague, Thomas, of Accomack & Keziah Scott, dau. Henry Scott,
    21 Feb. 1767, Solomon Scott sec.

Teackle, Abel Upshur, of Accomack & Rachel Gascoyne, 7 July, 1790,
        John Guy sec. Con. of William Harmanson, Gdn. of Rachel.
Teackle, Caleb, of Accomack, & Elizabeth Harmanson, dau. George
        Harmanson, 17 Dec. 1771, William Floyd sec.
Teackle, George & Fanny B. Bowdoin, 8 Aug. 1801, Peter Bowdoin sec.
Teackle, John, Jr. & Anne Upshur, 17 Dec. 1783, Griffin Stith sec.
        Con. of Thomas Upshur as to Anne.
Teackle, Littleton D. & Elizabeth Upshur, 27 May, 1800, John Stratton
        sec.

Terrier, John C. & Elizabeth Dixon, 24 Oct. 1827, Smith Nottingham
        sec. Con. of Thomas S. Brickhouse, Gdn. of Elizabeth.

Thomas, Benjamin & Elizabeth D. Broughton, dau. Isaac Broughton,
        dec. 14 Dec. 1829, Rowland Dowty sec.
Thomas, Benjamin & Elizabeth H. Warren, dau. John Warren, Sr., 1
        Apr. 1842, John Warren, Sr. sec.
*Thomas, George L. J. & Mary Ann Ward, dau. Arthur D. Ward, 17 Sept.
        1850.
Thomas, Harrison & Elizabeth Downing, 23 Mar. 1793, Elijah Baker sec.
Thomas, James & Elizabeth S. Turner, dau. Edward R. Turner, 24 Nov.
        1842, Edward R. Turner sec.
Thomas, John B. & Ann C. Dunton, 19 June, 1822, John Hanby sec.
        Con. of William Dunton, father of Ann C.
Thomas, John B. & Miss Harriet G. Holland, 1 Mar. 1826, Edward
        R. Boisnard & Nathaniel Holland sec.
Thomas, John W. & Sophia E. Dunton, dau. Maj. William Dunton, dec.
        19 Sept. 1836, Samuel W. Dunton sec.
Thomas, Joseph W. & Ailsie T. Floyd, wid. Shepherd B. Floyd, 7
        Oct. 1830, William J. Campbell sec.
Thomas, Levin J. & Sally Core, 21 Dec. 1813, John C. Mapp, sec.
        Con. of John Core, father of Sally.
Thomas, Levin J. & Harriet P. Matthews, wid. Levin R. Matthews,
        8 Aug. 1836, John W. Tankard sec.
Thomas, William & Polly Smith, 4 Apr.'1795, John Dixon sec.
Thomas, William & Frances Nottingham, ward of Jacob Nottingham,
        Sr., 1 July 1822, Jacob Nottingham, Sr. sec.

Thom, William Alexander & Anne Parker, 11 Apr. 1844, Miers W.
        Fisher sec.

? Thomson, Isaac & Leah Stevens, 22 Sept. 1792, Jacob Frost sec.
? Thompson, Isaac & Margaret Carter, dau. Ezekiel Carter, 9 Aug.
        1824, Ezekiel Carter sec.
Thompson, Isaac & Lilly Stephens, Free Negroes, 26 Dec. 1839,
        Henry Morris sec.
?Thompson, Jacob & Sukey Morris, 26 May, 1795, Thomas Lewis sec.
?Thompson, Jacob & Tamar Stevens, 26 Sept. 1800, Johannes
        Johnson sec.
? Thompson, Jacob, Jr., son of Jacob, Sr., & Mary Baker, dau.
        Thomas Baker, 20 Dec. 1827, Jacob Thompson, Sr. & Thomas
        Baker sec.
? Thompson, Raleigh & Peggy Collins, dau. little Peggy Collins,

dec., 2 May 1835, John S. Parker sec.
? Thompson, Robert & Eliza Watson, 25 Jan. 1819, Elijah Floyd sec.

Thruston(Thurston,Thurstain), Abner & Betsey Williams, 26 May, 1812,
    Peter Williams, Jr. sec. Con. of Peter Williams, father of
    Betsey.

Thurstain(Thruston,Thurston), Abner & Elizabeth Williams, dau. Peter
    Williams, dec., 25 Jan. 1782, John Tyler sec.

Thurston(Thruston,Thurstain), Azariah & Mary Ann Williams, dau.
    Samuel S. Williams, 24 June, 1826, Samuel S. Williams sec.
Thurston, Azariah & Susan A. Williams, dau. Capt. Samuel S. Williams,
    27 June, 1842, Leonard B. Nottingham sec.
Thurston, Azariah & Leah Fitchett, wid. Christopher Fitchett, 30
    Nov. 1848, Thomas K. Dunton sec.

Thurmer, Robert & Anna Catharine Westerhouse, dau. William West-
    erhouse, 12 Oct. 1756, Dickie Galt sec.

Tilney, Jonathan & Sarah Marshall, 22 June 1742, Thomas Cable sec.

Timmons, Michael & Mary Sabra, 18 May 1799, William Havard sec.

Toleman, William & Polly Heath, 9 June, 1792, Charles Stevenson
    sec.

Tomkins, John & Ann Custis, wid. 19 Feb. 1747, George Kendall sec.

Topping, David & Rosey Stott, 11 Apr. 1801, William Bain sec.

Townsend, Angelo & Mrs Adah Parrot, wid. George Parrot, 18 Oct.
    1823, Gilbert Townsend sec.
Townsend, Angelo A. & Martha Ann Eliza Holcroft, dau. William
    Holcroft, 13 July 1832, William Holcroft sec.
Townsend, Nathaniel B. & Rebecca M. Joynes, dau. Edmund Joynes,
    dec., 27 Mar. 1829, Henry B. Kendall sec.

Travis, Dennard & Rebekah Costin, 14 Sept. 1808, William S.
    Evans sec. Con. of Matthew Costin, father of Rebekah.
Travis, Dennard & Susan Whitehead, 26 June 1821, John Whitehead
    sec.
Travis, Elliott & Polly Herbert, 16 July 1813, Thomas Graves sec.
    Con. of B:Griffith, & certificate that Polly is of age.
Travis, Elliott & Anna Elliott, 13 Aug. 1821, William Goffigon
    sec.
Travis, Elliott & Mary Warren, 5 Jan. 1846, Leonard Warren sec.
    Con. of Joseph Warren, father of Mary.
Travis, James & Sally Dunton, 10 Nov. 1792, Henry Giddens sec.
*Travis, John & Charlotte Whitehead, wid. Stephen Whitehead, 9
    Sept. 1850.
Travis, Meshack & Adah Wilkins, dau. John Wilkins, Sr. 26 Dec.
    1825, John Wilkins, Sr. sec.

Travis, Meshack & Elizabeth Wilkins, dau. John Wilkins, Sr., 8 Dec.
    1828, Thomas Hallett sec.
Travis, Shadrack & Mrs Sukey Nottingham, 13 Nov. 1826, Bowdoin
    Costin sec.
Travis, Thomas & Sally W. Brickhouse, 12 June 1843, Leonard B.
    Nottingham & James B. Wilson sec. Con. of Susan Travis,
    mother of Thomas & of Thomas S. Brickhouse, father of Sally
    W.
Travis, William & Sally Odear, 13 Apr. 1818, Abram Costin sec.
*Travis, William & Elizabeth Costin, ward of Thomas K. Dunton, 11
    Nov. 1850.

Trehearn, Curtis(Custis) & Harriot A. Johnson, dau. Polly Johnson,
    9 Dec. 1833, Peter P. Mayo sec.

Trower, Douglas & Elizabeth Fitchett, 10 Sept. 1821, Thomas Hallett
    sec. Con. of William Dixon, Gdn. of Elizabeth.
Trower, John & Sarah Smith, dau. Richard Smith, 11 June, 1791,
    Richard Smith sec.
Trower, John & Delitha Belote, 19 Oct. 1805, James Johnson sec.
Trower, John & Elizabeth S. Fitchett, 23 Dec. 1846, John T. Hallett
    sec. Con. of Leah Fitchett, mother & Gdn. of Elizabeth.
?Trower, Luke & Bethany Jefferey, ward of Nathan Drighouse, 13
    Nov. 1826, Nathan Drighouse sec.
Trower, Luke & Ann Collins, Free Negroes, Ann wid. of Victor
    Collins. 18 Feb. 1845, Joshua P. Wescoat sec.
Trower, Robert & Nelly Costin, 31 Oct. 1795, David Topping sec.
Trower, Robert S. & Sally A. James, ward of John S. James, 6
    June 1838, John S. James sec.
Trower, William & Sukey Williams, 6 Sept. 1815, John Spady sec.
Trower, William H. & Susan Ann Tyson, dau. Thomas Tyson, 15 Dec.
    1849, Thomas Tyson sec.

Truitt, Solomon, of the County of Sussex, Penna., & Frances
    Smith, wid., 24 Apr. 1751, Matthew Warren sec.

Tunnil, John & Nancy Taylor, 31 May 1803, James Travis sec.

Turpin, Capt. John & Sally Gascoyne, 27 Oct. 1789, John Upshur,
    Jr. sec. Con. of Thomas Upshur, Sr., as to Sally.
Turpin, John & Nancy Willet, 9 Oct. 1809, Henry Walker sec.
Turpin, John D. & Elizabeth Willett, 15 Jan. 1819, Thomas H.
    Turpin sec.
Turpin, John S. & Maria S. Powell, 10 Apr. 1847, Lafayette
    Harmanson sec.
Turpin, Thomas & Lear Willet, 1 Dec. 1812, John D. Turpin sec.

Turner, Brandon & Leah Savage, 21 Oct. 1803, Samuel Minson sec.
? Turner, Custis & Sally Drighouse, dau. Nathan Drighouse, 15
    Nov. 1831, Nathan Drighouse sec.
Turner, Edward & Mary Addison, dau. Littleton Addison, 26 Oct.
    1781, Littleton Addison sec.
Turner, Edward R. & Margaret Brickhouse, 27 Dec. 1820,

Lawrence Enholm sec. Con. of George Brickhouse, father of
"Pegey" Brickhouse.

Turner, James & Patsey Wyatt, 27 Apr. 1818, William Matthews sec.

Turner, James & Nancy Haggoman, ward of Benjamin Dunton, 2 Sept.
1829, Benjamin Dunton sec.

Turner, James E. & Elizabeth S. Knight, dau. William Knight, dec. 29
May 1838, Reubin Goody sec.

Turner, James E. & Matilda Ann Ames, dau. Samuel Ames, 28 Jan.
1849, Levin T. Ames sec.

Turner, John & Sally Pitts, dau. John Pitts dec., 23 Apr. 1790, John
T. Turner sec. Con. of Sally Pitts as to Sally.

Turner, John G., ward of Joshua B. Turner, & Margaret Ann Joynes,
dau. Edward Joynes, 26 Nov. 1834, Joshua B. Turner & Edward
Joynes sec.

*Turner, John E. G., widower, & Nancy Savage, wid. William M. Savage,
19 Aug. 1852

Turner, Joshua & Bridget Turner, 18 Apr. 1815, Joshua Garrison sec.

Turner, Joshua B. & Sally S. Scott, wid. John N. Scott, 2 Feb. 1829,
Nathaniel West sec.

Turner, Nathaniel & Anne Dunton, 1 Oct. 1805, Joshua Garrison sec.

Turner, Revil & Betsey Palker (Parker?) 26 Aug. 1790, Teackle
Turner sec. Con. of Thomas Addison, Gdn. of Betsey
"Parlker"

Turner, Teackle & Nancy Sandford, 13 July 1790, Michael Matthews
sec.

Turner, Teackle & Peggy Mapp, 5 Feb. 1798, John K. Floyd sec.

Turner, Teackle J. & Ann P. Wescoat, 5 Dec. 1826, Jacob Nottingham,
Jr. sec.

Turner, Theophilus & Sophia Turner, dau. Edward Turner, dec. 22 Dec.
1759, Hezekiah Dowty sec.

Tyler, Benjamin & Polly Bell, his ward, 9 Aug. 1824, Richard Bell
sec.

Tyler, John & Catharine Moore, 7 Jan. 1778, William Wilson sec.

**Tyler, John & Betsey Speakman _____ 1802.

Tyler, John & Peggy Spady, 14 Dec. 1818, Thomas Vichus sec.

Tyler, Thomas & Ann Bishop, 1 Jan. 1800, William Wilson, sec.

Tyson, John & Mary Widgeon 14 Dec. 1787, Elijah Baker sec.

Tyson, John & Sally Knight, 21 Dec. 1814, Nathaniel Widgeon sec.
Con. of John Knight, father of Sally.

Tyson, John & Susan Widgeon, 2 Feb. 1820, Nathaniel Widgeon sec.

*Tyson, Luther & Rosena T. Ridley, dau. William W. Ridley, dec.
27 May 1851

Tyson, Nathaniel & Judith Wilkins, dau. John Wilkins, Sr., 19
June 1761, John Lewis Fulwell sec.

Tyson, Robert & Elizabeth Stoit, dau. Benjamin Stoit, 23 Dec.
1848, Joshua Nottingham sec.

Tyson, Samuel & Frances Godwin, ward of Shepherd B. Floyd, 17
July 1828, Shepherd B. Floyd sec.

Tyson, Thomas & Nancy Widgeon, dau. Nathaniel Widgeon, 20 Mar.
1823, Nathaniel Tyson sec.

Tyson, Thomas & Sarah E. Nelson, dau. John Nelson, Jr., 30 May 1842,
James S. Wilson sec.

Tyson, William & Anne Biggs, 23 Dec. 1817, John Biggs sec. Con of
Nancy Biggs, mother of Anne.

Underhill, Daniel & Mary Tompson, wid. 27 May 1761, Thomas Underhill
sec.

Underhill, Edmund E. W, & Polly S. Nelson, dau. Southy Nelson, dec.,
12 Aug. 1833, James M. Savage sec.

Underhill, Michael P. & Maria J. Nelson, dau. Southy Nelson dec. 1
Dec. 1834, Thomas O. Hunt sec.

Underhill, Thomas & Susanna Evans, dau. Arthur Evans, dec. 14 Nov.
1767, Edmund Glanville sec.

Underhill, Thomas & Susanna Barlow, 13 Aug. 1793, Michael Matthews
sec.

Underhill, William & Mary Westcoat 9 June 1807, Robert Sanford sec.

Upshur, Abel, of Accomack, & Elizabeth Gore, dau. Daniel Gore, dec.
15 Nov. 1779, Edward Robins sec. Con. of Alexander Stockley,
Gdn. of Elizabeth.

Upshur, Arthur B. & Elizabeth G. Carpenter, 27 Apr. 1811, Thomas
Nottingham sec. Con. of Rickards Dunton, Gdn. of Elizabeth.

Upshur, George P. & Peggy E. Parker, dau. Severn E. Parker, 25
June, 1836, Severn E. Parker sec.

Upshur, George L. & Sarah A. Parker, 8 Feb. 1844, Alfred Parker sec.

*Upshur, George son of Susan, & Mary Pool, dau. Hessy, Free Negroes,
22 May 1852

Upshur, John & Margaret Michael, wid. William Michael, 17 Mar.
1781, John Stratton, Sr. sec.

Upshur, John, Sr. & Rosey Robins, 23 July 1794, Arthur Rogers sec.

Upshur, John, Jr. & Elizabeth Brown Upshur, 22 Oct. 1798, Custis
Kendall sec.

Upshur, John Brown, of Accomack, & Mary Elizabeth Stith, dau.
William Stith, dec. 11 May 1802, William B. Savage sec.
Con. of Isaac Smith, Gdn. of Mary Elizabeth.

Upshur, Thomas & Anne Stockley, ward of Nathaniel & Mary Beavans,
29 Jan. 1761, David Edmunds sec.

Upshur, Thomas T. & Elizabeth T. Smith, dau. Isaac Smith, 8 Apr.
1842, Isaac Smith sec.,

Upshur, William M. & Elizabeth White, 2 Sept. 1805, John Addison
sec.

Upshur, William S. & Anne S. Wilson, 28 May 1827, Peter P. Mayo sec.

*Upshur, William B. & Catherine T. Neale, dau. Elizabeth T. Neale,
3 Nov. 1851.

Vawter, William & Margaret Bonewell, 12 July 1746, Luke Johnson
sec.

Vermillion, Guy & Sinah Jacob, wid., 15 May 1782, George Parker,
Jr. sec.

Vichus(Viccous), Thomas & Sally Freshwater, 14 Dec. 1818, John

Spady, Sr. sec.

Viccous,(Vichus), John & Esther Clegg, dau. Clark Clegg, dec., 4
    Oct. 1792, Stuart Saunders sec.

Waddey, Edward R. & Harriet Nottingham, ward of William Nottingham,
    Jr. 19 Oct. 1824, William Nottingham, Jr. sec.
Waddy, John R. & Hannah White, 29 Jan. 1801, William Gillet sec.
Waddey, Thomas & Adah Carpenter, 1 Nov. 1788, William Hornsby sec.
Waddey, William E. & Mary E. Griffith, ward of John H. Griffith,
    12 Nov. 1849, John H. Griffith, sec.

?Wakefield, Peter & Lusey Weeks, 7 Sept. 1794, Nathaniel Holland
    sec.

Waltham, John, of Accomack, & Anne Michael, wid. 26 Dec. 1759,
    James Peterkin sec.
Waltham, John & Susanna Johnson, dau. Obediah Johnson, dec., 10
    Feb. 1778, Jonathan Smith sec.
Waltham, William & Sarah Johnson ____ (not dated) Michael
    Dunton sec. Con. of Priscilla Johnson, mother of Sarah,
    dated 23 Feb. 1780.

Walter, John & Susanna Stott, wid. 8 Dec. 1767, William Dunton sec.
Walter, Solomon & Sarah Read, 18 Dec. 1819, Arthur Roberts sec.
Walter, Solomon & Patty Wescoat, wid. John Wescoat, 29 May 1835,
    Miers W. Fisher sec.

Walch, William & Mary Moore, 16 Dec. 1819, Charles Dillion sec.

Waples, Joshua & Betsey Costin, 12 Dec. 1803, William Costin sec.

Ward, Alexander W. & Jennet S. Turner, 13 Dec. 1813, James San-
    ford sec.
Ward, Alexander W. & Anne Bell, 11 Apr. 1831, William H. Bell sec.
    Con. of Anthony Bell, father of Anne.
Ward, Golden & Peggy Savage, 24 Aug, 1786, Seth Powell sec. Con.
    of Delither Savage, mother of Peggy.
Ward, James & Betsey Abdell, 19 Mar. 1806, Stephen Ward sec.
Ward, James & Susan Smith, 16 Nov. 1819, Jacob Pettit sec.
Ward, James H. & Mary Robins, dau. Arthur Robins, 27 Dec. 1841,
    William B. Upshur sec.
*Ward, James G. & Margaret Ann Ross, dau. John Ross, dec. 20
    Oct. 1852
Ward, John A. & Tinney Trader, 23 Dec. 1803, James Benson sec.
*Ward, Joseph & Sarah Isdell, ward of Joseph Ward, 12 Aug. 1850.
Ward, Littleton & Anne Bell, dau. William Bell, 21 Dec. 1787,
    William Belote sec.
Ward, Michael & Ann Johnson, 16 Mar. 1822, Michael R. Savage sec.
    Con. of John P. Johnson, father of Ann.
Ward, Michael & Mary Turner, 9 Sept. 1839, John Segar sec.

Ward, Robert B. & Peggy Heath, 26 Mar. 1804, Thomas Johnson, Jr. sec. Con. of James Heath as to Peggy.

Ward, Samuel & Malinda Mears, dau. John Mears, 9 Mar. 1836, James S. Carpenter sec.

Ward, Stephen & Elizabeth Harrison, 2 Apr. 1774, Elijah McLauchan, sec. Con. of William Ward, father of Stephen & of Salathiel Harrison, father of Elizabeth.

Ward, Stephen & Nancy Cook, 6 June 1791, Abner Thurston sec.

Ward, Stephen & Adah Hickman, 2 Mar. 1797, John Abdil sec.

Ward, Stephen & Betsey Edmunds, 19 Mar. 1806, James Ward sec.

Ward, Tully S. & Jane Brickhouse, 10 July 1815, George Brickhouse, Sr. sec.

Ward, William & Elizabeth Johnson, 8 Aug. 1786, Littleton Ward sec.

Ward, William & Catharine McCready (not dated - Bundle marked "1786-7" Robert Nottingham sec.

Ward, William & Agnes Melvil, 7 Jan. 1797, Charles Carpenter, Jr. sec.

**Ward, William H. & Mary Isdell, 13 Feb. 1850

Ware, William & Barbara Batson, 5 Feb. 1722, Abraham Bowker & John Elligood sec.

Warrington, George & Nancy Barrett 20 Dec. 1808, Thomas Widgeon sec.

Warrington, George & Sally Toleman, 8 Jan. 1816, Jeptha Johnson sec.

Warrington, John & Elizabeth Willis 18 June 1810, Joseph Warren sec.

**Warrington, William & Margaret Warrington, 6 Dec. 1821

Warren Argoll & Elizabeth Marriner, wid. 15 Feb. 1809/10, Robert Wiggon (Widgeon) sec.

*Warren, Calvin L. & Mary E. Roberts, dau. Edmund Roberts, dec. 30 June, 1852

Warren, Devorax & Esther Abdil, 12 Apr. 1802, William Rooks sec.

Warren, Devorax & Sabra M. Dix, dau. Levin Dix, 18 Jan. 1836, Levin Dix sec.

Warren, Henry & Rose Mary Campbell, dau. Nicholas Campbell, 28 July 1772, John Gleeson sec. Rose Mary Campbell born 1749

Warren, Hezekiah & Adah Kellam, 4 Dec. 1794, William Thomas sec.

Warren, Hilary & Anne Mary Dixon, wid. 11 July 1764, Richard Smith sec.

Warren, Hilary & Hannah Rafield, 11 Dec. 1787, Isaac Bell sec.

Warren, Hillary & Juda Wilkins, 13 Oct. 1806, William Speakman sec.

Warren, Hillary & Esther Widgeon 14 Feb. 1814, John Tyler sec.

Warren, James & Esther Parsons, dau. Marriot Parsons, dec. 8 Mar. 1832, Stephen Wilkinson sec.

Warren, James & Sally Parkerson, dau. George Parkerson, 28 Dec. 1846, Joshua Nottingham sec.

Warren, John & Sally Wood, 16 Oct. 1813, Patrick Rooks & Jacob G. Parker sec.

Warren, John P. & Catherine Kellam, dau. Charles Kellam, dec., 18 Apr. 1832, Jacob Waterfield sec.

Warren, John P. & Nancy Darby, wid. John Darby, 22 Jan. 1808, John R. Fisher sec.

Warren, John & Polly Floyd, 11 June 1838, John W. Elliott sec.

Con. of Sally Floyd, mother of Polly.

Warren, John, son of Patrick, & Tabitha M. Bell, dau. Anthony Bell, dec., 1 Jan. 1848, John Warren sec.

Warren, John & Emily Mister, dau. Gilbert Mister, 12 Feb. 1849, Gilbert Mister sec.

Warren, Joseph & Martha Lune, dau. Arthur Lune, ____ 1707, John Savage & Joshua Cowdry sec. (badly damaged)

Warren, Joseph & Peggy Evans, 7 Jan. 1812, William S. Evans sec.

Warren, Joseph & Elizabeth Travis, dau. Shadrack Travis, 11 Dec. 1843, Shadrack Travis sec.

Warren, Patrick & Betsey Williams, 12 Mar. 1810, William Downs sec.

Warren, Patrick, Jr. & Elizabeth Ann Scott, ward of William S. Floyd, 16 July 1838, William S. Floyd sec.

Warren, Peter & Mary Waterson, 13 Feb. 1750, John Flood sec.

Warren, Peter & Rose Johnson, wid. 3 Nov. 1774, Griffin Stith, Jr. sec.

Warren, Seth & Betsey Caple, 31 Oct. 1809, Edward Johnes sec.

Warren, Seth & Betsey Jones, 21 Dec. 1809, John Warren sec.

Warren, Thomas & Esther Viccus, 2 Dec. 1801, Stuart Saunders sec.

Warren, Thomas & Ann Floyd, ward of Thomas Hallett, 8 June, 1840, Thomas Hallett, sec.

Warren, Thomas P. & Eliza E. Henderson, dau. William Henderson, 20 Oct. 1842, Walter Belote sec.

Warren, William & Anne Wheeler, 26 July 1788, William Stith sec.

Warren, William & Fanny Clegg, 1 Jan. 1811, Walter Luker sec.

Warren, William & Peggy Travis, 12 Feb. 1821, Peter Williams sec.

Warren, William & Rosey Bradford, 16 Jan. 1830, Benjamin Tyler & William Speakman sec.

Warren, William, of Hilly., & Anne Dix, wid. Isaac Dix, 28 Dec. 1835, James Warren sec.

*Warren, William H. & Angeline Moore, wid. William D. Moore, dec., 16 Aug. 1852

Watson, Besial & Pattsey Dennis, 7 Aug. 1805, Major Dennis sec.

Watson, Bezel & Nancy Dennis, 25 Jan. 1815, Archibald Dennis sec.

Watson, Besey & Jenny Dennis, 14 Apr. 1816, William Satchell sec.

Watson, Edmund & Rosanna Andrews (not dated) William Harrison sec.
Con. of Sarah Abdell, mother of Rosanna, dated 27 Dec. 1786

Watson, Edmund & Peggy Thomas, 3 Feb. 1801, William Thomas sec.

Watson, Edmund & Peggy Westcot, 2 Aug. 1802, Thomas Dowty sec.

**Watson, George & Susanna Wilkins _____ 1805

Watson, Moses & Director Twiford, 1 Jan. 1730, George Nicholas Turner sec.

Watson, Revel & Nancy Tankard, 15 July 1794, George Holt sec.

Watson, Revel & Eckay Joliff, 8 July 1811, Kendall Addison sec.

Watson, William & Elenor Johnson, 17 July 1800, Benjamin Watson sec.

Watson, William & Nancy Major, 4 Sept. 1821, William Savage, Sr. sec.

Waters, Edward & Margaret Waters, 18 Aug. 1731, John Custis sec.

Waters, Thomas & Susanna Stringer, 20 Apr. 1799, William Wilson sec.

Waters, William & Mary Bayaton, 4 Oct. 1707, Andrew Hamilton sec.

Waters, William & Margaret Robins, 26 Mar. 1728, John Robins,Jr. sec.
Waters, William & Rose Harmanson, 10 May, 1739, Joseph Cottman &
     John Maddox, of Somerset County, Md. sec.
Waters, William & Anne Jacob, dau. Robert Clark Jacob, 13 July,
     1790, Robert Clark Jacob sec. (badly damaged.)

Waterfield, George & Margaret Fatherly, dau. John Fatherly, dec.
     24 Dec. 1849, Major Taylor sec.
Waterfield, Jacob & Susanna Harrison, 11 June 1748, George Holt
     sec.
Waterfield, Jacob & Sarah Joyne, 21 Feb. 1791, Elijah Watson sec.
Waterfield, Jacob & Zipporah Crocket, dau. Thomas Crocket, 14 Aug.
     1843, Teackle J. Turner sec.
Waterfield, Jacob & Sally Turner, dau. James Turner, (Occ.), 4
     Sept. 1843, James Turner (Occ) sec.
Waterfield, John, Jr. & Mary Dunton, 12 Feb. 1754, Isaac Dunton
     sec. Con. of Rickard Dunton, brother of Mary.
Waterfield, John & Elizabeth Brickhouse, 14 June 1803, John Brick-
     house, Jr. sec.
Waterfield, Meshack & Jane Salts, 14 June 1785, William Waterfield
     sec.
Waterfield, Meshack & Rachel Benthall, 15 Jan. 1790, John Water-
     field sec.
Waterfield, Meshack & Priscilla Bool,31 Jan. 1797,James Dalby sec.
Waterfield, Meshack & Sally West, 15 Feb. 1812, David Topping sec.
Waterfield, Southy & Peggy Wilkins, dau. William Wilkins, dec. 28
     Dec. 1771, William Trower sec.
Waterfield, Thomas & Mahala Heath, 13 Oct. 1816, Kendall Addison
     sec.
Waterfield, William & Nancy Hunt, dau. Azariah Hunt, dec. 8 June
     1779, Michael Dunton sec.

Watt, James & Mason Kendall, 22 Mar. 1707/10, William Kendall,Sr.
     sec.
Watts, David & Margaret Simkins, 5 Sept. 1799, Coventon Smith sec.
Watts, John Wilkins & Rachel Fitchett, wid. 25 May 1765, John
     Smaw sec.
Watts, John W. & Sarah Boyd , 24 Nov. 1794, Nathaniel Wilkins sec.

?Webb, Aaron & Catherine Drighouse, 31 Dec. 1811, James Carter sec.
Webb, Charles & Sinah Sample, Free Negroes, 7 June 1791, William
     Satchell, Jr. sec.
Webb, James & Margaret Isdale, his ward, 8 Oct. 1821, Matthew H.
     Dunton sec.
Webb, James & Louisa Bell, dau. John Bell, dec., 9 Oct. 1843,
     James S. Carpenter sec.
*Webb, Levin & Mary Matthews, Free Negroes, 31 Dec. 1851.
Webb, Southy & Anne Miles, 26 Oct. 1795, John Carpenter sec.
*Webb, Southey & Hessey Virginia Hargiss, 16 Aug. 1852

Weeks(Wickes), Cornelius & Nancy Howell, Free Negroes, 2 Sept.
     1848, George B. Dunton sec.
? Weeks, Daniel & Nancy Morris, 6 July 1803, Abraham Lang sec.

? Weeks, Ely & Molly Collins, 8 Aug. 1817, John Sample sec.
? Weeks, Gilbert ' Lucy Sisco, 22 Nov. 1834
? Weeks, Jacob & Tinsey Gardiner, 21 Sept. 1813, James Weeks sec.
? Weeks, James & Peggy Stephens, 8 May 1810, Richard Johnson sec.
? Weeks, John & Mary Weeks, 20 Aug. 1817, Sam Bevans sec.
Weeks, John & Jane Brickhouse, ward of said John Weeks, Free Negroes,
    13 Apr. 1846, Charles J. D. West sec.
? Weeks, Levi & Peggy Stephens, 6 Jan. 1809, James Travis sec.
    (badly damaged)
? Weeks, Nathaniel & Abigail Thompson, 23 Dec. 1822, Severn Weeks sec.
? Weeks, William & Comfort Weeks, 5 Mar. 1822, Samuel Beavans sec.
? Weeks, Zerobabel & Nancy Beavans, 3 Jan. 1793, Reubin Reed sec.

Weisiger, Joseph K. & Mrs Catharine S. Jones, 23 Dec. 1846, John
    S. Parker sec.

West, Abel & Bridget Hutson, 27 Dec. 1808, Teackle Roberts sec.
West, Charles & Joanna Dunton, 16 Feb. 1798, Littleton Major sec.
West, Charles J. D. & Elizabeth R. Pitts, dau. M. S. Pitts, dec.
    14 Mar. 1836, John G. Turner sec.
West, Edward & Martha Vandegrot, 6 Mar. 1726, Gawton Hunt sec.
West, Joseph & Anne Johnson, wid., 1 Sept. 1766, Littleton West-
    cote sec.
West, Joseph & Catharine Snead, wid. Thomas Snead, 13 Mar. 1781,
    John Furbush Turner sec.
West, Joseph & Nelly Martin, 5 Nov. 1817, James Johnson sec.
West, John C. & Elizabeth Snead, 6 Jan. 1801, William Gillet sec.
?West, John & Nancy Becket, 21 Aug. 1805, William Drighouse sec.
West, John T. & Sally Smith, ward of Walter W. Widgeon, 11 Dec.
    1837, Walter W. Widgeon sec.
West, Nathaniel & Mary Smith Dolby, 20 Nov. 1810, Arthur B.
    Upshur sec.
West, Nathaniel & Mary Turner, 29 Aug. 1812, Richard Johnson sec.
    Con. of John Turner as to Mary.
West, Nathaniel L. & Eliza Ann Harrison, dau. James Harrison,
    18 Sept. 1843, William P. Ridley sec.
West, Samuel & Margaret Fitchett, 12 Sept. 1815, Johannes Johnson
    sec.
West, Thorowgood & Susanna Eshon, 14 Jan. 1786, Nathaniel Holland
    sec.
West, Thomas & Margaret Nottingham, 7 Apr. 1814, Samuel Coward
    sec. Note signed by William E. Nottingham & Thomas Copes
    stating that Margaret Nottingham is of lawful age.
? West, Toby & Thamar Thompson, 22 Dec. 1820, Job. Upshur sec.
West, William & Mahala Collins, dau. John Collins, dec. Free
    Negroes, 16 Feb. 1828, Robert Powell (F.N.) sec.

Westerhouse, Abraham & Anne Andrews, 15 Feb. 1770, John Thomas
    sec.
Westerhouse, Reubin & Sarah Scott, dau. William Scott, 11 Nov.
    1766, John Waterfield, Jr. sec.
Westerhouse, William & Margaret White, wid. 23 July 1745, Isaac
    Nottingham sec.

Westerhouse, William & Leah Mapp, wid. 13 Mar. 1759, Thomas Watts sec.
Westerhouse, William & Anne Jacob, dau. Abraham Jacob, 12 Dec. 1764,
    Edmund Glanville sec.

Wescoat(Wescott,Westcoat,Westcote), Edmund & Polly Dunton, 19 May,
    1796, Michael Dunton sec.
Wescoat, Edmund & Adah Abdell, 25 Sept. 1805, George Meholloms sec.
Wescott, Edmund P. & Elizabeth Bunting, 26 July 1819, William
    Bunting sec. Con. of Nancy Bunting,mother of Elizabeth.
Wescoat, George & Mary Ann Johnson, dau. Thomas Johnson,Jr. dec.,
    26 Dec. 1828, Harrison T. Rayfield sec.
Wescoat, George M. & Rosey Savage, wid. George L. Savage, 22 Jan.
    1850, Joshua P. Wescoat sec.
Wescoat, Hezekiah P. & Susan Savage, 24 Dec. 1816, Michael Savage
    sec.
Wescoat, Hezekiah P., Jr., & Rosey J. Andrews, 14 Dec. 1847,
    Fredrick B. Fisher sec.
Westcote, John & Esther Floyd, wid., 6 Apr. 1774, John Upshur sec.
Wescoat, John & Rosey Westcot, 9 Feb. 1801, Edmund Wescoat sec.
Westcoat, John & Patsey Harden, 8 Apr. 1806, Esau Godwin sec.
Westcote, Joshua & Mary Pitts, dau. Major Pitts, dec., 14 Sept.
    1771, Robert Polk sec.
Wescoat, Joshua P. & Ellanor Dowty, ward of Benjamin Thomas, 20
    Dec. 1848, Lafayette Harmanson sec.
Westcote, Littleton & Mary Jacob, dau. Philip Jacob,dec., 1 Sept.
    1766, Zerobabell Downing sec.
Westcoat, Major & Polly Dowty, 11 July 1812, Thomas W. Badger, sec.
*Wescoat, Nathaniel & Margaret E. A. Scott, 19 Sept. 1853
Wescoat, William & Sally Bloxom, 9 Dec. 1789, John Bloxom sec.

Whaley, Joshua & Leah Wheeler, 25 Nov. 1778, William Graves sec.

Wheeler(Wheelor), James & Elizabeth Rippin, dau. John Rippin,dec.,
    8 Dec. 1778, William Rippin sec.
Wheeler, James & Elizabeth Saals, 3 Sept. 1781, Isaac Moor, Jr.
    sec.
Wheeler, James & Naomi D. Brickhouse, ward of William W. Scott,
    14 Dec. 1835, William W. Scott sec.
Wheeler, John & Edith Luke, dau. Daniel Luke, 14 July 1772,
    Joseph Dolby sec.
Wheeler, John & Anne Scott, 13 June 1777, John Harwood sec.
Wheeler, John & Margaret Garret, dau. Amos Garret, 24 Nov.
    1778, Joshua Wheeler sec.
Wheeler, John & Kesiah Snale, 24 Apr. 1782, Henry Snaw sec.
Wheelor, John & Betsey Odear, 22 June 1805, Marriot Willis sec.
Wheeler, John T. & Elizabeth Ann Dowty, ward of James Dowty,
    8 Oct. 1838, James Dowty sec.
Wheeler, Thomas & Betsey Wilson, 21 May 1803, George Scott sec.
Wheelor, Thomas & Peggy Seaton, 11 June 1810, Henry Snaw sec.
Wheelor, Thomas & Agnes Wilkins, 8 June 1811, Nathaniel
    Wilkins sec. Con. of Susan Wilkins, mother of Agnes.

White, Edward T. & Mahala Ann Savage, 4 Dec. 1839, James H.

White sec. Con. of Mahala Savage, mother & Gdn. of Mahala Ann.

White, George D. & Margaret Waterfield, 18 Dec. 1816, Thomas Waterfield, sec. Con. of Laban & Peggy Stott, Gdns. of Margaret
Waterfield.

White, James H. & Ann Wilkins, dau. John Wilkins, Jr., 30 Aug. 1837,
Thomas Smith, Jr. sec.

White, John & Sarah Deale, wid. 29 Jan. 1789, William Hays sec.

White, John & Susey Cary, 10 Nov. 1806, Johannes Johnson sec.

White, Joseph & Peggy Jacob, dau. Hancock Jacob, 10 Jan. 1775,
Severn Nottingham sec.

White, Obedience & Nancy Heath, 29 Oct. 1813, Robert A. Joynes sec.

White, Teackle & Elizabeth Pitts, wid. George Pitts, 28 May 1789,
James Sanford sec.

White, Teackle S. & Margaret Ward, 29 Nov. 1815, Obedience White
sec.

White, Teackle S. & Susan Kellam, dau. Charles Kellam, 24 Apr. 1827,
Teackle J. Turner sec.

White, Teackle S. & Margaret J. Harmanson, 20 May 1843, George T.
Belote sec.

White, Thomas & Esther Cowdry, wid., 4 Nov. 1745, Peter Norley
Ellegood & William Bishop sec.

White, Thomas &   Polly Thompson, 17 Aug. 1812, William
Matthews sec.

White, Thomas & Esther Abdel, 26 Aug. 1823, Abbot Belote sec.

White, Thomas & Polly Robins, 2 Nov. 1818, John R. Fisher sec.

White, William & Rachel Jacob, 17 Oct. 1771, William Jacob sec.

White, William & Sarah L. Sanford, 3 Dec. 1811, John C. West sec.
Con. of James Sanford, father of Sarah L.

White, William,Sr. & Elizabeth H. Dunton, 23 May 1814, George
Savage sec.

White, William & Elizabeth Eshon, 25 July 1818, John Bull sec.

White, William & Emeline Savage, 20 Jan. 1840, John C. Mapp,Jr.
sec. Con. of William K. Savage, father of Emeline.

Whitehead, John & Sucky Smith, dau. James Smith, 11 May 1790,
James Smith sec.

Whitehead, John & Sally Goffigon, 5 Jan. 1813, John Griffeth sec.
Certificate from Abraham Costin that Sally Goffigon is more
than 21 years of age.

Whitehead, John & Elizabeth Bain, 25 Nov. 1816, Caleb B. Upshur
sec.

Whitehead, Stephen & Charlotte Downes, wid. Capt. Daniel Downes,
24 May 1831, William Whitehead sec.

Whitehead, Thomas & Ann Milbourn, dau. Thomas Milbourn, 11 May
1829, Thomas Milbourn & William Whitehead sec.

Whitehead, Thomas & Emeline Jones, 28 Nov. 1836, Benjamin
Griffith & Jesse J. Simkins sec. Con. of Jesse J. Simkins,
Gdn. of Emeline.

Whitehead, William & Lucretia Spady, 6 Aug. 1789, Jacob Spady sec.

Whitehead, William & Margaret Warrington, 3 Dec. 1821, William
Parsons sec.

*Whitehead, William S. & Sally P. Evans, dau. Thomas S. Evans,
8 Dec. 1851.

Wickes(Weeks), Edmund & Lucy Brickhouse, Free Negroes, 27 July 1839,
    Leonard B. Nottingham sec.
Wickes, Gilbert, son of Maria, & Lucy Scisco, dau. Rachel, Free
    Negroes, 20 Nov. 1834, Edmund Wickes & Maria Wickes sec.
Wickes, Isaac & Lauretta Powell, Mulattoes, 26 Nov. 1839, Leonard
    B. Nottingham sec.
?Wickes, Jacob, son of Betsy, & Sukey Simkins, dau. Dilly Simkins, 16
    Feb. 1827, Short John Collins sec.
Wickes, Spencer & Sally Becket, Free Negroes, 22 Dec. 1836, Luther
    Nottingham sec.
? Wickes, Thomas & Rachel Ann Sasco, ward of Isaac Stephens, 12 Oct.
    1830, Isaac Stephens sec.
?Wickes, William & Betsey Wickes, 10 Oct. 1826, William Sample, sec.

Widgeon, George F. & Elizabeth Spady, 13 Jan. 1834, George P. Fitchett
    sec. Con. of Thomas S. Spady, father of Elizabeth.
Widgeon, John & Adah Westerhouse, 1 May 1765, Rickards Dunton sec.
Widgeon, John & Anne Floyd, dau. Matthew Floyd dec., 24 Mar. 1770,
    Thomas Widgeon sec.
Widgeon, John & Esther Ellegood, wid., 22 Aug. 1772, William
    Johnson, Jr. sec.
Widgeon, John & Bridget Robins, 19 Jan. 1792, Kendall Belote sec.
Widgeon, John & Priscilla Heath, 10 Mar. 1817, John Taylor sec.
Widgeon, John & Maria B. Nottingham, 3 Mar. 1818, Thomas Jacob sec.
Widgeon, John, Jr. & Susan Taylor, dau. Betsy Moore, formerly
    Betsy Taylor, dec., 5 Dec. 1831, Abram Moore sec.
Widgen, John S. & Sarah Ann Jacob, dau. Hancock Jacob, dec., 16 Oct.
    1834.
Widgeon, Capt. John & Elizabeth Widgeon, wid. Severn Widgeon, 30
    Sept. 1844, Robert B. Nottingham sec.
*Widgeon, Joseph S. & Margaret E. Mister, 28 Dec. 1852
Widgeon, Joseph & Peggy Russel, 11 Dec. 1787, Richard Savage sec.
Widgeon, Levin & Susanna Wilson, dau. William Wilson, dec. 13 Nov.
    1777, Southy Nelson sec.
Widgeon, Littleton & Lovey Timmons, 9 Mar. 1807, Moses Marman sec.
Widgeon, Littleton & Tinney Biggs, wid. Christopher Biggs, 2 Feb.
    1839, John T. West sec.
Widgeon, Nathaniel & Susanna Knight, 11 Dec. 1802, William Wilkins
    sec.
Widgeon, Robert & Nancy Wingate, dau. Southy Wingate, dec., 23 Dec.
    1828, John Tyson sec.
Widgeon, Robert & Susan Jones, 21 May 1840, Douglas Trower sec.
Widgen, Severn & Rachel Willis, dau. Josiah Willis, 25 Nov. 1778,
    John Scott sec.
Widgen, Severn & Molly Knight, 30 Apr. 1791, John Knight, Jr., sec.
Widgeon, Severn & Elizabeth Salts, dau. John Salts, dec., 1 Jan.
    1828, Thomas Tyson sec.
*Widgeon, Southy & Mary Susan Nottingham, dau. Joseph D. Notting-
    ham, 18 Dec. 1851.
Widgen, Thomas & Anne Stockley, wid. 3 Mar. 1759, Edward Widgeon
    sec.
Widgeon, Thomas & Esther Nottingham, 19 Nov. 1805, Joseph
    Nottingham sec.

Widgeon, Thomas & Elizabeth Bell, 11 Jan. 1807, Thomas Dunton sec.

Widgeon, Walter W. & Susan Smith, dau. George Smith,Sr., dec., 12 Nov. 1832, Thomas Griffith sec.

Widgen, Westerhouse & Nancy Fitchett, 5 Aug. 1789, John Dennis sec. Con. of Daniel Fitchett,as to Nancy.

Widgeon, Westerhouse & Nancy Costin, 3 Mar. 1798, Francis Costin sec.

Widgeon, Westerhouse & Sally Widgeon, 11 July 1796, Elijah Baker sec.

Widgeon, Westerhouse & Elizabeth Dunton, ward of Shepherd B.Floyd, 11 Feb. 1828.

Widgeon, William & Rachel Pitts, 18 Apr. 1761, John Gleson sec.

Wilson, Arthur & Nancy Wheelor, 20 Dec. 1806, Leroy Oldham sec.

Wilson, Edward H. C. & Sally Stratton, 5 May 1818, Jacob G.Parker sec.

Wilson, Edward B. & Elizabeth S. S. Floyd, dau. Shepherd B. Floyd, dec., 20 Dec. 1834, Kendall Groten sec.

Wilson, Harold L. & Leah L. Savage, 6 Han. 1814

Wilson, Henry P. C. & Susan E. Savage, 15 June 1824, Peter Bowdoin sec.

Wilson, James & Mary Tyson, 18 Dec. 1816, John Tyson sec.

Wilson, James & Sukey Spady, ward of H. B. Kendall, 12 Sept. 1821, Henry B. Kendall sec.

Wilson, James S. & Elizabeth A. Dix, wid. William A. Dix, 30 Aug. 1842, John Bishop sec.

Wilson, James B. & Anne H. Brickhouse, dau. Thomas S. Brickhouse, 25 Nov. 1843, Robert J. Nottingham sec.

Wilson, John, Sr. & Rosy Goffigon, 8 Dec. 1813, Abram Costin sec.

Wilson, John C. & Mary Ann Savage, 9 May 1818, Caleb B. Upshur,sec.

Wilson, John S. & Nancy Tilghman, 26 June 1821, Dennard Travis sec.

Wilson, James S. & Keturah Churn, 1 Jan. 1833, George Holt,Jr. sec.

Wilson, Littleton & Margaret Floyd, 9 Oct. 1815, Shepherd B.Floyd sec.

Wilson, Littleton & Polly Wilkins, wid. John Wilkins, 8 May 1837, George P. Upshur sec.

Wilson, Moses & Sally Wingate, 8 Mar. 1803, David Topping sec.

Wilson, Moses & Betsey Dunton, 3 Feb. 1813, Shepherd B. Floyd sec.

Wilson, Moses & Adah Knight, orph. of William Knight & ward of Thomas Tyson, 28 Dec. 1830, Thomas Tyson sec.

Wilson, Samuel & Peggy Custis, 25 Mar. 1760, Levin Gale sec. Con. of Anne Tompkins as to Peggy.

Wilson, Spencer & Frances Watts, dau. Thomas Watts, dec., 22 Sept. 1774, William Waltham sec.

Wilson, Spencer & Nancy Stott, Born 15 Nov. 1767 - 17 May 1788, Michael Dunton,Sr. sec. Con. of John Stott, brother of Nancy

Wilson, Spencer & Susanna Andrews, 17 Sept. 1778, John Wheeler sec. Con. of Ann Westerhouse, mother of Susanna Andrews.

Wilson, Stockley _ Sarah Wilson, 21 Sept. 1785, Henry Warren sec.

Wilson, Stockley & Smart Wilkins, 19 Apr. 1787, Argil Wilkins sec.

Wilson, Stockly W. & Mary W. Rayfield, 17 June 1822, John Rayfield sec. Con. of John Rayfield, father of Mary W.

Wilson, Thomas & Anne Scott, dau. Zerobabel Scott, dec., 26 Dec.

1787, Richard Nottingham sec.

Wilson, Thomas & Elizabeth Cobb, 8 June 1824, William Kellam sec. Con. of Southey Cobb, father of Elizabeth.

Wilson, William Bishop & Nancy Freshwater, 17 May 1790, Marrot Willis sec.

Wilson, William W. & Peggy Custis Tompkins, 14 Jan. 1795, Thomas Parramore, Sr. sec. Con. of T. Tompkins, father of Peggy C.

Wilson, William & Molly Spady, 10 Feb. 1795, Azariah Williams sec. Con. of Abraham Spady, father of Molly.

Wilson, William, Jr. & Adah Pratt, 18 Nov. 1797, Charles Dillon sec.

Wilson, William & Polly Wilson, 23 Dec. 1814, Thomas G. Scott sec.

Wilson, William & Margaret Kellam, 26 Jan. 1835, Matthew D. Moore sec.

Wilson, William & Ann Harrison, wid. Isma Harrison, 14 Dec. 1835, Charles Dillion sec.

Wilson, William T. & Polly Frost, 8 Oct. 1839, William W. Wilson sec.

Williams, Archibald & Margaret B. McIntosh, 22 July 1847, Jackson B. Powell sec.

Williams, Azariah & Anne Costin, 14 Aug. 1787, Benjamin Griffith sec.

Williams, Azariah & Susan C. Clay, 17 Jan. 1821, Matthew Floyd sec. Con. of Peter Williams, Gdn. of Susan.

Williams, Benjamin & Margaret Barnes, 26 Jan. 1829, John Spady, Jr. sec.

Williams, Benjamin & Sukey Clegg, dau. William Clegg, dec. 1 Jan. 1838, John Spady, Jr. sec.

Williams, Benjamin & Sally Ann Jacob, dau. William Jacob, dec., 30 Aug. 1843, Joshua P. Wescoat sec.

Williams, Christopher & Nancy Moore, dau. John Moore, 11 Sept. 1826, John Moore sec.

Williams, Custis F. & Elizabeth Griffith, 4 July 1839, Elias Roberts sec. Con. of Sally Griffith, mother of Elizabeth.

Williams, Edward & Sarah Saunders, dau. Richard Saunders, 7 Aug. 1778, Richard Saunders sec.

Williams, James & Susey Matthews, 23 Dec. 1801, Thomas Lewis sec.

Williams, James & Sukey Costin, 14 Sept. 1812, William Jarvis sec. Con. of William Costin, Sr., father of Sukey & of Southy Goffigon, Gdn. of James.

Williams, James D. & Lavinia A. W. Dunton, ward of John E. Nottingham, 10 Dec. 1838, John E. Nottingham sec.

Williams, James & Nancy Harrison, dau. Nathaniel Harrison, 4 Feb. 1840, Newton Harrison sec.

Williams, John & Edith Nottingham, dau. Thomas Nottingham, Sr., 11 Aug. 1775, Thomas Nottingham, Jr. sec. Con. of Samuel Williams & Thomas Nottingham.

Williams, John & Margaret Johnson (not dated-Bundle marked 1786-7) William Stith sec.

Williams, John & Margaret Glanville, 17 Aug. 1787, Severn Nottingham sec.

Williams, John & Margaret Goffigon, 12 June, 1793, Hillery Hunt sec. Con. of Nathaniel Goffigon, Gdn. of Margaret.

Williams, John & Nancy Hughes, 24 Dec. 1800, Charles Fitchett sec. Con. of William Stokely, Gdn. of Nancy.

Williams, John, Jr. & Peggy Powell, 25 Aug. 1804, Thomas Dowty sec.

Williams, John Green & Nancy Hitchens, 12 July 1805, James Travis sec.

Williams, John L. & Elizabeth Powell, 21 Nov. 1812, Thomas Dowty sec.

Williams, John & Esther Roberts, dau. Teackle Roberts, dec., 28 Dec. 1829, Benjamin Dunton sec.

Williams, John & Mary Dillion, dau. Charles Dillion, 29 May 1833, Charles Dillion sec.

Williams, John A. & Sally Trower, dau. Douglass Trower, 18 Feb. 1846, William T. Fitchett sec.

Williams, John W. M. & Corinthia V. J. Read, 21 Dec. 1846, John H. Winder sec. Con. of Margaret L. Read, mother of Corinthia.

Williams, Peter & Elishe Dixon, 14 June 1791, Thomas Downs sec.

Williams, Peter & Betsey Trower, 14 Nov. 1808, Joseph Warren sec.

Williams, Peter & Polly Hickman, 7 Apr. 1811, George Powell sec. Con. of Elizabeth Hickman, mother of Polly.

Williams, Peter & Nancy Clay, 28 Feb. 1816, Thomas Powell sec.

Williams, Samuel & Sarah Haggoman, 7 Nov. 1853, George Harmanson sec.

Williams, Samuel & Sarah Dunton, 4 Dec. 1764, Levin Dunton sec.

Williams, Samuel & Margaret Nottingham, dau. Thomas Nottingham, 12 Dec. 1772, Thomas Nottingham sec.

Williams, Samuel & Sukey Dixon, 14 June 1799, Peter Williams sec.

Williams, Samuel & Peggy Burris, ___ Jan. 1806, Levin Nottingham sec. Con. of William Jarvis as to Samuel Williams.

Williams, Samuel & Eliza Mills, dau. Jacob Mills, dec., 22 Mar. 1833, Gilbert Mister sec.

Williams, Seth & Rosy Roberts, dau. Teackle Roberts, dec. 20 Dec. 1831, Stephen Wilkinson & James Williams sec.

Williams, Thomas & Elizabeth Timmons, 21 July 1800, William Salisbury sec.

Williams, Capt. Thomas N. & Anne S. Nottingham, 12 Feb. 1814, William Nottingham, Sr. sec. Con. of William Nottingham, Sr. father of Anne.

Williams, Thomas & Sally A. Luker, 6 May 1814, Walter Luker sec.

Williams, Thomas & Rachel Willis, dau. Josias Willis, dec. 14 Jan. 1822, Josias Willis sec.

Williams, Thomas B. & Sarah Ann P. West, dau. Nathaniel West, 30 May 1836, Smith S. Nottingham sec.

Williams, William & Mary Nottingham, 29 Apr. 1786, Thomas Eilson sec. Con. of Thomas Nottingham, Sr. father of Mary.

Williams, William & Lear Goffigon, 3 Aug. 1795, John Goffigon sec.

Williams, William & Ann Jacob Dunton, 16 Dec. 1806, Hancock Dunton sec.

Williams, William H. & Adah Widgeon, ward of Walter W. Widgeon, 26 Sept. 1833, Walter W. Widgeon sec.

Williams, William N. & Rosina B. Dunton, ward of John E. Nottingham, 1 Aug. 1842, John E. Nottingham sec.

*Williams, William N. & Virginia U. Fitchett, dau. Daniel Fitchett, 8 Sept. 1851

Wilkins, Benjamin & Elishe Willis, 26 July 1775, John Widgeon sec.
    Con. of Josiah Willis, father of Elishe.

Wilkins, Custis F. & Frances McCowan, dau. Nancy McCowan, 27 Apr.
    1835, Elijah Nottingham sec.

Wilkins, Eleazer & Rachel Griffith, dau. Nathan Griffith dec., 17
    June 1772, Hezekiah Griffith sec.

Wilkins, George F. & Anne Snead, 27 Dec. 1817, William Satchell sec.

Wilkins, George F. & Margaret B. Williams, ward of Margaret
    Williams, 28 May 1825, Margaret Williams sec.

Wilkins, James & Hetty Harman, 9 Dec. 1822, James Saunders sec.
    Con. of Edwin Godwin as to Hetty.

Wilkins, Joakim & Delitha Hunt, 14 Dec. 1801, William Jones sec.

Wilkins, John & Catherine Custis, wid. 7 Sept. 1748, Henry Snaw sec.

Wilkins, John, Jr. & Susanna Stratton, 18 May, 1752, Thomas Stratton
    sec. Con. of Susanna Stratton, mother of Susanna.

Wilkins, John, Blacksmith, & Smart Stockley, dau. Woodman Stockley,
    dec. 10 Jan. 1764, John Wilkins, Jr. sec.

Wilkins, John, Jr. & Mary Pettitt, wid. 13 June 1769, John Blair
    sec.

Wilkins, John & Sarah Hunt, dau. Thomas Hunt, 30 Dec. 1769, Obediah
    Hunt sec.

Wilkins, John & Susanna Carpenter, 15 Nov. 1786, Charles Carpenter
    sec.

Wilkins, John & Elizabeth Elliott, 31 Mar. 1794, William Scott, Jr.
    sec.

Wilkins, John S. & Elizabeth Wilkins, 10 Nov. 1795, Thomas Wilkins
    sec. Con. of William Wilkins, father of Elizabeth.

Wilkins, John & Betsey Goffigon, 9 Nov. 1803, David Rippin sec.

Wilkins, John, Jr. & Mary Spady, 3 July 1810, Levin Nottingham
    sec. Con. of Southy Spady, father of Mary.

Wilkins, John B. & Polly Williams, 22 May 1824, James Wilkins sec.

Wilkins, John, Jr. & Catherine Evans, wid. John Evans, 22 Dec.
    1832, Samuel W. Dunton sec.

Wilkins, John M. & Margaret Susan Williams, ward of James
    Saunders, 13 Jan. 1836, James Saunders sec.

Wilkins, Dr. John T. & Elizabeth A. Roberts, 5 Nov. 1844, Alex.
    W. F. Mears sec. Con. of Sally Roberts, mother of
    Elizabeth.

*Wilkins, Leonard T. & Sallie E. Downing, 18 May 1852

Wilkins, Major & Adah Fathery, 22 July 1769, John Evans sec.

Wilkins, Major & Mary Guy, wid. _____ 1778 - George Harmon sec.

Wilkins, Nathaniel & Susannah Wilkins, dau. William Wilkins,
    21 Dec. 1779, William Wilkins sec.

Wilkins, Nathaniel & Nancy Joynes, 24 Aug. 1818, Abram Costin
    sec.

?Wilkins, Peter & Elishe Collins, 19 Sept. 1795, Thomas Webb sec.

Wilkins, Richard & Elizabeth Wilkins, dau. Watkins Wilkins, 10
    July 1764, John Wilkins sec.

Wilkins, Robert & Elizabeth Harmanson, dau. Henry Harmanson,
    4 Nov. 1793, Nathaniel Holland sec.

Wilkins, Robert & Nelly Jones, dau. Nathaniel Jones, dec.,
    26 Dec. 1827, James Wilkins sec.

Wilkins, Robert E. & Mary Ann Fitchett, 11 Nov. 1844, Daniel Fitchett
    sec. Con. of Daniel Fitchett, father of Mary Ann.

Wilkins, Robert & Elizabeth Parsons, dau. Marriott Parsons, 7 Dec.
    1841, George F. Wilkins sec.

Wilkins, Severn & Rosy W. Elliott, dau. John Elliott, dec., 3 Apr.
    1832, James Saunders sec.

Wilkins, Southey S. & Keturah G. Dunton, 27 Mar. 1843, John S.
    Wilson sec.

Wilkins, Thomas M. & Sarah Saunders, 22 Dec. 1840, Victor A.
    Nottingham sec. Con. of James Saunders, father of Sarah.

Wilkins, Walter L. & Patsy F. Nottingham, ward of Thomas J.
    Nottingham, 22 Dec. 1832, Thomas J. Nottingham sec.

Wilkins, William, Jr. & Agnes Stratton, dau. John Stratton, Gent.
    dec., 9 Nov. 1758, Nathaniel Stratton sec.

Wilkins, William & Elizabeth Johnson, wid. 11 Aug. 1773, William
    Scott.

Wilkins, William & Frances Benthall, dau. William Benthall, 29
    Sept. 1778.

Wilkins, William, Jr. & Peggy Scott, dau. William Scott, 11 Jan.
    1790, William Scott sec.

Wilkins, William (O.P.) & Margaret Speakman, 5 Mar. 1793, James
    Floyd sec.

Wilkins, William, (O.P.) & Sarah Fitchett, 25 Jan. 1802, William
    Hanby sec.

Wilkins, William & Susanna Godwin, 9 Dec. 1802, Nathaniel
    Widgeon sec.

Wilkins, William & Nacy Trower, 26 Sept. 1815, Thomas Dixon sec.

Wilkins, William W. & Elizabeth C. Kendall, 26 June 1843, Robert
    E. Wilkins sec. Con. of Elizabeth W. Kendall, mother
    of Elizabeth C.

Wilkins, William S., son of William E. Wilkins, & Emily S. Spady,
    dau. Rosey S. Costin, 25 June 1844, William E. Wilkins
    & Rosey S. Costin sec.

Willy, George & Elizabeth Jones, dau. Richard Jones, dec., 12
    Dec. 1835, Nathaniel J. Winder sec.

Wilkinson(Wilkerson), Stephen & Anne Speakman, wid. 3 Feb. 1790,
    Robert Fitchett sec.

Wilkinson, Stephen & Betsey Warren, 25 Dec. 1811, William Warren
    sec.

Wilkerson(Wilkinson), Stephen & Sally Biggs, 26 Feb. 1827,
    Christopher Biggs sec.

Willis, Custis & Polly Fitchett, 26 Apr. 1812, Peter Bowdoin sec.

*Willis, Custis & Emily S. Moore, dau. Angeline B. Warren, 23
    Nov. 1852

Willis, George & Jenny Jackson, dau. Jonas Jackson, 26 Dec.
    1791, William Smith sec.

Willis, Jacob & Comfort Willis, wid. Jonas Willis, 18 Dec.
    1789, George Willis sec.

**Willis, Jacob & Agnes Graves _____ 1794.

Willis, James & Lucretia Moore, dau. John Moore, 24 Dec. 1821, John
    Moore sec.

Willis, John & Elizabeth White, 18 Feb. 1788, Severn Widgon sec.

Willis, John & Peggy Clegg, 25 Jan. 1800, John Frost sec.

Willis, Josiah & Elizabeth Rippin, 24 Dec. 1823, Thomas Smith,Jr.
    sec. Con. of Thomas Rippin, father of Elizabeth.

*Willis, Leonard J. & Mary S. Cottingham, dau. Henry Cottingham,
    20 Dec. 1852

Willis, Marrot & Sally Freshwater, 23 Apr. 1790, Severn Widgen sec.

Willis, Parker & Sarah Goffigon, 15 Dec. 1795, Samuel Costin sec.

Willis, Parker & Elishe Costin, 27 July 1797, Richard Nottingham sec.

Willis, Thomas & Ann Knight, 1 Nov. 1792, Westerhouse Widgeon sec.

Willis, Thomas & Elishe Graves,11 Feb. 1794, Littleton Jones sec.

Willis, Thomas & Susan Jones, dau. Nathaniel Jones, dec., 1 Jan.
    1836, John Spady, Jr. sec.

Willis, William & Margaret Ellegood, __ Sept. 1775, Richard
    Nottingham sec.

Willis, William & Smart Dunton, dau. Elias Dunton, dec. 3 Jan. 1788,
    John Stott sec.

Willis, William & Sally Burke, 23 Dec. 1824, Moses Turner sec.

Willis, William & Kessy Stripe, wid. Peter Stripe, 29 June, 1830,
    James Williams, Sr. sec.

Willis, William & Polly Nottingham, wid. Joseph Nottingham, 30 Nov.
    1836, Smith Nottingham, sec.

Willitt(Willet,Willett), Douglass & Henrietta Johnson, dau. John
    Johnson, dec. 21 June 1760, Amos Johnson sec.

Willet, Douglas & Betsey Savage, 13 Jan. 1796, Thomas Dunton sec.
    Con. of Abel Savage, father of Betsey.

Willett, James R. & Edy Wheeler, 21 Mar. 1827, Arthur A. Wilson,
    sec.

Wingate, Daniel & Comfort Willis, 27 Dec. 1815, John Floyd sec.
    Con. of Marrot Willis, father of Comfort.

Wingate, George & Mary Miller, 22 June 1786, James Wilson sec.

Wingate, Jacob & Nice Wilson, 11 Mar. 1796, Matthew Floyd sec.

Wingate, James & Nancy Scott, 13 Jan. 1812, Benjamin Griffith sec.

Wingate, James & Mahala Clegg, dau. Major Clegg, dec., 1 Jan.
    1833, Nathaniel Dalby & Thomas Whitehead sec.

Wingate, John & Sarah Watson, 27 Feb. 1760, Azariah Hunt sec.
    Con. of Robert Watson, father of Sarah.

Wingate, Severn & Nancy Moore, dau. Abram Moore, 1 Jan. 1833,
    George Holt, Jr. sec.

Wingate, Southy & Peggy Costin, 11 Jan. 1808, John Spady sec.

Wingate, Thomas & Arady Dear (Odear), 1 Aug. 1789, John Stoyt
    sec. Con. of William Dear, father of Arady.

Wingate, William & Amey Tylor, 24 Dec. 1807, John Spady sec.

Winder, John H. & Sally C. Snead, 4 Nov. 1816, Caleb B. Upshur
    sec.

Winder, Nathaniel J. & Margaret S. Bowdoin, 21 Nov. 1821,
    Peter Bowdoin sec.

Winder, Richard H. son of Sarah U. Winder, & Elizabeth L. Custis, ward of James J. Ailworth, 2 Feb. 1849, Sarau U. Winder & James J. Ailworth sec.

Window, Levin & Elizabeth Ann Andrews, 28 May 1838, Edward J. Joynes sec. Con. of Shepherd Andrews sec.

Wise, John, Jr., of Accomack, & Sarah Batson. wid., 2 Jan. 1765, Custis Matthews sec.

Wise, Johannes & Peggy Dunton, 23 Jan. 1799, James Travis sec.

Wise, Tully & Mary Bowdoin, 11 Feb. 1795, John Eyre sec.

Wise, Tully R. & Mary Fisher, 7 Dec. 1797, John Macgowan sec.

Wise, Tully R. Anne K. Evans, dau. John K. Evans, 18 Nov. 1834, William L. Savage sec.

Wise, Zachariah & Cassey Dalby, 21 Jan. 1801, Severn Nottingham sec.

Wise, Zachariah & Fanny Bishop, 10 Jan. 1814, Teackle Roberts sec.

Wisely, Ronald & Ann Fitchett Dixon, 8 Aug. 1808, Jacob Miller sec.

Wood, William & Bridget Batson, 7 June 1760, John Harmanson sec.

Wood, William & Rebecca Scott, 12 Jan. 1786, Kendall Godwin sec.

Woodard, John & Rebecca Chandler, 12 June 1708, Capt. John Luke sec.

Worser, Jacob & Esther Trower, 1 Oct. 1811, James Jacob sec.

Wright, John & Betsey Dunton, 17 Feb. 1802, John Simkins sec.

Wright, Thomas & Margaret Belote, dau. George Belote, 16 Dec. 1793, George Belote sec.

*Wyatt, Arthur M., of Accomack, & Mary V. Downing, 6 Dec. 1852

Wyatt, James W. & Virginia Fitchett, dau. William Fitchett, Sr., dec., 30 May 1845, Calvin H. Savage sec.

Wyatt, John R. & Elizabeth Jane Kellam, dau. Stewart Kellam, dec. 21 Dec. 1846, John B. Smith sec.

Wyatt, William, of Accomack, & Margaret Smith Tankard, 4 Nov. 1811, Isckar Lewis sec. Con. of John Tankard, father of Margaret S.

Wyatt, William & Sally Sturgis, wid. William Sturgis, 18 Sept. 1827, Edward A. Joynes sec.

Yatman, John & Elizabeth Ayres, 18 Oct. 1803, Sturt Saunders sec.

Yerby, George T. & Charlotte H. Jacob, ward of Peter S. Bowdoin, 5 Apr. 1824, Peter S. Bowdoin sec.

Yerby, William & Mary Satchell, 23 Nov. 1782, Laban Johnson sec.

Young, Ezekiel & Sally Luker, wid. Walter Luker, 3 Jan. 1822, James Young sec.

Young, George H. & Nancy Ward, 10 Feb. 1809, Golding Ward sec. Con. of Littleton Ward, father of Nancy.

Young, John & Sukey Johnson, 22 May 1794, Major Pettit sec. Con. of Obedience Johnson, father of Sukey.

Young, Littleton W. & Elizabeth P. Savage, wid. William T. Savage, 24 June, 1831, James Young sec.

Young, Richard & Patsey Abdell, 26 Oct. 1797, Westerhouse Widgeon sec.

Young, Thomas & Elizabeth Trower, 13 Aug. 1810, William Costin sec. Con. of John Trower, Sr., father of Elizabeth

Young, Dr. Thomas W. & Margaret S. Downing, dau. Dr. Edmund W. P. Downing, 24 May 1842, George Brickhouse sec.

Young, William & Mary Darby, 21 Jan. 1748, Peter Hog sec. Con. of John Darby, father of Mary.

----

* Indicates that name appears more than once on same page.

Abbot, Margaret 26

Abdel,(Abdell,Abdeel,Abdil,Abdill),
    Esther 107;Kesiah 38;Margaret
    50

Abdell,Adah 106;Bekah 79;Betsey
    101;Elizabeth 15;Leah 52;
    Mary 79,80;Margaret 80;
    Nancy 49*;Patsey 116;
    Rachel 13;Rosey 63

Abdeel, Betsey 6; Mary 29;Kesiah
    82; Nancy 11

Abdil,Esther 102

Abdill, Polly 15

Abell, Paggy 9

Addison, Anne E. 61;Harriet 69;
    Jane 0. 5;Louisa W. 45;
    Margaret 10,49;Margaret W.
    21;Mary 98;Nancy 95;Nancy S.
    84;Peggy 11,89;Priscilla 10;
    Rosey 55;Rosey W. 84;Rosanna
    81

Aimes(Ames),Nancy 64

Ames(Aimes),Ann 77;Catharine 52;
    Catherine C. 12;Eskey 53;
    Mary 45;Mary P. 16;Margaret
    12;Matilda Ann 99;Sarah S.
    22

Andrews,Adah 25,28,35,62;Anne 105;
    Druscilla 92;Eliza 78;Eliza-
    beth 50,67; Elizabeth Ann 115'
    Esther 89;Hannah 53;Juliet J.
    56;Lavenia 78;Rachel 24,54;
    Rosey J. 106;Rosanna 103;
    Sally 94;Sarah 23,37,61,94;
    Susanna 81,109;

Anderson,Anne 88;Betsey 18;Molly
    44

Annis, Mary 81

Anthony,Nancy 74;Peggy 83

Armistead,Elizabeth 47

Arnold,Anne 91

Ash,Anne 80

Ashby,Caty 44;Julia 79;Polly
    55

Ayres,Elizabeth 115

Badger,Elizabeth P. 7;
    Margaret G.28

Bagwell,Margaret 78

Bain,Elizabeth 107

Bailey(Bayly),Esther 38

Baker,Ibby 86;Jane 60;Mary
    75,96;Rosey 74;Susanna
    19

Ball,Delia 82

Baptist,Maria S. 54

Barecraft(Bearcraft),Betsey
    34;Catharine 49;Eliza-
    beth 1

Barnes,Anne 90;Margaret 110;

Barlow,Elizabeth 16,22,61;
    Mary 21,52;Sally 62;
    Susanna 100

Barret,Amy 31;Molly 61;
    Nancy 102;Sally 85

Batson,Barbara 102; Bridget
    115;Sarah 115

Bayly(Bailey),Anne W. 86

Bayaton,Mary 103

Bearcraft(Barecraft,Bar-
    craft),Elizabeth 40;
    Mary 68;Sally 31

Beavans(Bevans,Bivins,
    Bibbins),Comfort 18;
    Kesiah 82;Nancy 18,82,
    105;Rachel 47

118

Becket,Diana 66;Juliet 61;Kesiah
58;Leah 87;Mary 66;Maria 87;
Nancy 105;Rosey 8;Rosy Ann 90;
Sally 108;Sukey 18

Bedell,Elizabeth C.57

Belote(Beloat),Anne 17;Delitha 98
Elizabeth 44,52,55,56;Esther
78;Esther A. 31;Mary 12;Mar-
garet 2,57,115;Nervilla 50;
Rachel 83;Sally 73;Sarah 26;
Susanna 92;Tabitha 83;Tabitha
S. 41

Beloat(Belote),Nancy 15;Susanna
21,77

Bell,Abigail 22;Adah 38;Ann 81,
101*;Anne S. 51;Betsey 69;
Bridget 45;Vatherine 78;
Charlotte 79;Elizabeth 19,
109;Elizabeth Jane 32;Eliza J.
77;Esther 31,63;Hannah 59;
Keziah 43;Louisa 7,104;
Lucretia 42;Mary 26,43,50,61,
86;Mary Robert 14;Mary Susan
80;Margaret 80;Margaret Jane
80;Molly 70;Nancy 39,50;Polly
38,80,99;Rebecca 77;Sally 10,
59;Sarah 27,67,82;Susan 43;
Susey 7;Sukey 28; Tabitha M.
103

Benthall,Elishaba 38;Frances 47,
113;Leah 36;Mary 57;Patience
17;Rachel 104;Sinah 27

Benson(Benston)Ann 40; Catharine
71;Rachel 23

Benston(Benson),Ann 29;Betsey 8;
Sally 27

Bevans(Beavans,Bivans,Bibbins),
Adah 18;Emily 26;Mary 4;
Rachel 8;Sukey 5

Bibbins(Beavans,Bevans,Bivans),
Mary 70

Biggs,Alichia 94;Anne 100;
Elizabeth 66;Margaret 26;

Sally 113;Susan 69;Susan
Ann 59;Tinney 108

Bingham,Ann 26;Betsey 4;
Charlotte 16;Elizabeth 26;
Jenney 41;Lusey 66;Margaret
35;Polley 51;Tamar 18;
Tinsey 36

Bird(Byrd),Polly 9;Sally 50;
Susan 37

Birch, Levinia 23

Bishop,Anne 95,99;Caroline 63;
Fanny 115;Gracy 24;Polly
52;Sarah 47

Bivans(Beavans,Bevans,Bibbins),
Betsey 5

Blair,Kasiah 16

Bloxom, Polly 17;Polly B. 52;
Sally 106

Bloodsworth,Betsy 61

Bonewell(Bonwell),Margaret
100;Margaret S. 15;Mary
Ann 65

Bool,Adeline 15;Kesiah 13;
Leana 37;Martha 22;
Margaret Ann 6;Nancy 83;
Patsey 2;Peggy 10,17;Pris-
cilla 104;Ritta 84;Sarah
Ann 65;Susan 91;Violetta
62

Booth,Sally 93

Boswell, Elizabeth 11

Bowdoin,Elizabeth 56,89,
Elizabeth U. 89;Fanny B.
96;Louisa 30;Mary 45,115
Margaret 75;Margaret S.
114;Sarah 82

Boyd,Sarah 104

Braiser,Zillah 79

Francis,Comfort 18;Mary 91;Sally 38;

Freshwater, Elisha 61; Mrs 93;Nancy
    65,93,110;Polly 51;Sally 8,16,100,
    114;Sarah 67;Susan 34

Frost, Mary 40;Peggy 69;Polly 110;
    Rachel 31;Sally 32

Fulwell, Elizabeth 36;Margaret 58

Gadd, Mary J. 66

Gale, Lucy 79;Mary 17;Peggy 36

Gardner(Gardiner),Emma E. 89; Mary
    Stead Pinckney 69;Sarah S. 2;
    Tinsey 105

Garris,Elizabeth 95;Sarah 19

Garrison,Ann D. 24;Sarah 27

Garrett(Garrat), Edna 63;Elizabeth
    19;Margaret 106

Gascoigne(Gascoyne), Anne 52;Peggy
    94;Rachel 96;Sally 98;Sarah 7

Gault, Anne M. 71;Frances 37;Leah
    50;Lucy 15

George, Catharine 83

Giddens,Elizabeth 52;Fanny 33;
    Molly 92;Sally 80

Gilden(Gildon),Agatha 52;Elizabeth
    31,74;Mary 49;Mary A. 8;Susan 11

Glanville,Margaret 110

Gladston,Mary 59

Godferry,Mary 28

Godwin,Ann 52;Eliza 92;Elisha 52;
    Emily 25;Frances 99;Mary 83,94;
Margaret Ann 62;Nancy Grey 39;
    Sally 27,81;Sally Ann 50Susanna
    60,80,113;Tabitha M. 53

Goffigon,Amelia 90,Anne 13,
    56;Betsey 112;Bridget
    69;Elizabeth 8,30,52,88;
    Emily 39;Esther 39;Esther
    W. 87;Frances 14,48,87;
    Lear 111;Mary 19;Mary Ann
    85;Mary E. 54;Maria 67;
    Martha 33;Margaret 110;
    Nancy 47;Polly 39;Rosey
    66,109;Sally 11,39,107;
    Sally F. 50;Sarah 66,
    114;Susan 39;Susan Ann
    55;Tabitha 8,15

Gooday,Levicy 1

Gooldsburry,Elizabeth 36

Gore,Elizabeth 100

Graves, Agnes 64,113,Anne
    53; Elizabeth 9;Elishe
    114;Margaret 53;Molly
    19;Rachel 80

Green,Anne 44;Elizabeth
    85;Esther 30;Margaret
    84;Sarah 80

Grice,Abigail 7;Agnes 27;
    Susanna 57

Griffin,Betsey 22;Louisa
    20;Peggy 27;Sally 79

Griffith(Griffeth),Anne
    24,40,92;Angeline 65;
    Caty 90;Elizabeth 20,
    33,41,110;Elizabeth A.
    33;Fanny 40;Frances 68
    Lilly 70;Mary 73,88;
    Mary E. 101;Margaret 19;
    Nancy 59;Rachel 46,112;
    Sally 53,54;Sarah Ann 68;

Groten,Drusilla 65;Nancy 85

Gunter,Ann W. 21;Catharine
    P. 6;Mary Ann 91;Margaret
    A.J. 6

Guy,Ailsey 71;Elizabeth 74;

Liverpool,Adah 5;Sally 34;Sarah 5

Long,Leanna 2

Lucre(Luker,Luke),Delitha 47

Luker(Lucre,Luke),Caroline S.F. 68;
Elizabeth N. 12;Sally 115;Sally
A. 111;Susanna 77

Luke(Lucre,Luker),Anne 14,57;Betsey
48;Edith 106;Jane 25;Jenney 19;
Molly 33;Peggy 76,82;Sally 95

Lune,Martha 103

Lyon,Margaret A. 95

McCowan,Betsy 90;Caty 94;Frances
112

McCready(McCrady),Catharine 102;
Molly 59;Nancy 53;Sally 73

MacDaniel(McDaniel),Mary 42;Polly 31

McDonald,Mary 47

McGregor,Nancy 73

McIntosh,Margaret B. 110

McMeth,Jenney 23

Mac_____,Rebecca 50

Major, Anne 71;Betsey Purnal 54;
Elizabeth 78;Margaret 50;Nancy
74,103;Peggy 17

Maley, Margaret 47

Mapp,Adah 46,Adriana 49;Betsey 83;
Elizabeth 59;Esther 53;Jane 4;
Leah 55,106;Mary 14;Margaret 44;
Margaret C. 44;Peggy 99;Sarah 9,
78;Susanna 53

Martin,Elizabeth A. 67;Mary 15;Nelly
105

Marshall,Elizabeth 57;Sarah 54,97

Marriner, Elizabeth 102

Mason,Henry 86

Maslin(Mazlin,Mazeline),Susan E.
63

Massey,Elizabeth 2

Matthews(Mathews),Ansley 70;
Bridget 15;Catharine 36;
Elizabeth 15,37,57;Eliza J.
95;Esther 14;Harriet P. 96;
Kesiah 71;Mary 104;Mary Floyd
34;Margaret 31,54,60;Margaret
A. 31;Margaret S. 84;Nancy 47;
Peggy 24;Rosey 27;Susan 31,61;
Susey 110

Mayo,Louisa M. 84

Mazlin(Maslin,Mazeline),Lucy 95

Mazeline(Maslin,Mazlin),Mary J.
63

Mears,Adah S. 76;Catharine 22;
Elizabeth 25,88;Elizabeth A.
3;Elizabeth J.M. 84;Eliza-
beth W. 17;Esther 34;Lovey
48;Mahala F.55;Malinda 102;
Mary 10,13;Mary J. 55;
Margaret F. 17;Sargaret S.
11;Rosey P. 39;Sally B. 79;
Susan 71;Susan S. 37

Mehollomes(Meholloms),Lurana 9;
Mary 13;Margaret 9;Nancy 17,
88;Sarah 89;Susan T. 39;
Tamar 16

Melborne(Milbourn),Arinthia 65

Melvil,Agnes 102

Michael,Anne 101;Comfort 84;
Mary Blaikley 89;Margaret
42,100;Patience 16;Peggy 54;
Sarah 59

Mifflin,Anne 31,79

Miles,Anne 104;Polly 44;

Parramore,Harriet B.D. 55;Henrietta
49;Margaret A. 71;Rosey 45;Sarah 19

Parrot,Adah 97

Parvin,Maria 13

Peake,Betsey 17

Peaton,Nancy 86

Pearson,Adah 92;Elizabeth S. 78;
Emeline 73;Mary 55;Nancy 62;Tamar
41

Peck,Sally 4

Pettitt(Pettit),Adah 73,81;Amy 1;
Anne 82;Elizabeth 9;Mary 112;Nancy
73;Rachel 94;Susan 32

Phaben,Anne 14,Esther 70

Pigot,Ann 14;Elizabeth 58,61

Piper,Agnes 17

Pitts,Anne Mary 30;Elizabeth 107;
Elizabeth R. 105;Leah 73; ANNE
89;Mary 106;Margaret 47;Nancy 5;
Polly 13;Rachel 109;Sally 99;
Sarah D. 18;Tamar 40;Vianer Gray
49

Pool,Adah 54,66;Absel 41;Betsey 91;
Kesiah 92;Mary 100;Peggy 2,71;
Sally 91;Sarah 66

Poulson, Anne B. 13;Lucy 23

Powell,Ann 39;Ann N. 62;Anne W. 87;
Barbary 67;Betsy 21;Elizabeth
58,75,111;Hannah 33,88;Hannah
Bell 2;Lauretta 108;Mary Ann 14;
Maria S. 98;Margaret L. 76;
Nanny 29;Pamala E.J. 5;Peggy 32,
111;Rachel 79;Sally 16,77,86;
Sarah 30,52

Pratt,Adah 110;Anne 17;Mary 19;
Molly 40;Nancey 18,48;Rosey 77;
Sally 45;Susey 65

Preeson,Ann 42;Esther 3;
Margaret 57;Susanna 11,
38

Press,Caroline 91;Molly 5;
Susanna 47;Tabby 35

Ra_____,Anne 24

Rafield(Rayfield)Hannah 102

Rasin,Susanna 95

Rascoe(Rasco),Elizabeth 4;
Mary 63;Sarah 83

Rayfield(Rafield),Elizabeth
10;Lavenia 15;Mary S. 76;
Mary W. 109

Read,Ann 5;Ann Maria 18;
Chilametha 66;Corinthia
V.J. 111;Elizabeth Jane
83;Emily 83;Juno 66;
Leah 91;Margaret S. 76;
Penda 62;Sally 64;Sarah
101

Reeve,Mary 23

Respess(Rispas,Rispass),
Esther 1

Reynolds,Harriot 84;Susanna
76

Richardson,Elizabeth 6;
Eliza:64; Fanny 35;
Kessy 89;Margaret 27;
Nancy 7,79;Pamela 62;
Polly 14,95;Rachel 7;
Sally 10;Sukey 61

Ridley,Elizabeth 40;Esther
11;Esther P. 11;Mary
Ann P. 30;Rosena T. 99

Rippin,Anne 75;Elizabeth
106,114;Esther 36;Fanny
16;Margaret 26;Molly 43;
Polly 21;Susanna 40

Tamar A. 2

Scarborough,Susan 29

Scisco(Sasco,Sisco),Juliet Ann 14; Lucy 108

Scott,Anne 47,89,106,109;Ann Mary 86;Eliza Ann 60;Elizabeth 7; Elizabeth Ann 103;Elizabeth N. 59;Elizabeth Susan 36;Elizabeth S. 24;Elishe 65;Esther 7,42; Fanny 15;Hannah 93;Hannah E. 60;Keziah 95;Leah 40;Mary 54, 82,89;Mary Ann 14;Mary Juliet 18;Maria 81;Margaret 34,38; Margaret E.A. 106;Nancy 10,86, 114;Peggy 93,113;Rachel 45; Rebecca 115;Rosey 16,43;Sally S. 99;Sarah 94,105;Sarah Ann 93;Sophia 63;Sukey 95;Susanna 61

Seaton,Elizabeth 91;Peggy 106

Segar,Diana D. 39

Seymour,Rosey D. 77;Sarah 72

Shepherd,Betsey 18;Ibby 35

Sheerwood,Mary 22

Shores,Rose 52

Sickles,Rebecca 88

Simkins,Ann 13;Elizabeth 36; Elisa 53;Elmira 88;Fannie O. 33;Mary 76;Margaret 104;Peggy 30;Sabra 24;Sally 56;Sukey 108; Susan 28

Sisco(Sasco,Scisco),Lucy 105

Snaw,Anna 51;Elizabeth G. 77;Elishe 8;Nancy 88

Smith,Ann 3,11,83;Anna 25;Ann T. 35; Ann W. 76;Betsey 24;Betsey Floyd 55Catharine 37;Elishe 73;Elizabeth 70,82;Elizabeth G. 20;Elizabeth T. 100;Frances 23,98;Lucy Jane 10;

Lydia 72;Mary Anne 27;Maria 80;Margaret A.S. 78;Nancy 12, 29,34;Peggy 6,44;Polly 96; Rosy 69;Salley 89,105;Sally Wilson 44;Sarah 98;Sarah A. 79;Sukey 50,107;Susan 25,101, 109;Susanna 25,84,92

Snale(Snail,Snails),Kesiah 106; Olive 79;Sally 41

Snead,Adah 93;Anne 112;Catharine 42,105;Elizabeth 69,70,105; Mary B. 29;Sally C. 114

Spady,Adah 89;Ann 10,67;Arinthia S. 26;Betsey 23,30;Catharine 65;Elizabeth 108;Elizabeth S. 87;Emily S. 113;Harriet 67; Lavenia 65;Leah 16,41;Louisa C. 39;Lucretia 107;Mary 112; Margaret 20,72;Margaret E. 93; Molly 110;Peggy 95,99;Rosey E. 65;Rosy S. 19;Sarah 86;Sukey 22,109

Speakman,Anne 113;Betsey 99; Elizabeth 4;Elizabeth Spady 17; Lavenia Ann 48;Mary 93;Margaret 113;Susan Ann 29;Tinney 8

Spires, Elizabeth 7

Stakes,Mary 34;Polly 74

Stevens(Stephens)Abigail 5;Ann 36;Arinthia 16;Betty 76; Betsey 18;Leah 96; Mary 66; Mary Ann 36;Sally 5;Tamar 96

Stephens(Stevens),Abigail 41; Caty 91;Elizabeth 20;Leah 87;Lilly 96;Matilda 8; Patience 74;Peggy 105*; Rachel 21;Sabra 18

Stevenson,Judith 4

Stewart(Stuart),Ann S. 27; Elizabeth 67;Peggy 74

Stith,Elizabeth 71;Elizabeth

Harriet 16;Joanna 43;Lavinia 4;
Leah 90;Mary 11,64;Mary Ann 88,
97;Mary G. 42;Mary S. 32;Margaret 43,
51,78;Margaret B. 112;Margaret Susan
112;Margaret S. 70;Nancy 34,40,75;
Peggy 36;Polly 112;Rachel 12;Sally
37,41,69;Sarah 34,58;Sarah Green 90;
Sukey 98;Susan 33,97;Susey 70

Wilkerson,Eliza 18

Willis,Ann 15,34;Comfort 113,114;
Elizabeth 79,102;Eliza 65;Elishe 54,112;
Emily 55;Frances 94;Lucretia 9;Nancy
34;Peggy 90;Polly 7,71;Rachel 108,111;
Sarah 11;Susanna 78,92

Willet(Willett),Elizabeth 21,66,98;Lear 98;
Nancy 98

Wingate,Caroline 29;Emily 36;Nancy 13,108;
Rosey Ann 54,57;Sally 71,109;Sarah Ann
13,36

Winder,Charlotte L. 70;Sarah C. 57; Sarah U.
115;Susan C. 37

Window,Leah 23

Wise,Anne 72;Eleanor D. 21;Frances 36;Leah
54;Mary 30;Mary R. 34;Margaret H. 92;
Sarah 92

Wood,Margaret 65;Rebecka 30;Sally 102

Woodward,Weltha 31

Wright,Sally 62

Wyatt,Elizabeth 58;Patsey 99;Sally 77

Yetman,Elizabeth 29

Young,Elizabeth B. 62;Elizabeth P. 84;
Elizabeth W. 14;Mary A.T. 52;Sarah
A. H. 3

www.ingramcontent.com/pod-product-compliance
Lightning Source LLC
Chambersburg PA
CBHW031128020426
42333CB00012B/282